CROSSED PURPOSES

Ralph Folds has lived and worked at Walungurru Community in the Northern Territory for twelve years. A graduate of Adelaide and Flinders Universities in South Australia and the Northern Territory University, he has been involved in indigenous education for sixteen years, in roles including training indigenous adult educators and community administrators and as a school principal.

CROSSED PURPOSES

THE PINTUPI AND AUSTRALIA'S INDIGENOUS POLICY

RALPH FOLDS

UNSW PRESS

A UNSW Press book

Published by
University of New South Wales Press Ltd
University of New South Wales
UNSW Sydney NSW 2052
AUSTRALIA
www.unswpress.com.au

National Library of Australia
Cataloguing-in-Publication entry:

Folds, Ralph.
Crossed purposes: the Pintupi and Australia's indigenous policy.

Bibliography.
Includes index.
ISBN 0 86840 691 0.

1. Pintupi (Australian people).
2. Aborigines, Australian — Government policy. I. Title.

305.89915

Printer Griffin Press

Cover photograph Katingura, Pintupi tribesman. Courtesy of the
Archival Heritage Collections, State Library of South Australia.
PRG 1218, Series 3. Part 1, 1361M. Photographer: Charles P.
Mountford.

All photographs used in this book were taken by the author unless
otherwise indicated.

CONTENTS

To Shimona Rosamund Napaltjarri Pollard
Growing Up Strong

The author's royalties from the first print run are to be used to fund Pintupi children's Christmas parties through the Waḻungurru Tjaatji.

ACKNOWLEDGMENTS

This book would not have been possible without the compassion and generosity of the people of Walungurru community. In what must surely be a triumph of hope over experience they continue my slow education in what they consider responsible behaviour. It is these relationships, forged in the shared history of tumultuous settlement life, that have sustained me through my time in Walungurru.

With special thanks to Napangati, Nangala kutjarra, Nampitjinpa kutjarra, Tjapaltjarri, Tjakamarra, and all those others who contributed stories and ideas that helped with the writing of this book. Also to Fred Myers and Peter Thorley who read drafts of the book and provided me with valuable advice.

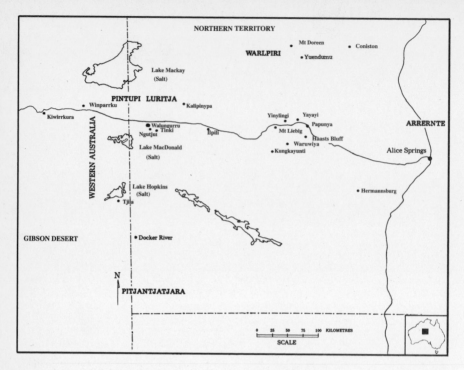

Regional map showing language groups and places mentioned in the text.

Road into Walungurru, 1994.

INTRODUCTION

The worst imperialisms are those of preconception.
(W E H Stanner 1979, 30)

At the end of a long, dusty, red road winding through desert country, its pristine wilderness marred only by the occasional shredded tyre, squashed can or rusted car body, you suddenly hit a 'rubbish line'. You have almost reached your destination, the litter more pronounced the closer you come to the settlement, until you enter a scene that could almost be post-apocalyptic in its squalor. Decaying houses and shelters built from galvanised iron, tarpaulins and other convenient bits and pieces apparently sprout haphazardly from what appears to be a wrecking yard. In places pools of stagnant water — or worse — collect for mangy dogs to drink and children to play in while among these ruins dispirited people are portrayed going about their lives as best they can.

Such snapshots, captured for short television or magazine 'info-tainment' features, are the only pictures most people get of the alien settlements scattered in the distant regions of our own 'backyard', and through these upsetting pictures preconceived stereotypes of remote indigenous life are immediately and convincingly confirmed. The settlements look like ghettos and the evidence of degradation seems to be everywhere. Yet these images, on which so much indigenous policy is confidently formulated, actually reveal very little, either about the people for whom these settlements are home or their relationship with other Australians.

This book is an exploration of that relationship, written for those who wonder how policies like social justice and reconciliation engage with the lives of remote indigenous Australians. It draws on voices from two generations of Pintupi who were part of an epic journey that started in the 1930s when some began moving from their desert homelands towards newly established western outposts.

As part of the assimilation policy those Pintupi then living at Haasts Bluff (see map) were moved en masse to the settlement of Papunya, opened in 1960. Over the next decade many more Pintupi were trucked there from their desert homelands to live under the 'civilising' influence of the Welfare Ordinance. The 1970s saw the advent of more enlightened indigenous policies and in 1981 Pintupi at Papunya finally returned to their own country to establish Walungurru.

The author's voice is that of a participant with Pintupi at this settlement but, as a white Australian, I am an outsider to the indigenous society I describe. However, this book is as much an exploration of western society as manifest at the interface with an indigenous culture and in this context I am an insider, having spent from 1988 until now (2001) managing a government institution at Walungurru.

A fit between well-meaning policies, aimed at banishing disadvantage, and their indigenous clients is often taken for granted. It is reinforced by much of the literature characterising remote indigenous societies as disempowered, collapsing due to the erosion of traditional culture through contact with the West. In 1988, as a relative newcomer to indigenous settlements, I confidently drew on this perspective when I left my job as a lecturer at Batchelor College, an indigenous tertiary institution near Darwin, bound for a school in the little-known desert settlement of Walungurru, far to the west of Alice Springs. As I departed, the deputy principal of the College, who had long experience with desert settlements, wished me well and offered a piece of advice. 'For the first six months', he told me, 'don't make any changes, just use the time to learn as much as you can about the place'. I agreed this was a wise course to take.

And yet, within a few days of my arrival, armed with my preconceptions of a society eager to be rescued from the despair of the colonised, I had resolved that my urgent mission as Walungurru School Principal was to empower Pintupi through self-management. I was encouraged in my rescue mission by those charged with training the future Pintupi teachers: the trainees were, they told me, ready, willing and able to take over the school and needed only the formal qualifications to take charge officially. Giving myself three to five years to complete the task of so-called Aboriginalisation, I set about reorganising the school to give the self-management program the highest priority.

What was best for Pintupi seemed so obvious to me that I failed to ask them about their own aspirations. I mistook their apparent acquiescence to my blueprint as agreement, not realising that my eager plans were listened to without demur because I seemed to be just another zealot, there for the short term, assailing them with his own particular brand of salvation.

One of my first actions was to announce that I would give the trainees a taste of the empowerment so long denied them: I told them they could run the school by themselves for a week, without the usual untoward interference from outsiders. The response to this wonderful opportunity was less enthusiastic than I expected. One of the trainees, to my shocked surprise, suggested she might also take a holiday like the whitefellas.

As I was risking my reputation with my employer in order to give them a precious taste of self-management, I was somewhat dismayed by their reaction to this first attempt at supporting their aspirations. However, the teacher trainers reassured me. They informed me that Pintupi were suffering from 'profound colonisation', brought on by long-term disadvantage and discrimination, and while they certainly wanted to run their own school without whitefellas, more training was needed to build confidence and overcome malaise.

In time, living and working with Pintupi forced me to confront my most cherished preconceptions. I came to acknowledge a strong, self-confident people, people in sharp disjuncture at every turn with the assumptions of indigenous policy, yet who tapped the advantages on offer with great deftness and immense humour. This change in my thinking came about through much patient explanation from Pintupi friends and colleagues, who taught me the high value they place on a way of life often described merely by reference to its 'deficits'.

Even more powerfully, I was instructed by the inevitable conflicts that flared up between Pintupi and me as the administrator of a western institution with goals and accountabilities very different from their own. It is largely through engaging in the inevitable rigorous exchanges of cultural expectations that I came to understand a little about the clash between western and Pintupi logics of life

The view I express in this book is of a competent indigenous society, still resilient at the periphery, while at the centre the dominant society self-confidently regards its policies as critical to the physical and emotional well-being of a disintegrating culture. A perspective where indigenous people are vigorously shaping their own lives, rather than having them determined by the 'dominant' society, does not, apart from some notable exceptions, feature widely in Australian indigenous studies or anthropological literature. For this reason I looked further afield for my theoretical framework, to the extensive literature on globalisation that describes many thriving small-scale societies around the world which, like the Pintupi, are taking what they need from the West rather than merely allowing themselves to be westernised or globalised.

When I first articulated a view of modern Pintupi society based on an appreciation of its strengths, rather than drawing on the long-entrenched deficit model, I struck an immediate chord with many whitefellas who had lived for some time with Pintupi or other Western

Desert people. I was also assailed by others, often with a more fleeting acquaintance, who complained that I lacked compassion for the 'plight' of the Pintupi because I did not emphasise inequalities such as their 'appalling health statistics', implying that I cared about them only as interesting cultural artefacts, not as fellow human beings. Because this is an easy smokescreen to use in avoiding serious consideration of the premise, developed later in this book, that valuing disparate societies is much more complex than merely doing comparative statistical analyses, I feel this interpretation cannot be ignored.

As someone who has, over the years, lost many friends and acquaintances here, I have been far from untouched by the human reality of statistical inequalities, and I doubt that anyone who lived for any length of time with the welcoming Pintupi could remain detached from them as people. It was precisely my engaging with Pintupi as a society of fiercely independent individuals leading sustaining lives, rather than as dehumanised numbers in a report, which slowly caused me to question my own deep-seated preconceptions. It is their great vitality that inspired me to write this book.

CHAPTER 1
THE 'LAST CONTACT' PEOPLE

In the bush days we were naked. We were hunting without any clothes or trousers.
It was good the way we went around then. We were happy.
(Pinta Pinta Tjapanangka 1989, 10)

Pintupi are the so-called 'last contact' people (the last to come out of the desert), many of whom continued to live their lives relatively untouched by the encroaching flood of western civilisation until the 1960s. In large part this was because their homeland, in the recesses of the western deserts of Australia's central arid zone, was considered by whites to be 'one of the most inhospitable inhabited areas in the world' (Thomson 1964, 401).

The early white explorers of these deserts, men such as Carnegie, Warburton and Giles, describe them in horrific terms, as ghastly regions, godforsaken wastes, the worst deserts in the world, racked by furnace winds and likely to send men mad if they managed to survive them. Greenway observes that explorers ringed these deserts with names of 'past tragedy and present warning' such as Lake Disappointment, Mount Misery, Mount Despair, Mount Deception, Mount Destruction, Mount Hopeless, Mistake Well and Madman Outcamp (1973, 74–5).

Pintupi know these same regions as the very centre of their universe. Their heroic ancestors in the *Tjukurrpa* (Dreamtime) created their features, fashioning an undulating sea of steep red sandhills and dense spinifex plains interrupted by quartzite hills which appear blue on the horizon at midday, all under an immense turquoise sky.

Pintupi country is exceptionally dry, its water lies deep underground,

Above Ingrid and Norel Nakamarra, two of Nampitjinpa's granddaughters, taken in 1989.

Below Carissa Nampitjinpa and Shimona Napaltjarri, two of Mimala's grandchildren, taken in 2000.

only rarely available on the surface. After sudden downpours clay pans fill and water gushes from the hills, but for long periods water is found only in a few rockholes, soaks and wells dug so deep the precious contents had to be passed through several hands to the surface. In 1896–97 the explorer David Carnegie trekked almost 3000 miles on constant look-out for waterholes, without ever finding a single one on his own. He explained that had his party not taken captive and 'to a small extent used rough treatment to some natives so caught, we could not by any possibility have succeeded in crossing the desert' (1989, 133). Carnegie's real regret was taking horses because, unlike camels, these demanding beasts needed to drink at least once a day.

This unpredictable country did not allow its inhabitants to settle for long into unchanging or comfortable routines of life at any one place, or with any particular group. Pintupi had to be ready to seize the varied opportunities that came along. In the hot summers, before the storms, when people in the open without water may die in a matter of hours, they tapped the few sources of reliable water. What they regarded as 'big water' was a mere cleft in a rock containing a brackish pool, a hand-hewn well or even damp earth from which water could be steadily wrung. These supplies were usually secure, but if they dried up the group retreated by night to an alternative source.

Timing was critical: the desert is capable of inflicting severe casualties on those who fail to take advantage of its opportunities at exactly the right time. If Pintupi waited too long at one failing water supply, they were weakened even before they set out for another. If the next one they sought had dried up, they waited under shade during another scorching day until late afternoon, to set out again, a cycle they sometimes repeated several times. Occasionally there was just not enough water and death from dehydration occurred, but only after enormous efforts to find water. Stories abound of those who staggered on with their bark sandals long shredded, and the soles of their feet worn to a bloody pulp.

If it became clear that it was not possible for everyone in a group to survive one of these nocturnal treks the harsh logic of desert life dictated that some had a better chance than others. The men forged on ahead looking for water, while the women came along after with the old people and any children. The children, rather than the old people, were given any remaining water and if the group was a very long way from their destination the elderly were reluctantly left behind, often by way of a mutually understood deceit, a promise to return quickly. In a society where relationships between family members must reflect the value placed on total support, Pintupi could not tell their relatives they were leaving them behind to die and the old people could not have borne the shame of the truth.

After such deaths, distant classificatory brothers and sisters of the deceased returned later to collect and protect the bones and set fire to the surrounding countryside, after which closer relatives could return. Pintupi recall that the penalty for those who failed to perform this duty was death by spearing at the hands of a revenge party. Whatever the harsh pattern of life imposed by the desert environment, total caring for relatives has never been optional in their society, which is based on a complex and flexible polity of relatedness.

As the anthropologist Fred Myers points out, '[w]hat seems important about the Pintupi is not that they "adapt", but that they create such societal intensity while managing to conform to the ecological constraints of a harsh region' (1986a, 292). To be looked after without reservation by one's *walytja*, or relatives, is the very opposite of being alone, and so fundamental to Pintupi that it also came to underpin their ideas about their relationship with whitefellas.

The late summer rains, carried on tropical monsoons from the Indian Ocean, sweep in from the west in the form of localised squalls and storms. Preceded by walls of blinding dust rolling across the desert, the downpours drench one area while leaving others completely untouched. In the watered area the desert springs to life, insects and small animals emerge from the red sand to feed and quickly breed in greening spinifex. Vegetable foods and fruit grow to maturity from this single prolonged drenching while adjacent, unwatered areas remain grey and apparently lifeless.

Across the immense, flat landscape, Pintupi could see these deluges funnelling to earth from patches of darkened sky and smell the rain as it teemed down. The downpours brought new opportunities, to hunt in sandhill country with its ephemeral water, to perform important ceremonies and renew links with kin. Like their adventurous supernatural heroes from the *Tjukurrpa*, Pintupi travelled widely during the rainy time and forged bonds of relatedness with many other groups. Custom dictated that Pintupi men should go far away to seek a wife and live with her and her relatives in their country.

The late summer wet season also brought danger because opportunities to travel made the settling of scores possible. Pintupi often attribute deaths to sorcery, and punishment for this was meted out at the hands of revenge groups of warriors who had been danced invisible by ceremony. However, the outcome of such expeditions, where the target was also well armed and confident in his own country, could never be assured.

Tjungarrayi recalls that many years ago, well before he first met whitefellas, he was hunting to the south of Lake MacDonald (see map) when he came across the footprints of a revenge party sent to kill him, before they discovered his own. Brushing away his tracks he stalked the killers until nightfall, when they made camp. Before dawn he sprang on them, spearing two of the assassins as they stumbled for their weapons, before retreating into the desert night. The surviving members of the revenge party rushed after him but never found him, and eventually they limped back in the direction of their own country.

Despite the hardships and dangers of life in the desert, Pintupi do not recall a life of despair or even of hunger. In 1957, during a period when the summer rains had failed to materialise for several years, Dr Hargrave, the medical officer who accompanied a Welfare Patrol to determine the health status of Pintupi, reported that, 'Considering the poor conditions these people must have endured during the past summer ... they were in an excellent state of nutrition and health' (1957, 4).

'Last contact' people, like Mick Namararri Tjapaltjarri, said they rarely suffered prolonged hunger:

> We would make a fire, eat and move from camp to camp, through this country here. As we went we would eat, drink water and sleep, after making a fire. We ate and ate and ate, then our stomachs would be full. After eating we would sleep. Then, as the sun rises we would get our spears and spear throwers and hunt for kangaroos. (1989, 13)

Pintupi were not, as many believe, tied to an arduous routine of life based on an endless search for food. They had mastered the desert and they did not place a high value on their technical knowledge of flora, fauna or the physical geography of the country. These basic survival skills were taken for granted, and only whitefellas find them astounding.

> In addition to their extraordinary knowledge of the water reserves, a knowledge that allows them to be complacent in the face of the land's most hostile moods, they have a reserve of food in the form of lizards ... This knowledge too assures their survival even during long drought. (Thomson 1975, 85–6)

While they do not particularly value their ability to survive in the desert, it is important to Pintupi to be at home in a country, not merely to be able to live in it, but to know its origins in the Dreaming. This is real knowledge and, like everything else in Pintupi society, it is bestowed by others: by those who 'hold' or 'look after' on those who are 'held'. From their nurturing relatives Pintupi learned the meaning of their world: the claypans, rockholes, soakages, wells, particular trees, hills, 'footprints' and places of storms created in the Dreamtime. Important places are *Tjukurrpa purrkaringanyi*, where the Dreaming 'slowed down' and Dreamtime heroes became the landscape and are visible to people on a material plane. These sacred places are still alive and Pintupi say that if you walk on a sacred mountain it may shake violently underfoot, as it is disturbed.

The Dreaming provided for Pintupi according to their needs, not just to survive but to feel at home in a world fashioned by their supernatural heroes for their own purposes. Boomerangs are not man-made from lifeless lumps of wood, rather they are pre-fashioned and 'hidden' within trees. Neither are spears created by Pintupi, they are already fully formed in *mulyati* (spearwood), just waiting to be taken and used. As one of the 'last contact' generation, Pinta Pinta Tjapanangka recalled how they could seize ready-made implements and use them almost immediately:

> I pulled out a spearwood tree, shaped it and smoothed the edges. Then I heated it to make it straight. Then I got up and followed and tracked and finally saw a red kangaroo. Holding my spear I rose and followed, always moving quickly across. I threw the spear, 'finish!' (1989, 11)

'WE FOLLOWED THE *PULAWA* (FLOUR)'

> In becoming their own voyagers, the Aborigines claimed, coaxed and fought an opening into an incomprehensible world. Many died, and many others were ruined; those who survived found they could not go back; and it does not seem that many even wanted to. Nowhere, as far as I am aware, does one encounter Aborigines who want to return to the bush, even if their circumstances are very miserable. They went because they wanted to, and stay because they want to. (W E H Stanner 1979, 49)

Pintupi probably first encountered whitefellas during the expeditions of Carnegie and Warburton in the 1870s, when Carnegie captured a few individuals (1989, 133). Inexplicably for a people who were thought to be primitive and unchanging and most unlikely to have met whites before, Carnegie found a steel axe fashioned from a horse-shoe and he saw metal implements including an old tent peg in Pintupi camps (1989, 140). Along with other indigenous people, Pintupi were considered primitive and uninterested in innovation merely because they had long perfected their elegant technology. Indigenous tools are, as Stanner explained, '... brilliantly simplified rather than "simple" or "primitive" ... a perfected invention' (1979, 162). And, long before they met whitefellas, Pintupi established domestic cats turned feral as *Ngaya Tjukurrpa* (Cat Dreaming) and hunted them for food, medicine and the status of tracking and killing this cunning predator.

There was increasing contact with western society from the 1930s. Pastor Albrecht from the Hermannsburg Mission believed that it was important for the survival of indigenous people for them to stay in the bush and he regularly took food and gifts to the 'Western tribes'. Haasts Bluff (Ikuntji), located 215 km north west of Alice Springs, was established as a meeting place by evangelists from the mission and, by 1935, a substantial number of indigenous people, including a group of Pintupi, had moved into the area.

From the 1940s more strangers began travelling west from Alice

Springs and Pintupi grew fearful of their intentions. An official at that time was quoted as stating, 'I'm not going to allow the Aboriginals to drive the Whites out of the country. I'm going to see that the Aboriginals are taught a lesson'. The prevailing view at the time was 'Cattle make money; Aboriginals do not' (Davis et al. 1977, 35).

Rumours about Pintupi abounded. Many whites believed that they were ferocious savages and few, apart from the missionaries and prospectors, went willingly into the desert (Davis et al. 1977, 21). A spear was sometimes more than a match for a pistol, especially at night. 'Last contact' Pintupi liken their former spear-throwing prowess to the effectiveness of a bullet, Pinta Pinta Tjapanangka recalled, '*Wakaṉu ma punkatjiṉgaṉu* (I made the spear strike at long distance with great force)' (1989, 11).

Disturbing stories filtered through to Pintupi from other areas. Indigenous people were shot on sight along the Canning Stock Route and to the south there were accounts of people being fed poisoned meat. At Coniston Station well, in 1928, men, women and children were hunted down and shot en masse during a punitive raid. From a number of detailed accounts, such as that of Billy Nolan Tjapangaṯi (1989), one of the intruders in the desert he met as a child, at a water-hole called Tjila, was a whitefella Pintupi called Kuṉki, the 'white murderer'. Kuṉki travelled through the desert on camels, shooting at Pintupi whenever he saw them, especially targeting their children, to supplement his diet with 'Aboriginal meat'.

Fear of this cannibal spread throughout the desert and all white strangers were feared. Any whitefella they met might be Kuṉki because it was impossible for Pintupi to distinguish between the explorers, prospectors, missionaries, adventurers, doggers, murderers and inspectors, partly because 'all of them carried rifles and revolvers, to procure game and as protection against possible attack' (Davis et al. 1977, 34). A pastor travelling in the desert came across a family group who 'ran away from us, but they were shaking so much from fear that they could hardly run at all' (21).

In the 1950s Pintupi attracted official attention and patrols were mounted by the Welfare Branch to 'assess their needs', though it was reported that Pintupi must have found it difficult to understand why they were visited so frequently if this was the only motivation (Davis et al. 1977, 23). These visits profoundly affected Pintupi even if they did not actually see the patrol. They saw the tracks in the desert sand made by patrol vehicles, and some knew that whitefellas and their precious supplies of food had passed that way. A few followed these strange footprints eastwards.

Two expeditions mounted by anthropologist Donald Thomson in 1957 found nomadic people he called 'Bindibu' who retained their traditional pattern of life (1975). Thomson expressed concern that explorers and others stole their sacred objects and the horses and camels drank water holes dry (1975, 7, 135). Despite such disturbing encounters and stories, Pintupi still had a great interest in whitefellas and their resources, and a few had even been to the ration station at Haasts Bluff.

RATIONS

> I saw a group of these desert dwellers at Mt Doreen recently in the dirty ragged trappings of civilisation. My heart goes out to them. (Donald Thomson 1975, xi)

Word of a ration station at Haasts Bluff, established by the Lutheran Mission far to the east of their own country, which dispensed new foods and other elements of a hitherto unexplored world, excited and attracted Pintupi in increasing numbers. A party from the station, travelling with camels and hunting dogs in 1955 around the Kintore Range, met Pintupi and told them about the rations. Consequently, a large group of about 30 'nomads' walked in to the station during the following year (Davis et al. 1977, 14).

Rations, including sugar and flour, were carried in saddlebags on donkeys, horses and camels to Pintupi living out towards Western Australia. Charlie Tjungarrayi Watuma was employed by the mission to take food to the 'bush mob', and he rode out on camels to find them. He recalled that on one such expedition a small group of people were located at Wili rockhole, to the east of where Walungurru settlement is now located. Pintupi camping there were reported to be 'happy to see the food' and they subsequently moved to Mt Liebig to be closer to its source.

Pinta Pinta Tjapanangka was a young man participating in *Tjulpurrpa* (ceremonies which are open to women and children) at an important site called Winparrku, when whitefellas rode up on horses. Pinta Pinta described his group as *nikiti pini* (many naked people) and they called the whitefellas *warrawarra* (witchetty grubs) because of the colour of their skin. His group was amazed at the sight of these 'witchetty grubs', but they stood their ground, although one or two of them gathered up their spears. They were given flour by the strangers but they did not know what it was, so they hid it rather than eat it. After the whitefellas rode off on their horses they tasted it, tentatively, then they ate it raw, without knowing it could be made into damper.

Pintupi were wary of the whitefellas but their fears were overcome by great loads of tucker, including 'hundred pound' bags of flour. In a society that placed high value on generosity no individual could accumulate much of any resource, and the sheer quantity of food utterly astounded them. It was beyond belief, Pinta Pinta Tjapanangka said, it was 'too much'.

Pintupi stories describing first contact emphasise the food given to them and their subsequent interest in whitefellas. Explaining the reason for travel to the ration depot at Haasts Bluff, Tjungarrayi, an emigrant from these times, says:

> We followed the *pulawa* [flour]. We went for tucker and trous [trousers]. We got pulawa — *tii* [tea], *tinamita* [tinned meat], *lumara* [sugar]. We didn't care for country then, all we could think about was that tucker. We talked about it all the time and so we went and got it. (pers. comm.)

They were exploring a new world, visiting far-flung cattle stations and missions. Benny Tjapaltjarri relates how he travelled from a place called Kalipinypa to Hermannsburg Mission by foot, a distance of some 500 km (1989). He was given some Christmas cake by the missionaries, but was not encouraged to take up permanent residence so he walked back to his own country. Later he went to Haasts Bluff where he had relatives and his bush days ended forever.

Pintupi often describe the movement to settlement as 'following *walytja*', to rejoin kin who had already left their own country. This was the motivation of a Pintupi man, Katingura Tjungarrayi (cover photo), who often camped around the present site of Walungurru settlement, his own country. Katingura had never seen a white man when he came across strange tracks in the sand, made by graders working on road-building to provide access for a rocket range across the Western Australia border. Katingura crept closer, but when he heard the distant roar of the machines he ran away, terrified, convinced the graders were *mamu* (devils).

From other Pintupi, Katingura heard exciting stories about an old whitefella (Pastor Albrecht) who had visited them at a place called Ilpili, to give them flour and other presents, and promised to return. It was reported at the mission of Hermannsburg that:

> Pintupi mob, never seen white men, they were frightened ... For a lot of them he [Albrecht] was the first white man they saw, didn't know why he came, most white people came for trouble. They couldn't understand flour, what this one, might be ashes ... Pintupi liked it [flour] straight away, wasn't ashes after all. (Quoted in Henson 1992, 59–60)

With his two brothers, Katingura followed their missing *walytja* east to a depot at Ilpili to await the missionary. For the first time they saw whitefellas, although from a safe distance, and gradually they grew bolder. Finally, shaking with fear and anticipation, Katingura accepted food from one of the whitefellas, passed to him around the trunk of the tree he hid behind.

At Ilpili they were joined by other Pintupi who had heard word of the impending return of the old whitefella who had brought them miraculous gifts of food and was looking after their relatives in the east. At last Albrecht arrived and he shook hands with the tremulous

Pintupi, gave them food and asked them if they wanted to join their families at the ration station. Without hesitation Katingura and the others agreed, and they walked naked beside the Pastor astride his camel as he led them to Haasts Bluff. Katingura could not know that he was leaving his ancestral lands for the last time. Like most of his pioneering countrymen, forging an entry to the whitefella world for the first time, he would be a casualty of the attempt.

Katingura and his brothers camped with their *walytja* around Haasts Bluff, at various soakages and rockholes, eating rations and starting to wear clothes for the first time, but still following most of their normal pursuits, such as hunting, singing and participating in ceremonial life. With so many people gathered together at Haasts Bluff, these ceremonies could be bigger than ever before.

For Pintupi to live in large groups at one place for a lengthy period was without precedent, and while groups in the desert separated after conflict they now stayed together because of the food. Spearings took place more frequently and fighting was often on a large scale, with payback killings rife because they were easier to perpetrate than in the bush. At Haasts Bluff a man marked for death was camped in close proximity, rather than far off in the desert, and, therefore, had much less chance to escape.

There were other changes. The attraction of the rations prevailed against the custom of going far away to get a wife. After Katingura's wife, a Warlpiri woman, died giving birth to Cameron Tjapaltjarri, he took a second wife, this time a Pintupi woman from his own group. This 'second mother' grew Cameron up as her own child, so Cameron had 'two mothers' as well as his three fathers, Katingura and his two brothers, the three Tjungarrayi.

At Haasts Bluff Albrecht offered a weekly ration of flour, sugar, tea and some baking powder, but only for the elderly, children and women. In doing so he wanted to support them so that they would not need to go to Alice Springs, but not so much that they would become totally dependent on whitefellas. Albrecht believed that, while indigenous people should not suffer from hunger, the 'indiscriminate distribution of food would discourage the healthy men and women from going out for bush tucker — that, in his opinion, could only have a pauperising influence on their community life' (Henson, 1992, 170). This reflected widespread concern about rationing. As Tim Rowse observes, by the late 1930s the belief that rationing not only sustained, but also corrupted, had begun to contribute to a crisis of policy (1998, 33).

Tjungarrayi recalls how the rationing system worked: 'Old people got tucker and we hunted. We got "pocket money" for dingo (scalps).' Able-bodied men like Tjungarrayi received no handouts in their own right, but had to bring in dingo skins and scalps, which could be sold for cash or bartered. Within a day they exhausted their whitefella food, so they went off hunting *rumiyaku, kiparaku, maluku* (for goanna, for bush turkey, for kangaroo). In effect, their diets continued to be their traditional staples, supplemented at regular intervals by whitefella food from the station.

Meat was not distributed, on the grounds that it would encourage the men to become idle, and 'roo ears' had to be produced before rations were given out, to demonstrate that people were supporting themselves through hunting. Few people had rifles so the men were kept busy following their traditional hunting pursuits, both to feed themselves and to obtain rations. Pintupi were discouraged from settling in one place, and even after rationing stopped they were brought their money, which they immediately exchanged for food off the back of a store truck. One of the drivers from this time reported that if there was any change it would simply be thrown away, as Pintupi returned to lives where money had not yet come to have any use or meaning (Rowlings, pers. comm.).

Pastor Albrecht was certainly an assimilationist, but he had known indigenous people for decades and appreciated the vast cultural differences that stood in the way of that ambition. He knew what policy-makers then, and since, have ignored: that no matter how attractive or laudable changes in indigenous society seem at the time they cannot just be legislated or programmed into existence. His own timetable for change was generations rather than years or decades and he believed that any speeding-up would be counter-productive (Henson 1992, 227).

This anomalous relationship with a benevolently paternalistic whitefella, who had an understanding of their culture and was always generous in his dealings with them, is how Pintupi first experienced and conceived their relationship with whitefellas. The traditions established from this first-contact experience reverberate to the present, with the beliefs engendered then about their relationship with whitefellas still colouring interactions on their contemporary settlements.

As Rowse points out, rationing did not demand a bridge between donors and receivers, to explain why the rationing took place, because '[i]ndigenous recipients could preserve their own understandings of why they were rationed ...' (1998, 5). In the view of Katingura and the others, Albrecht was 'holding' them, just as the older generations of Pintupi 'hold' those who come after them, contributing to their welfare without impinging too far on their autonomy. This became the model and standard against which all whitefella actions are judged.

PROTECTION AND ASSIMILATION

It is the policy of the Government to promote and direct social change among aborigines in the Northern Territory in such a way that they will eventually become indistinguishable from other members of the Australian community ... (Northern Territory *Annual Report* 1958–59, 40)

From the 1920s to the early 1940s government policy was one of pro-tection. The aim was to 'serve the best interests of the aboriginal com-ing into contact with white civilisation while permitting the white pioneer successfully to settle in available pastoral country' (*Report on the Administration of the NT* 1932, 7). While it was acknowledged that towns were attractive to indigenous people and that 'the running of stock on tribal ground induces the owner to drive aboriginals from cer-tain waterholes' (7), the subsequent migration was greeted with con-sternation. In Central Australia reports that the desert was 'emptying of Aborigines' heading for Alice Springs, including an (erroneous) report in 1937 that the northern part of the country Pintupi had lived in was now empty, were described as a 'shocking state of affairs' (*Report on the Administration of the NT* 1937, 10).

This so-called 'Aboriginal problem' was particularly alarming in Central Australia because indigenous people there were thought to be especially keen to seek respite from the forbidding terrain they inhab-ited (*Report on the Administration of the NT* 1933, 5). Reducing the rations available to people coming in to Alice Springs was one response, and another was extending to Central Australia, in the face of fierce opposition, the policy requiring pastoral employers to main-tain their Aboriginal employees' dependants (*Report on the Administration of the NT* 1932, 7).

The merit of reserves, in which indigenous people could live, and to which those evicted from townships could be sent, soon became apparent (*Report on the Administration of the NT* 1936, 9). It was widely believed that without them 'Alice Springs would be flooded by two thousand primitive natives, unable to support themselves, begging for food, creating pestilences because they would not have the rudi-ments of civilized living' (Gartrell 1957, 15).

In their new-found enthusiasm for reserves, town interests began to rival those of the pastoralists, as Pastor Albrecht discovered to his sur-prise when he sought to establish the Haasts Bluff block for Pintupi and other groups. Albrecht's victory came at the end of a protracted, and largely futile, struggle to win minimal funding for indigenous people in the bush, in which he persisted because he saw towns as 'graveyards for Aborigines' (Henson 1992, 151). He commented on his unexpected success that, '[t]his is the only known occasion in Australian history where the Aborigines have been preferred before bullocks' (268).

The benefits of the reserves were now lauded, 'in areas where there are most full-bloods (Western Australia and the Northern Territory) the proportion of half-castes is lowest ... this appears to show the wisdom of maintaining inviolate reserves where the natives are entirely free and unmolested' (*Report on the Administration of the NT* 1944–45, 5). Soon governmental determination to curtail the drift to town overrode Albrecht's considered compromise between supporting people in the bush, and not undermining their way of life by creating welfare dependency.

Albrecht found himself challenged by the same government officials who had previously denied his meagre requests for welfare. Now they were the ones insisting that more must be done for people on the reserves, and he was the recalcitrant. Surely, the officials argued, the ration should be extended to all sections of the settlement, not just the old, infirm and children.

Albrecht was reminded that reputation was of prime importance:

> ... what would interested parties in the south think if they heard the government was supporting Aborigines at the rate of only 3s 8d per person per week? Albrecht must have wondered if his ears were deceiving him. It was only the sheer economy of his proposal for Haasts Bluff that had narrowly won official approval for it three short years before. (Henson 1992, 170)

The equality argument was used by government against the social argument based on the value of indigenous lifeways, and the compromise sought by Albrecht became an acute embarrassment. Money was no longer an obstacle, rather largesse had become the badge of honour. The ration depot was to be replaced by a settlement at Papunya, providing three meals a day, training, a hospital and a central school. Albrecht was astounded, 'they are going to the other extreme; before nothing was done, now it is to be a showplace' (Henson 1992, 171).

The ascendancy of the equality argument was conceived in terms of generosity, as all indigenous policies have been. Assimilation was a 'positive policy' which recognised for the first time that indigenous people were capable of being equal. The indigenous residents at Papunya were to be the beneficiaries of training and other assistance, 'privileges not enjoyed by other Northern Territory citizens', with Papunya developed as a 'supervised transitional community' (Davis et al. 1977, 140). Here the orchestrated destruction of indigenous culture was described as 'social, economic and political advancement for the purpose of assisting them and their descendants to take their place as members of the Commonwealth' (*NT Annual Report* 1957–58, 36).

There was to be no overt compulsion, the settlement was supposedly not intended as a prison camp, even though a group of Pintupi who walked out after good rains had fallen to the west were promptly rounded up and trucked straight back again. That was merely done for their own good, because making them 'wards' to curtail their travel lust and civilise them in settlements meant ensuring access to health services and higher standards of housing.

None of this was seen as racist. On the contrary, racism was supposed to be eliminated by overcoming the problem of indigenous people not being accepted on the basis of social and economic inequality

(*NT Annual Report* 1949–53, 24). Surely, channelling resources to overcome this inequality could not be considered racist?

Successive policies of protection and assimilation were the two schools of thought on 'the Aboriginal problem': quarantine them in reserves or move them to settlements and assimilate them. Protection was a holding action where 'the aboriginal may here continue his normal existence until the time is ripe for his further development' (*NT Annual Report* 1938, 2), while assimilation was justified, not so much by ignoring the human costs, but by massively inflating the real benefits of 'civilisation' to a very different society.

PAPUNYA

> We live by a plan of life. The law ratifies it; much of our scholarship justifies it; some of our historians canonise it; the schools teach it as mores; the churches by and large condone it; commerce and industry follow within it ...The innermost rationale of our policy towards the Aborigines draws and will continue to draw on the same sources. (W E H Stanner 1979, 302–3)

For Pintupi like Katingura and his *walytja* living around Haasts Bluff, the arrival of trucks to take them to the new settlement of Papunya was greeted with consternation. Pastor Albrecht was looking after them, not these other whitefellas, and they wanted him to come and talk to them, to tell them whether or not it was safe to go. When they were told that no more food would be provided at Haasts Bluff they reluctantly climbed onto the trucks.

They left Haasts Bluff without their dogs because the officials insisted, despite much protest, that they would not be allowed at Papunya. The next day Katingura and the others promptly walked back to Haasts Bluff and retrieved their dog packs, thus giving them the first victory in what was to become an enduring contest between the values of the two societies on Pintupi settlements.

The premise of the assimilation policy was that indigenous people were merely neglected and undeveloped members of the wider Australian community, and therefore only in need of some guidance and special assistance to take their place in western society. The notion that indigenous people were not inferior, after all, was a radical proposition at the time, and one that was not accepted by everyone. Central Australian explorer Gill expressed the position of many whites in the first half of the century when he described the 'primitive' people he encountered in the 1930s as 'clever hunters ... yet incapable of thinking objectively' (1968, 128). But while this new policy, and those coming after it, saw indigenous people as being able to do anything other Australians could, it did not conceive that many might have absolutely no interest in doing so. Assimilation policy ignored indigenous preferences, which led to the further mistake of assuming that it could actually work.

In theory, at least, the assimilation policy made few concessions to indigenous lifeways, even where the consequences were dire. Instead of dispensing rations to individual families, everyone was now fed together in a communal dining room, despite Pintupi avoidance relationships which made this proximity punishable. The fact that they were primarily meat-eating people did not influence the type of food they were given, even when their new diets contributed to the death of many of them. There was no consultation with the traditional owners of Papunya and sometimes this had lethal consequences. There were several different groups in residence, some of whom were strangers to the area. If a man from one of these visiting groups accepted a direction from a white boss to do a job like chopping down sacred trees the traditional owners would kill him. 'The European would not know why the Aboriginal was killed' (Davis et al. 1977, 159).

A people who prized their autonomy, and for whom, according to Davis, the idea of 'work as a voluntary act having some virtue in itself is quite foreign' (1977, 43), were now compelled to labour on a series of job creation schemes which had little purpose. Pintupi were angry. They had not gone to Haasts Bluff and Papunya to conform to the oppressive routines of whitefella work, and even the officials could see that the jobs they were given were 'so European from the moment of their conception that they were fore-doomed' (90–91).

However, enforced work was not the main Pintupi complaint. What really upset them was the change in their relationship with their whitefella bosses. In their view this was now not the nurturing one established by Albrecht; it had been transformed into one of denial and compulsion. This change was a great shock to Pintupi. As Myers explains, 'Theirs is a view of once a precedent, twice a tradition' (1982, 108), and Pintupi thought that they would always enjoy the relationship with whitefellas established in the desert and at the ration station. This included a personal, open relationship with whitefellas, in which they received food and other goods while retaining time for family life, hunting, travelling and performing ceremonies.

At Papunya that tradition was violated by officials who, as Rowse observes, did not take into account that they were 'dealing with another civilisation within whose codes they themselves were intelligible, if exotic, creatures' (1998, 32). Now Pintupi had to work for meal tickets, which were exchanged for food. After school children were fed, the adults lined up at the dining room and presented their tickets, without which no food was provided. They were closely supervised, scrutinised, and relentlessly and impersonally 'bossed' by whitefellas. They still remember the humiliation they felt at this unconscionable treatment; as Duguid noted, 'It did not occur to employers that routine and long hours of work, without apparent reason, were concepts utterly incomprehensible to tribal aborigines' (1963, 184).

In 1964 Papunya officials tried to encourage self-reliance by paying wages rather than food tickets, insisting that Pintupi now buy their own food. Because money and rations had always been separate, according to the tradition of their inviolable relationship with whitefellas, Pintupi responded angrily. To the astonishment of the officials, who thought that they could be made to do anything for food, Pintupi refused to eat in the dining room at all, the only indigenous group at the settlement to reject the new decree (Davis et al. 1977, 45).

The astounded officials saw the Pintupi response as further evidence of their entrenched primitiveness. They were clearly unable to come to terms with a money economy; it seemed that they completely failed to comprehend that they were actually losing nothing in the new arrangement. However, that explanation ignored the way that Pintupi had conceived their earlier relationship with whitefellas.

For Pintupi, whitefella bosses had long established their obligation to feed them, even if they were now given money themselves for that purpose. Money and rations had always been separate in the tradition of the long-standing relationship. Whitefella bosses were 'holding' them, which means showing primary concern for their welfare, and such a relationship does not countenance taking something away when giving a new benefit. To Pintupi, the officials were breaking the relationship by stealing from them.

In the face of betrayal, Pintupi began to use the word *mulyarratayimi* or 'angry time' for payday, which was when employees registered grievances about their pay. The issue was not just that they were paid very little, in their view no payment of money could recompense them for the freedom lost and the betrayal of their established relationship with 'bosses'.

Even if Pintupi found their relations with whitefellas at Papunya unsatisfactory, they still worried about their *walytja* left behind in the desert and, for their part, the officials were eager to bring them in. Those left behind in the bush also worried about their relatives in Papunya and the lack of people left in their desert homelands meant that 'their social life had been impoverished by the depopulation' (Long 1964b, 33).

After seeing the smoke of hunting fires and following footprints, patrol officers would hide their Land Rover on one side of a sandhill while their Pintupi companions walked around to the other side to their relatives, telling them about the food and inviting them to join them at the settlement. News of these expeditions reuniting *walytja* at a place to the east, where there was abundant food and water, circulated far and wide. Stories of water delivered from taps at Papunya captivated and delighted people who lived in exceptionally dry country, and this miracle brought forth a new wave of emigrants from the desert. No matter what they had heard, for desert people who had never seen a truck to climb aboard and travel at unparalleled speed to a country they had never seen, and a life unimaginable, was both remarkably adventurous and courageous. Pintupi have always been keen explorers.

The influx of relatives to Papunya turned voyage into permanent settlement. Pintupi had previously lived in small groups at different places across a vast landscape of desert, travelling around to visit relatives. With most relatives at Papunya there was little reason to travel, apart from visiting country again, and there is little evidence they wanted to do this at that time. As Tjungarrayi explains, 'We weren't thinking about country then' (pers. comm.).

The movement of many different groups of indigenous people to the settlement was observed by Stanner (1979, 47) to be a 'one-way movement', but for the Pintupi it was never based on the expectation of settling down in one place for ever. Residence for Pintupi is based on relationships, and these are always in flux; they do not travel to any particular place with the expectation of staying there for long, and they have never relinquished the right to make their own choices in this. For almost all Pintupi, 'They came in because they were hungry. They didn't know they could not go back' (quoted in Myers 1986a, 25).

'THOUSAND DIED'

Promoting changes in the Aborigines' diet and eating habits is one very important feature of the work of assimilation. A variation in diet is expected to bring about major improvements in health, and adoption of European eating habits should have the effect of making Aboriginal people more acceptable in the community generally. (NT Welfare Branch, *Annual Report,* 1971)

Pintupi are adventurers and sometimes that exacts a high price. Papunya offered tantalising benefits: free food, abundant water, and *walytja* in large sustainable groups, but despite this bounty there were many casualties, though some groups fared much better than others. Those who came in during 1963–4 were especially unfortunate; of the 72 new arrivals from the desert, 29 were dead by August 1964, a staggering death rate of 40 per cent in one year (Davis et al. 1977, 52).

Old people, especially the men, were the first casualties, despite being in excellent health when they arrived at Papunya, many having walked enormous distances to get there. They arrived in superb condition, lean and muscled, but within a few weeks they were sick and listless (pers. comm.). As for the children, from 1956–61 there were 45 deaths among infants (up to two years) at Papunya and Haasts Bluff alone (Tatz 1964, 131). A teacher at Papunya School in 1965 wrote of the plight of the children:

> I have never seen anything like it. They were dying, the poor souls. They were herded into the kitchen and given food they had never seen before, they threw vegetables on the floor. No one thought to get kangaroo for them. Children four years old were 20 lb [9.1 kg]. They were too sick to come to school and were dreadfully frightened and clung to their mothers. We had 9 year-olds in the infant room, petrified when we closed the door. We had toilet problems and they were very dirty and ragged. We showered them and gave them school clothes and tried to make them part of the school. They were lovely children, quiet and obedient but the other children picked on them. (Davis et al. 1977, 58)

Staff at Papunya reported the deaths, and other problems, to the Welfare Department hierarchy in terms of Pintupi being 'different in their degree of acculturation', but the Department was 'not persuaded to make allowances' (Davis et al. 1977, 23). After all, assimilation was always expected to create casualties in the short term, especially among the people from the desert heartlands who were thought by many to be '… socially backward, and hidden by a barrier of language which makes contact with Europeans difficult' (Lockwood 1964, 7).

For Katingura Tjungarrayi, Pinta Pinta Tjapanangka and the other Pintupi, the great wave of death and sickness rippling through their society was a disaster beyond all previous experience. According to Pinta Pinta, 'In the bush we weren't in poor health, no. We weren't always sick as we went. I only became sick when I sat with the white-man' (1989, 5).

Pintupi recall they were always *purrka* (tired), not surprisingly, given that they were suffering what was described as a 'universal history of disease' (Davis et al. 1977, 52). Tatz described the major health problems as infantile diarrhoea, gastroenteritis, respiratory infections, skin infections and failure to thrive in babies (1964, 126). Epidemics raged through the camps, and a people with a great horror of the dead, whose own custom was to move far away to a different country after a death, were ordered to return to the very houses where their own relatives had passed away.

Pintupi believed their *kurrunpa* (spirit), located in the pit of the stomach, had been *kurrunpa mantjinu* (snatched away) by having their handprints and photographs taken by officials and through their names having been written down. This knowledge by strangers of the 'essence' of a person was felt to be highly dangerous and produced a debilitating weakness. Survivors describe an agony of the spirit, a burning pain akin to that inflicted by a sorcerer.

Ngangkari (traditional doctors) found they were unable to cure their patients. *Ngangkari* have a *mapanpa*, or healing spirit, which they can send out to manipulate or retrieve a sick person's spirit, which may be dislodged or outside the body altogether. At Papunya, even the powers of the *ngangkari yala* (the doctor who always heals) were exhausted through overuse and drinking alcohol, which drove away the healing spirit. Doubts also arose about the ability of *ngangkari yala* to cure the new diseases brought by *walpangku pikatjarranu* (bad winds), blowing cold from the east (where whitefellas live). This failure was felt as a great loss to Pintupi at a time when they experienced unprecedented sickness.

Pintupi suffered *putulypa* (a great depression), some did not even go to the communal dining room for their food, and when they did they ate the scraps of meat and threw the rest away. The early morning wind is a messenger of illness and death for Pintupi and, time after time, they felt that peculiar cold and knew that yet another one of them had died. They cried out in shock as fire leapt from coals, 'like a wild snake', to ignite spinifex in the direction of the death.

Settlement officials guided visitors to the Pintupi camp by telling them to follow the wailing, the incessant high-pitched crying of 'sorry business' that continued day and night, week after week. Meanwhile, payback fights raged. The old men conducted their own 'autopsies', divining the cause by the shape of the smoke from the dead person's burning hair, while relatives wailed relentlessly. They could 'see' the murderer in that smoke and fashioned spears for their revenge, no matter what scientific explanations the white medical staff gave them.

Cameron Tjapaltjarri was a youngfella when his father, Katingura, was abruptly struck down by sickness and taken to the Papunya hospital, before being evacuated to Alice Springs. Within a few days the word came back that he was dead. Such events are etched into the memories of those Pintupi who lived through the first decade of contact; looking back, they now say 'thousand died', an unprecedented scale of destruction. Even the survivors were sick all the time, something they were not used to in the desert. The scattered nature of the population had prevented the spread of infectious disease, and individuals generally either recovered or quickly died. The chronic illnesses that dogged them at Papunya had been virtually unknown. Pintupi sat and wailed, crying not just for their dead but for themselves as a people, and with good reason. Chronic sickness and a high death rate were not just aspects of the initial shock of first contact, but decimated the old and the very young year after year.

In an insightful analysis of the basis of their former good health, the full importance of which has only recently been recognised, Pinta Pinta Tjapanganka said they did not need medicine in the desert, only good meat. Physical wellbeing was integral to their way of life, and was largely sustained by the food they ate. Pintupi did not have to endlessly medicate themselves or pick and choose between various foods to maintain health. That changed dramatically at Papunya. Staple Pintupi foods such as *rumiya* (goanna), *malu* (kangaroo), *wayuta* (possum) and *takanypa* (pig-footed bandicoot), together with desert seeds, fruit and vegetables, were abruptly replaced by low-quality, fatty, tinned meat, overcooked institutional vegetables and white flour.

David Carnegie noted that people he encountered in the bush in the 1870s loved salt and fat, ingredients essential for survival in the desert that were often in short supply there (1989, 226). Even so, Pintupi were forbidden to add salt to desert meat because of the *Tjukurrpa* (Dreaming) of the animal. At Papunya, they delighted in pouring handfuls of it into their stew and smothering both sides of their bullock meat with it. Fat is a prized part of food animals and those without fat are often considered not worth hunting. Later Pintupi would they say that the fatty meat at Papunya was *kuya* (bad), and while the flour was 'easy way' (compared with grinding it from seed), it sapped their strength. *Tjuupi* (honey ants) are the sweet of the desert and Pintupi women laboured for hours to find just a few, but the jam they replaced it with, opening a can with a rock and drinking the sugary contents at a sitting, weakened them. At the same time as Pintupi experienced this profound dietary change they also became sedentary, living together in close quarters while exposed to a host of lethal new diseases.

Throughout this period, Pintupi were ridiculed as 'myalls' (wild blackfellas) by the more westernised Kukatja, Warlpiri and Arrernte residents at Papunya. This was deeply felt, especially by those late arrivals, the so called 'new Pintupi', who moved to Papunya in the 1960s and whose lack of whitefella etiquette in the communal dining room was openly scorned by the other groups. John Greenway (1973, 282) witnessed the plight of a distressed Pintupi family, trucked straight from the desert and dumped in the middle of the settlement in 1966. They pleaded to be returned to their own country after receiving a drubbing from the other indigenous groups, but the official response was that, since they were at Papunya, they now had to be civilised, there was no going back. Memories of the treatment the 'last contact' Pintupi received at Papunya on the basis of their 'uncivilised' ways still linger. Even today some of those whose grandparents came from the heartland of Pintupi country to the west of Walungurru will claim to actually be from the east.

CONFRONTATION

Many whites [at Papunya] felt great hatred towards the Aborigines. Whites refused to shake hands with them for fear of catching diseases. Blacks were seldom allowed in government cars or any white car at all ... Aborigines know when you don't like them. (Geoffrey Bardon 1991, 15)

Papunya was described in a government report as encapsulating the history of Commonwealth policy towards Aboriginal settlements in the

Territory. That history involved 'a complex mixture of ideals, sustained efforts, misunderstandings, mistakes, paternalism and what can perhaps best be described as undue and unfortunate pressure' (Davis et al. 1977, 102). Even some officials at the Papunya settlement recognised that Pintupi had much to feel angry about.

Pintupi are demonstrative people, but they vented their anger in their camps rather than face their bosses, both because they worried about food being withdrawn and because Papunya was not their own country. According to their traditions strangers must not complain; if there is conflict, or they do not think they are being treated well, they should leave and go back to their own country. Yet there were limits to Pintupi acquiescence and sometimes the officials 'went too far' (Davis et al. 1977, 67).

Pintupi had not given up their weapons, such as spears, at Papunya, and when disarmed by officials they quickly fashioned more. In the face of these well-armed warriors from the desert, officials had to tread warily. Greenway reported on his visit to Papunya in 1966 that 'the few aborigines we saw around the settlement carried spears and ferocious scowls' (1973, 281). In March 1961 three staff members from Papunya went to a camp to follow up an act of 'cheekiness' and were attacked by the occupants (Davis et al. 1977, 37). The following day police arrived and they too were attacked and driven off. Subsequently a senior Welfare Department officer concluded that the trouble had been caused by the failure to meet basic needs, including the provision of blankets, money and food.

In 1970 there was a violent scene at the outstation of Lampara Bore when police and staff from Papunya tried to arrest a man for theft, and found themselves confronted by an angry mob (Davis et al. 1977, 38). Then 1972 was marked by the 'Papunya riot'; shots were fired and police reinforcements were rushed in to quell the disturbance.

The school run by the Welfare Department was another enduring arena of conflict. Officials at Papunya considered that little could be done to change the older generation, but pressure was brought to bear on them to send their children to school, in order to advance them from their 'present unsophisticated ways of living' (*NT Welfare Branch*, 1961, 26). Pintupi, however, believed that the men, rather than the children, should be taught first, as a participant at the time recalled:

> An old Tjampitjinpa [man] scolded me in no uncertain terms when I was demonstrating writing in the sand to some women. He told me that my husband should teach the men first, and they would decide whether the women and children would learn later. (pers. comm.)

A schoolteacher who taught Pintupi children at Papunya in 1963 described it in the following terms:

The kids were run down and caught and they were always trying to escape through the windows of the vehicle on the way to school. They didn't know about doors and were terrified when we closed them behind them. We spent most of our time washing and feeding the kids, malt at smoko time, dried black apricots from tins and fruit in the afternoon. We washed them and changed them into their school clothes, which we kept at school. We washed the clothes every few days to stop disease spreading. The kids were supervised all the time to make sure they ate their food and we took them to the toilets every half hour to get them used to the idea. We had no contact with parents whatsoever, except when they were angry. Parents confronted us when we cut their children's hair, but the kids had terrible scabies and lice. What else could we do? (pers. comm.)

Forced separation from their children perplexed and upset the parents, who were not used to being apart from them. In the early days, when the children were held at school, their mothers sat outside wailing and repeatedly asking what was happening to them inside the building. They would call and wail non-stop and, although they sometimes cried all morning, their children were kept from them at lunchtime, so they would not have to be hunted down and caught all over again (pers. comm.).

Repeated attempts to make the parents bring the children to school, which saw recalcitrant parents refused access to the communal dining room, failed completely (Davis et al. 1977, 58, 103). The school bell was the signal for children to scatter, or for their parents to put them on donkeys and send them trotting briskly off into the bush and out of reach.

Law was yet another area of intense conflict. Pintupi did not relinquish their own law when they went to Papunya, so there were two systems in place. In 1962 there was an early flashpoint when a superintendent announced that only one law would apply and he had weapons (mainly spears) gathered up and publicly burned. New ones were quickly fashioned and the traditional punishments continued unabated (Davis et al. 1977, 38).

The conflict was not so much over the possibility of being punished twice under different laws, but over which law would take priority. Katingura's son, Cameron Tjapaltjarri, described this to me as follows:

There were lot of accidents. Lots of [hand sign indicating drinking wine]. *Walypala* [whitefellas] stopped us [exercising our Law]. If someone were murdered *Yanangu* [Pintupi] would come running, hungry for punishment kulatatjarra [with spears]. *Walypala* would call the police and say, [to the murderer] 'Come in here. I'll hide you.' *Yanangu* would come for this one [indicating repeated spearing into the thigh]. Police would say 'No! That man has to go to jail.' *Yanangu* got angry. Have to punish first, then go to jail. When that man came back after *tjinguru* [maybe] one year, two year, still have to punish.

Such clashes of cultural expectations caused further alienation of Pintupi from settlement life. The NT Welfare Branch *Annual Report* of 1972 depicts Pintupi as being in a state of withdrawal 'to the western limits of Papunya's water reticulation system'. A people who had relied on their own physical prowess for their survival now 'just sat', facing their country far to the west. Yet, despite their apparent despondency, they were far from defeated.

Pintupi describe themselves then as *nyinapayi walytjatjarra* (sitting with their relatives), drawing on their primary source of sustenance and strength. Ironically, the authorities at Papunya mistook the kinship ties of *walytja* for something like the western family and thought that it should be preserved during the process of assimilation. They could hardly foresee that its resilient values would override their own attempts to create the changes they wanted, as they do to the present day.

When Pintupi who had not earned their meal ticket were excluded from the dining room, their *walytja* smuggled some of their own food to them, as they were obliged to do. When the teachers at Papunya school thought that local involvement in rounding up the children would improve attendance, they soon discovered, to their dismay, that external indigenous authority had no real hold beyond *walytja*. 'The Aboriginal Councillor would tell the children to get on the school bus, but they ignored him, that is until their own family was involved' (Heffernan 1977, 2).

Although they reeled from the deaths and sickness at Papunya, Pintupi still had much of what is important to them: shared identity, affinality, and ceremony and, as Myers shows (1986b, 433), these continued to represent the basis of their access to resources. If these priorities defied the ambitions whitefellas held for them, Pintupi had realised their value in new circumstances and were not about to give them up. In particular, kinship was the great strength they drew on and it survived because of their largely voluntary, banded migration. As Stanner, writing about the Aborigines he knew, observed, this particular aspect of contact history is of primary importance for the future of such societies, since it enabled them to maintain a 'self-will and vitality' (1979, 48).

SURVIVORS AND EXPLORERS

How does one deal with what changes and yet stays itself?
(W E H Stanner 1979, 42)

The 'last contact' people were, and still are, considered by many outsiders to be the most 'traditional' indigenous society of all. This is ironic because they have survived, not by resisting all change, but by embracing much of it.

Kayleen Nungurrayi, one of Cameron's daughters, with bush tucker, 2000.

When the so-called 'new Pintupi' arrived at Papunya in the mid-1960s, the officials were so shocked by their demeanour that they re-appraised their opinion of the other indigenous residents who, they now decided, had made considerable 'progress' after all. Pintupi were described as an 'inflexible, primitive people who may lack the capacity to make changes in their systems of belief and social organisation' (Davis et al. 1977, 28). This was thought to be their vulnerability, they needed to change in order to survive in the modern world but the slightest change would surely destroy them.

This judgement proved to be quite wrong. Pintupi are adept at mastering the challenges of all manner of forbidding environments and, like all Western Desert people, are in many respects open, outward-looking and innovative. Pintupi were the very opposite of the exotic 'lost tribe' of their popular portrayal. They were, and are, culturally and linguistically dynamic, constantly borrowing and adapting through their contact with other groups.

The way Pintupi understand the world facilitates this flexibility because it does not lock them into particular relationships, but provides a rationale for establishing new ones. For example, the Dreaming is not a rigid code to which their belief system is shackled, but it is progressively discovered, like a book gradually unfolding to the interpretation of 'readers' according to their changing needs. Myers shows that its 'management' by Pintupi includes its linking to new sites and their occupants, thereby legitimising social relationships with them (1986a). This was demonstrated in 1974 when some Pintupi wanted to move from Papunya to Kungkayunti (Brown's Bore), 136 km to the south-west. They justified their rights of residence there to the Luritja owners on the basis of a recent revelation of Dreamtime women having danced their way from Kungkayunti along a creekbed to their own country far to the west.

Pintupi celebrate the flexibilities of relationship above dogma, networking themselves to tap the diffuse resources of a range of groups in the desert. The high value assigned to negotiability proved its worth when they faced the white interloper, who offered attractive resources and complex challenges alongside appalling casualties. Just as it had been essential to share identity with other groups in the desert, to be 'countrymen' with them, they now sought ways to please and encourage a relationship with whitefellas.

While this contact with whitefellas brought enormous upheaval, Pintupi were never merely grim survivors, clinging to a receding past at Papunya. They already knew there was no going back to bush life, a change they would come to identify with the sudden disappearance of many of their traditional food animals. Pintupi believe that the very existence of these animals depended on themselves, they were literally 'wanting to be hunted'. As Mick Namararri Tjapaltjarri said, 'We ate them but we left them behind' (1989, 7).

Pintupi were exploring what life could be for them, what Stanner, who witnessed the settlement of many indigenous groups, calls 'exploring a potential of their structure, a people taking advantage of its flexibility' (1979, 47). Pintupi seized an opportunity they saw at Papunya and, although their gamble presented far more challenges than they could ever have foreseen, its possibilities did not altogether disappoint them.

The Pintupi response to the Australian state has largely been ignored but, as Nicholas Thomas has pointed out, the 'culture of colonialism' is also denied its complexity, just as it denies the complexity of those it seeks to subjugate (1994, 61). Despite the inflated rhetoric of the assimilation policy as 'deliberately planned social engineering programs ... in which culture conquest of a minority group is the theme' (Davis et al. 1977, 25), the practice was anything but coherent, thereby providing openings for the exercise of Pintupi creativity.

It was not easy for officials bent on 'civilising' the Pintupi to make any headway with a people habitually armed with deadly spears. Although the settlement was abundantly staffed, most officials soon gave up and preferred to spend their time in their air-conditioned cottages. 'Yes, a pity', John Greenway was told when he asked where the Papunya administrators were, but then the view was that 'the people were incorrigible and quite dangerous. Best to leave them alone' (Greenway 1973, 280).

In any case, there was no sustained agreement as to exactly how the desert dwellers could be transformed into dedicated, productive members of western society and Colin Tatz (1964, 271), who found an overwhelming 'irregularity of intent', concluded that policies were often incompatible. Jeremy Long (1964a, 81) commented that 'if one takes the position that deliberate efforts to change the attitudes and values of a people is not morally justifiable, then it may be desirable that settlement staff should not be equipped or motivated to set about the job systematically and efficiently.' While condemned by observers as hopelessly inefficient, it was rarely considered that indigenous people, not desiring to be assimilated effectively, subverted the policy to something more akin to the earlier policy of protection.

Pintupi were not assimilated, but they embraced many aspects of their new world as surely as they rejected others. While officials were complaining about their inability to change, the Pintupi dialect was moving towards the more widespread, and higher status, Luritja, while also incorporating some of the English needed to describe new concepts and technology, and to communicate with whitefellas. Pintupi readily accepted the whitefella names they were given, not just because of their utility in dealing with officials, but also because this allowed them to keep their real names secret and thereby protect themselves.

They were beginning to adapt to living in large groups, and the intense fighting that went on at Haasts Bluff gave way to less harsh regimes. For example, people no longer insisted that medical treatment be banned after punishment, and soon it became more acceptable for people to have their wounds dressed in the clinic rather than crawl away into the bush to either recuperate or die. Settlement also presented the opportunity for Pintupi to realise some of the ideals of their society. For example, Long (1964a, 78) noted that, prior to settlement, marrying the most acceptable partner according to Pintupi mores may actually have been less achievable than after, when the larger population allowed for social conformity.

Pintupi were not passive either in their changed material environment; they were part of a vast network of indigenous trading relationships that sprang up in response to the introduction of desirable new western goods (Graham and Thorley, 1996). In the 60s Pintupi turned to the use of cast-off metal to make *piti* (dishes) for carrying food and water, and used glass from the thick base of bottles, instead of stone, to produce knives with a razor-sharp cutting edge. A mere decade or so later they were seeking roads to their outstations and demanding bores on them, as well as vehicles. While Pintupi refused to live in the settlement housing (which was comprised of huts separated by barbed wire), they did not reject the idea of having houses per se, and salvaged scrap metal to build movable shelters to their own design.

The devastating casualties that occurred initially at Papunya belied a people eager to colonise new elements on their own terms, in ways which suited their own purposes. That Pintupi were blamed for everything that went wrong at Papunya was actually a measure of their success: rather than succumbing to their new environment they sought to control and use the vagaries of policy and its administration by instigating their own changes.

At first officials claimed that Pintupi would never be able to leave the settlement because they were incapable of mastering the technology of modern transport. Then they complained that they wanted not merely to get lifts in their cars and trucks, but '[they] always want to sit up front' and soon were asking to be allowed to drive the vehicles themselves (Davis et al. 1977, 22). Far from being daunted by transport technology, owning cars became the preoccupation of Pintupi, with card games enabling winners to accumulate enough money to buy one for their own family. While the authorities at Papunya lamented the way they sat around gambling and then 'wasted the money on motor cars' (38), Pintupi defied the preconception that they were incapable of adjusting to a money economy. They adjusted in their own way, subverting the 'proper' use of money, not to live in one place like whitefellas but to become mobile once again.

Certainly for Pintupi, as Robert Tonkinson observes with respect to another Western Desert group, the Mardu, located at Jigalong (1991, 169), mobility also meant more access to liquor and problems of drunkenness . Yet the use of alcohol should not be too readily attributed to a 'colonised status', 'alienation' or 'socio-economic deprivation'. For all its apparent dominance, the assimilation policy enforced merely a brief interlude of inertia in a vast history of travel. Now there were new possibilities to explore, and an adventurous people with family connections across the vast desert elaborated their journeying with renewed zeal.

Pintupi colonised cars to regain their mobility, creatively using a new technology to pursue their own plan of life. By the 1970s, cars were used for hunting, to get to ceremonies, and to visit relatives. In following these pursuits Pintupi were unrestrained by whitefella conventions of how a car should be used. For example, they mastered the art of driving on wheel rims after the rugged country shredded their tyres, while whitefellas were known to have perished because they did not even consider continuing with flat tyres. Pintupi just kept going over massive sandhills and flooded creeks, with many hands manoeuvring cars where even four-wheel drives could never go.

Cars also became useful instruments for expressing anger, being driven around Papunya loudly at high speed, though not altogether recklessly given the consequences of actually hitting anyone. The complete lack of official enthusiasm for Pintupi use of cars, kept alive briefly by Pintupi mechanics and then discarded, was (and still is) of no account to them in their adoption of vehicles. The task of repairing cars was also unconstrained by convention: when necessary cars were (and still are) simply flipped onto their sides or roofs to allow access to mechanical parts. Clutch parts shaped from mulga wood were found to briefly work, and windscreen washer pumps could be substituted for broken-down fuel pumps.

As Nicholas Thomas notes, '"Culture" is not tradition but what people do, whatever that happens to be' (1999, 10). Yet the 'misuse' of cars and money at Papunya earned Pintupi special scorn from the officials, who lamented simultaneously their lack of assimilation and the 'destruction' of a distinct culture. Hannerz explains that this denial of the validity and worth of anything drawn from the centre to be used in 'corrupted' ways by a society at the periphery is deeply ethnocentric: 'There is little question of cultural difference here, but rather of a difference between culture and non-culture, between civilisation and savagery.' Moreover, such a perspective of corruption 'posits a very uneven distribution of virtue' (1991, 109).

Despite, rather than because of, the multitude of training programs aiming to integrate them into the workplace, a successful industry sprang up. Pintupi like Willy Tjungarrayi, Pinta Pinta Tjapanangka and Uta Uta Tjangala produced paintings of such presence and power that they defied the stereotype of people who had been crushed by 'assimilation'. Thomas contends that it is the innovation in this art that is its most extraordinary feature, and that such an adaptation of wholly new media to produce work of 'palpable strength' is virtually without precedent in any art history (1999, 197–8).

Like other changes, the art industry was not, and could never be, imposed on Pintupi, but they demonstrated that they could be ruthless with their own culture. The idea of commercialising Dreamings initially provoked a storm of dissent between different generations and those with differing contact histories. They argued about what could be represented, yet realised ultimately that it was acceptable to paint *Tjukurrpa* because 'what is most secret can be least hidden if there is no real recognition' (Amadio and Kimber, 1988, 27). The debate was never just a matter of tradition versus the new, for sometimes tradition drove innovation, as when a famous artist passed away and his son reworked his own paintings to revolutionary new designs, lest relatives be reminded of the dead man.

LEAVING PAPUNYA

> Those Aborigines I know seem to me to be still fundamentally in struggle with us. Their struggle is for a different set of things, differently arranged, from those which most European interests want them to receive. Neither side has clearly grasped what the other seeks. (W E H Stanner 1979, 42–3)

Papunya was 'too lonely' — it was *ngurra kuya* (a bad place) because too many relatives died there, but that was not the main source of Pintupi discontent. They say they felt like strangers which, to the other indigenous groups, they were, because it was not their land. They wanted the power of access to the whitefella 'bosses' and their resources, but visitors cannot speak out, they must listen. Pintupi wanted their own place, where they could assume the role the owners of Papunya enjoyed. Cameron Tjapaltjarri explains it:

> *Walypala* (whitefellas) talked to themselves — they didn't talk to us. They didn't ask us for tea. We had to wait outside, not inside. They said, 'You mob sit down over there'. Not level. If Ya<u>n</u>a<u>n</u>gu (Pintupi) and *walypala* got in a fight the police would come straightaway. They didn't talk about it, they didn't say, 'Who started this fight?' They just took *Yana<u>n</u>gu* to jail. (pers. comm.)

If living at Papunya was unsatisfactory, leaving was immensely difficult. It was not just a matter of walking back into the desert and, while officials agreed Papunya was not suitable for them, they were rarely willing to actively assist their leaving. Ironically, it was 'dependency' on social security payments that helped set Pintupi free, allowing them to live in places other than Papunya while still getting a subsistence living. Their movement back to their own lands was certainly an escape from wardship, but it was not a refuge from welfare.

A few individuals, in the face of official ambivalence and private obstruction, started the exodus from Papunya. By 1966 a camp at Alumbra Bore had grown into a sizeable settlement, and two years later more than a hundred Pintupi left Papunya to live on the outstation of Waruwiya, some 60 km to the south west. They returned to Papunya a year later, to camp on its western fringe looking out towards their own country.

Pintupi were soon asking sympathetic whitefellas to help them leave again and the timing was now fortuitous, for in 1973 assimilation was out, self-determination in. Pintupi had never really believed that the services they wanted would ever be provided on their own far-distant country, but now there was an opportunity for a people who sought their own terms of life. As Rowse observes, 'Indigenous agency would now be rendered in terms of its moral plenitude and cultural authenticity rather than its ethical lacks and historic attritions' (1998, 41).

A submission to the government was prepared, calling for the 'relocation' of Pintupi, and on the strength of the request alone a few Pintupi moved to Yayayi some 25 km west of Papunya. Some were so keen to get there they simply walked out and soon there were 350 people living there and at Kungkanyunti. The officials saw these attempts to leave Papunya as holidays, or breathing spaces, for a people who did not fit settlement life. They were convinced that, although Pintupi went 'walkabout', they would inevitably come to their senses and return. Pintupi insisted that they wanted their own settlement built at Yayayi, not merely as an outstation or appendage of Papunya, but this was an idea not shared by the federal Department of Aboriginal Affairs (Stead 1986, 5).

With enthusiastic whitefella support, this was a period of unprecedented experimentation. Permission was sought from the old men for the women and children to be taught a vernacular literacy program and a *walytja* school was started at Yayayi. Whereas at Papunya Pintupi had controlled none of the material goods, they, rather than whitefellas, were now responsible for highly desirable items, such as trucks and tractors, and for the conduct of their financial affairs. The whitefellas who came to work with them were caught up in the heady rhetoric of the times. They saw themselves as advisers, rather than 'bosses', and thought that self-management was an indigenous concept and, if given the chance, Pintupi would soon be running a model settlement. Most became disillusioned and quickly left when Pintupi failed to conform to their expectations. They found it hard to explain the rapid destruction of the vehicles and damage to buildings, either to themselves or the government departments still staffed with the same personnel who had administered the old assimilation policy.

As Yayayi teetered, Papunya officials considered it was time for Pintupi to stop wasting resources and come to their senses. They openly scorned the idea of Pintupi running their own settlement and thought that the sooner they returned to Papunya the better. They assisted the process by withdrawing all support, decreeing that the Yayayi people 'must find their own way' to carry rations to their community (Davis et al. 1977, 91).

Pintupi responded by trying to run their own store, off the back of a remaining truck. But they found it impossible to make their relatives pay for the supplies, while everyone insisted on being involved in their distribution because a store belonged equally to all. Money from the sale of goods, including a hoped-for profit, was to be used to purchase the next load of food but, instead, there was less and less money available. Each time the truck returned from Papunya, it carried fewer goods for sale until there was no point to the exercise.

No one could complain that what had happened was wrong. Pintupi could not demand payment from their own relatives, 'community' interests could not come before obligations to *walytja*, but the people were hungry. There were calls for whitefellas to run a store, since they could act in ways Pintupi could never countenance, such as denying demands for 'bookup' (giving credit) in the interests of the collective, but funding was unavailable for such a purpose. Part of the rationale for outstations was indigenous self-management, not renewed 'dependency' on whitefellas.

By 1975 the federal government had changed again and the new imperative was to overhaul indigenous affairs outlays to eliminate extravagance and waste. Pintupi were told that, if they wanted food and medicine, they should go back to Papunya, where the resources had already been provided for them. But, although supplies and clinic visits were irregular, it was only the death of an important man in his prime that caused Pintupi to disperse. Autonomy had stumbled on self-management and the unprecedented problems of large groups of people living together, but it was only the death that ended Yayayi.

To officials at Papunya, Yayayi was just another wasteful failure, as they had predicted all along. For Pintupi, the idea that their constellations of *walytja* could live permanently together was utterly revolutionary. Pintupi have often been described as opportunistic in their approach to government policy, but rarely has there been acknowledgment of the constraints they face in managing their lives. In hindsight, this was a time of rapid transformation, in which Pintupi were exploring the possibilities of their own society in its relationship with the Australian state.

For all the problems, Pintupi found Yayayi a welcome contrast to Papunya where, by the early 1970s, more than 100 white staff, occupying a central core of houses and services, attempted to control every aspect of their lives. Even after government support declined at Yayayi they probably would have stayed on if it had not been for the death.

Most of the people at Yayayi never returned to Papunya, they moved even further in the direction of their own country, to places like Yinylingi, New Bore and Mt Liebig, even though there were no regular stores, clinics or schooling at these places.

Breaking into smaller groups and separating for a while to lessen the tensions of large-group living was not a failure to them, but part of their ancient pattern. They said that as long as they had water they were all right and they carted it to their new camps in jerry cans. Inevitably, some Pintupi drifted back to the fringe camps of Papunya, but most stayed put until they finally moved to Walungurru.

NGURRA PALYA (A GOOD HOME)

Wilurarra mulyati ngurrarangalatju nyinapayi. We are the ones who belong to the *mulyati* spear country in the west. (Pinta Pinta Tjapanangka 1989, 11)

At Papunya, Katingura had told his son, Cameron Tjapaltjarri, 'I can't tell you about this place, I don't know the Dreaming for it. This isn't my country. This might be Arrernte country, not ours'. So while Cameron lived on land he didn't know the Dreaming for, and therefore could never really feel at home in, he was told about his ancestral country at Walungurru, where his fathers and grandfathers had lived. He learned the knowledge of this country, the creation stories of places with names like Lingakura, Tinki, and Ngutjul, a special place because Katingura's father had passed away there.

A generation grew up hearing the songs and stories of a country they had never seen for themselves. The same children who drove the teachers at Papunya to despair with their apparent inability to learn memorised the epic of a vast country they had never once set foot in.

In their tradition of acquisition and adaptation to new forms and influences, Cameron and his peers devoured the knowledge they needed for the new world in which they were forging a place. Their education was partly a matter of hearing and learning more English, but compared with their own parents they also had more familiarity with the exotic ways of whitefellas from a much earlier age.

A lack of understanding of western society had always hamstrung their parents. The first generation to come in from the desert defined the alien culture in their own terms, a misrecognition that left them endlessly baffled. Pintupi like Katingura and Pinta Pinta Tjapanangka responded to the alien culture by attempting to envelop its representatives within their own *walytja*. They insisted to the bemused welfare officers, and other whitefellas they came to know in the desert, at Haasts Bluff and at Papunya, that they were relatives of theirs, true *walytja* and they tried to renegotiate the meanings of this relatedness in order to create exchange relations with whitefellas that were equitable in their own terms.

Their children, like Cameron Tjapaltjarri, were able to acknowledge the 'other', to recognise another way of life, even if many of the alien customs amazed and appalled. They came to understand that, for whitefellas, there were relationships that existed outside of family, that government had obscure obligations to Pintupi in general, as a people, rather than through relatedness.

As is so often the case, knowledge of 'how things work' in western society was not used according to official intentions, but to advance Pintupi ambition at the time, which was to break away decisively from the regime of life at Papunya. A big mob of men, women and children living on the fringes of Papunya evoked no government response when they asked to leave, but 530 km west of Alice Springs the same group, sustained by just one hand pump, could not be ignored indefinitely. As one official put it, 'When we saw the conditions [in 1982], we knew we had to do something' (pers. comm.).

Change in Pintupi society is usually surging far beyond, and away from, official descriptions of it. The movement of Pintupi back to their own lands, to the settlements of Walungurru and Kiwirrkura, was by no means an attempt to return to life as it had been in the bush. Tonkinson states that, for the Mardu, the outstation movement is an 'affirmation of the values encoded in tradition' (1991, 179), but this was by no means the sole inspiration for Pintupi.

They hoped to combine group autonomy and looking after Tjukurrpa with the government services they had at Papunya along with such other items they had come to regard as essential, including transportation and money for tucker. By the late 1980s Walungurru had grown to become a settlement of some 450 Pintupi and 20–30 whitefellas, serviced by a community council, a store, women's centre, church, an NT government school and federally-funded health clinic. But this adoption of western institutions and technology by Pintupi should not be mistaken, as it so often seems to be, for a desire on their part to live as whitefellas. Western knowledge does not automatically supersede their own.

Pintupi did not aspire to be autonomous in the sense of economic self-sufficiency or self-management. As they prepared to leave Papunya, they say with some puzzlement, the patrol officer Jeremy Long, who first met them in the desert, exhorted them to start looking after themselves rather than relying on government. But self-sufficiency was never their goal, they separated from Papunya to seek a new understanding with government bosses, not to dispense with the relationship altogether.

When they finally returned to their soft spinifex country, the older generation who had been born there threw themselves down and, stroking the red sand, sang the country in their delight. But for their children a return to country was not an end in itself, they had changed too much for that. Cameron Tjapaltjarri says that when they moved to Walungurru they wanted much of what they had at Papunya but, this time in their own country, they would take control, at least of the resources they needed. Whitefellas would work for Pintupi now, even though they would still call them 'bosses'. It would not be the pioneering 'last contact' generation, but their children, like Cameron, who would take the initiative, thereby revealing an unprecedented change in their society.

Gillian Cowlishaw noted the lack of recognition 'of the active part that Aborigines might have played in the retention or resurgence or even rejection of cultural forms ...' (1986, 10). In their movement back to their own lands, Pintupi demonstrated again that they were bent on fashioning their own circumstances of life, that they were not straitjacketed by their past, even if the integrity of their society is invariably recognised by outsiders only in their older traditions, rather than in any new forms.

Despite the stereotype belief that 'a sense of not belonging to contemporary Australian culture' is a devastating problem for indigenous people (for example, Pollard 1992, 13), it is precisely the forceful claim by Pintupi to their own autonomy and their insistence on difference that has sustained them. Indigenous 'autonomy' in the Pintupi case is by no means the disastrous failure that critics such as Howson (1996, 4) have described. 'Progress' is meaningful to Pintupi within their own cultural tradition and they pursued separation long before the advent of the outstation movement, and would have continued to do so regardless of resourcing. The premise that western policies determine indigenous lives is wholly misconceived.

Settlement life was, and still is, a challenging new world for Pintupi to explore and subjugate, an opening for which they express regrets only for the particular circumstances, such as the vagaries of the government bosses who went against them at Papunya, rather than the encounter itself. The few Pintupi who may remain in the bush are invariably referred to as *kuunyi tjuta* (poor things) by their compassionate compatriots. The nine 'new Pintupi', discovered in October 1984, near Lake Mackay, and who, with one exception, burned the tools of their old world and joined their relatives at the settlement of Kiwirrkura, were eagerly shown its new traditions: driving cars, football and playing cards.

It is one of the many ironies of contact history that while, for Pintupi, the encounter is in many respects a continuing voyage of discovery and an endless search for satisfactory exchange relations, it now evokes profound disquiet in many whitefellas. Certainly, government had a disastrous effect on Pintupi, destroying not only infants, children and old people, but also many strong, healthy adults who were in their prime when they went to Papunya.

However, while successive governments flounder around trying to fulfill the obligations and responsibilities they can only relinquish when Pintupi achieve 'equality', Pintupi themselves are creatively negotiating lives from the new opportunities at the interface with western society. As Howell explains, 'much as we flatter ourselves that an inevitable destruction follows in the wake of western ideas, products and practices, many ... small-scale societies are alive ... in most parts of the world, taking or rejecting western influences as they deem appropriate' (1995, 171).

It is a mistake to believe that two disparate societies should both be on the same path, just because historical circumstances have led to them sharing the same continent. Like those small-scale societies described by Howell, Pintupi are far from preoccupied with western ideas, or the well-intentioned advice they receive from outsiders, or the ambitions other Australians have for them. Instead, in their Western Desert settlements, Pintupi are forging their own vibrant contemporary society, imbued with its own unique forms and meanings.

Omay Christobel Nampitjimpa, one of Cameron's granddaughters, playing telephone, 2000.

CHAPTER 2
THE CONTEMPORARY
INTERFACE

Indeed if one tried to invent two styles of life, as unalike each other as could be,
while still following the rules which are necessary if people are to live together at all,
one might end up with something like the Aboriginal and European traditions.
(W E H Stanner 1979, 59)

This account of the contemporary interface of Pintupi and western
society is based on personal experience, arising from my own relationship
with Pintupi. Although, as the school Principal at Walungurru, my role
is viewed by the dominant society as the bearer of important social justice values, Pintupi dismiss institutional managers on their settlements as
mere 'bosses for paper', with little authority or influence over people.

This disdainful assessment of whitefella managers is inevitable when
western institutions, with their own particular forms of accountability,
are situated in a culture where the authority of 'bosses' is, as Myers
shows, 'sustained by generosity in providing access to valued resources
("looking after") rather than [through] withholding them for the
greater good' (1986a, 265).

When I arrived at Walungurru in 1988 some of the school funds
had been loaned to school workers and my first, rather invidious, task
was to collect the money in order to acquit the grant from which funds
had been accessed. Although most of the loaned funds were eventually returned, it was made clear that, far from occupying any high moral
ground in bringing the school finances under control so that new funding could be applied for, I was actually behaving very badly. As their
boss my concern should have been for their welfare, and by putting
the proper acquittal of institutional funds above this I had reduced my
status and authority.

Managers who withhold 'institutional' resources from Pintupi, as individuals, in order to fulfil their official purposes, are considered to be 'hard' bosses, careless of relationships through their unreasonable greed. 'Holding' assets in a western institution is always contested on a family-based Pintupi settlement and it is bosses who are held accountable on both sides. In an attempt to overcome this recalcitrance, and encourage proper behaviour, whitefellas are usually assigned skin-names that prescribe a relationship with Pintupi, beyond the domain of the western institution.

The frequently contradictory, sometimes vexed, yet always intimate character of my own relationship with Pintupi mirrors much of the contemporary interface between them and the non-indigenous society they confront. In every sphere of the relationship the differences have been profound, complex and generally intractable but, of the two societies, it is Pintupi who have usually managed to maintain a cheerful and confident exploration of the possibilities that contact between them offers.

PINTUPI COUNTRY — 'SITDOWN' COUNTRY NGURRA PALYA (A GOOD HOME)

> The Pintupi emphasis on extensive sociality among individuals, once rooted in the requirements of a hunting-gathering economy, has proven important to settlement life, sustained by the dependence on intermittent welfare payments ... settlement conditions have also allowed people to elaborate the ties of relatedness that are valued in and of themselves. There has been an increase of social production. (Fred Myers 1986a, 262)

Welfare is considered by David Pollard to be 'a disempowering experience engendering passivity' (1992, 15) for indigenous societies, because this is the case in western society, and movement away from welfare towards equality of employment is taken by the Council for Aboriginal Reconciliation as a measure of the success of social justice and reconciliation (1995, 22).

However, welfare actually enables many Pintupi to maintain their chosen lifeways, to follow their own preoccupations with *walytja* and maximise their economic and political autonomy. Altman notes that, 'The payment of welfare allows indigenous people to pursue their own prerogatives ... and this autonomy is often more highly valued than high cash income levels' (1987, 28). Indeed, King argues that '[t]he extent to which the state organizes culture ... depends on material conditions' and welfare disempowers the state in this regard (1991, 17–18).

Many Pintupi are on welfare, but they are far from passive recipients of it. They are shaping representations of themselves in their relationship with government in ways that fit their own view of the world and serve their own purposes. As Thomas shows:

Hunting fire at White Tree Outstation, near Walungurru, 2000.

[C]olonial discourse has, too frequently, been evoked as a global and trans-historical logic of denigration, that has remained impervious to active marking or reformulation by the 'Other'; it has figured above all as a coherent imposition, rather than a practically mediated relation. (1994, 3)

Although unrecognised by the dominant society, Pintupi have developed their own patron–client explanation of their relationship with the state, traced by Myers to the hierarchical relationships that dominated traditional life, in which 'the capability of seniors to "look after" dependents in a material sense was the moral basis of their authority' (1980, 313). At Haasts Bluff, Pintupi believed they were 'held' by Pastor Albrecht, while at Papunya the letter, though certainly not the spirit, of the duty of whitefellas to 'look after' them continued, as it has right down to the benevolent policy of social justice, with a few anomalous attempts to encourage Pintupi self-reliance. The relationship is seen by many in the wider society as too costly, and inherently one-sided, but Pintupi have also paid, including the untold costs of half a generation wiped out at Papunya.

Of course, the Pintupi view of the relationship is frequently challenged by government representatives. They impress upon them the fact that the money they receive comes from taxes paid by people who, unlike most Pintupi, are working. However, such attempts to reduce whitefella responsibilities are seen as nothing but a perfidious attempt to deny the relationship the dominant society itself has defined. Whitefellas had demonstrated a readiness to 'hold' them as a people, just as each generation of Pintupi 'holds' the next, when they set up ration stations and carted unprecedented quantities of food into the furthest reaches of the desert.

Now this relationship is defined by the dominant society as 'dependency' and many other Australians rail against it, complaining that groups like the Pintupi are not looking after themselves, and should show gratitude for the assistance given them by becoming more like proper members of western society. Or the federal government announces, without ever once discussing the matter with Pintupi, that it is only by eliminating welfare dependency that our two societies can be reconciled.

Pintupi have kept their part of the bargain, living in settlements under various arbitrary administrations and participating, in a somewhat desultory fashion, in the plethora of programs devised for them. They naturally consider it treacherous of government to try and foist the responsibility for their physical well-being back onto them, especially now that the traditional life they were enticed away from is utterly irretrievable. Attempts to change the arrangement they believe was mediated with whitefellas have always been greeted with dismay, and the explanation that whitefellas are becoming 'lazy'.

Cowlishaw argues that 'The indigenous gloss which anthropologists put on such interpretations ... [as] "looking after" is in danger of becoming another stereotype which positions Aborigines as people who misapprehend their obligations and the realities of the modern world' (1999, 325). But Pintupi are modern people who have interpreted their contemporary world in their own way, and they angrily denounce arguments that permit governments to deny their responsibilities to them.

The desire of the wider society that Pintupi should begin to take more responsibility for themselves is dressed up in self-congratulatory terms, such as releasing them from the 'bonds of dependency'. Yet Pintupi have themselves rejected any felt loss of control over production, or dependency, attributed to other indigenous societies (for instance, Bell 1993, 102–3). Instead, they have elaborated their own traditions and through these they couch 'dependency' in terms of the debt which the government incurred by taking them in from the desert and which it is fully expected to continue to repay. Mick Dodson, the Aboriginal and Torres Strait Islander Social Justice

Commissioner condemns 'the master/subject relationship which has long characterised non-indigenous relationships in this country' (1994, 129): this is precisely the relationship Pintupi encourage, since, in their polity, the 'masters' have many obligations to them. They experience no more feelings of dependency than someone in the wider society living on the proceeds of a profitable if somewhat unpredictable investment.

Therefore, far from welfare destroying their relationship with government, it actually perfectly matches their own understanding of how it should be. As Tonkinson notes, Western Desert indigenous people see power in Australian society as inexplicable (1991, 160); yet although Pintupi do not understand its workings, they are not at all puzzled by their particular relationship with the state, for which they have forged their own logical explanations.

'Pintupi children have a great deal of autonomy'

Pintupi boys playing on roof, 1995.

Francine Nampitjinpa out visiting, 1996.

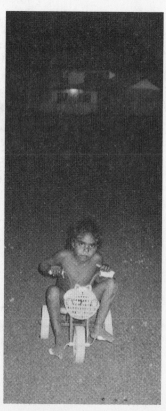

GROWING UP STRONG

> ... how they have adapted themselves to that bitter environment so that they laugh deeply and grow the fattest babies in the world. (Donald Thomson 1975, 4)

A car pulls up at the dusty airstrip at Walungurru settlement, where a plane is waiting to take teenage Pintupi students to an indigenous boarding school in Alice Springs. Three whitefellas, the author, another teacher and the pilot, are waiting by the plane. The relatives of a boy who is supposed to be going on the plane get out of their car and walk towards it, but the boy hangs back, head down, reluctant.

Mother: *Tjungarrayi* [skin-name]! *Ngalyarra! Wala wala!* Come quickly!
(The boy's head hangs even lower, and he shuffles his feet in the sand without moving away from the car. The boy's relatives begin to coax and cajole him.)

Mother: (to author) Other boys going?

Author: Yes. He'll have three friends from here. Come on *Tjungarrayi* get on the plane, *malpa tjuta, kuka palya, kungka tjutaku* [you will have friends, good meat and girlfriends].

Mother: (laughing) *Palya* [Good]. *Kulini Tjungarrayi* [Do you hear that *Tjungarrayi*]?
(The boy, still hanging back, gives a perfunctory shake of his head.)

Pilot: Well! Looks like he doesn't want to go.

Mother: (angrily) *Ngalyarra. Walypalalu pungkunta* [Come on, or the whitefella will hit you].

Author: (to pilot) She's saying we'll hit the kid if he doesn't go.

Pilot: What!
(The boy picks up a rock.)

Mother: *Mulyarra paluru* [He's angry].
(The boy throws the rock in the direction of, but a fair distance from, the group waiting for him.)

Teacher: He's a 'cheeky' one.

Mother: (proudly) *Yuwa* [Yes], and this one (pointing to her other, younger son).
(The family begins to walk back to the car.)

Mother: (to son) *Ananyilatju. Nyuntu ngaangka nyinanyi* [We're going without you. You can stay here].
(The boy begins to cry noisily, rubbing his eyes.)

Mother: *Kuunyi. Ngulurringu* [Poor thing. He's frightened].

Author: *Yuwa* [Yes].

(The family gets back into their car and start the
engine. The boy stands nearby, his crying reaching a
new pitch. He lies down in the sand dejectedly, cover
ing his head with his arms.)

Mother: (compassionately) *Pakara kalpakati* [Get up and
climb in].
(The boy climbs in the car, and they drive back to the
settlement.)

The above description could just be that of a recalcitrant teenager
whose sulky resistance is allowed, perhaps through the short-sighted-
ness of his parents, to preclude him from the best chance he has to get
a secondary education, a critical ingredient in the social justice package
offered to him. Yet Pintupi caregivers, who consistently give in to their
children's demands for compassion, are neither short-sighted nor
neglectful. On the contrary, they carefully 'grow up' the next generation, a process which does not simply happen by itself, but which
demands their close attention.

Pintupi parents have a perfectly clear idea of the society into which
they are socialising their children, and the personal qualities they will
need to prosper within it. Their parenting is not mistaken, or perverse,
merely because it does not match the expectations of outsiders. It is
designed to produce adults who are good Pintupi citizens, who will
be successes in their own society. It is a source of constant amazement
to most whitefellas that, while Pintupi caregivers want their children
to have mainstream benefits (such as a western education), they will
not compromise their ability to function in their own society to gain
these.

'Growing up' children means 'holding' them and, while there is no
lack of rules applied to this important task, there is no place for overt
discipline or control where the will of one generation is pitted against
that of the next. In their intense nurturing, caregivers are proud of
their strong, 'cheeky' children, even though their autonomy often precludes them from many of the benefits of 'equality'. The sight of a
grandparent bringing children to school, only to take them back home
if they protest, is not unusual. Similarly, children playing on the roofs
of settlement buildings rarely provoke adults to intervene, even though
they would not only be grief-stricken, but also severely punished by
other relatives, if an injury occurred.

The urgent preoccupation of schools and health services is on outcomes which match those of other Australians, but for parents to override the wishes of a child in trying to achieve them usually creates far
more problems than it solves. Known from birth by skin-names signi-
fying a place within the web of kinship relationships, children express

anger and grief when their will is thwarted, compelling relatives to intervene forcefully on their behalf. Not to do so would be to show a shameful denial of relationships, which in Pintupi society offer unqualified support and acceptance.

ACHIEVING STATUS

> Those nomad aborigines taught me so many things outside my own line of reasoning. (Bill Harney 1995, 150)

Long-term whitefella residents on Pintupi settlements are sometimes considered to be honorary members of the Pintupi families who adopt us. We have negotiable obligations as family members and, for their part, Pintupi extend their own custodianship to include us.

Pintupi woman:	(to author's seventeen-year-old daughter who has lived on the settlement since she was six) *Napanangka* [skin-name]! Have you been some where? *Tjinguru* [Maybe] Alice Springs.
Napanangka:	*Wiya* [No]! I've been here — studying.
Pintupi woman:	(disbelievingly) *Ilta* [True]?
Napanangka:	(sadly) *Yuwa* [Yes].
Pintupi woman:	*Ngurrangka* [in your house]. *Rawa lingku* [For a long time] — like jail.
Author:	She's studying so she can go to university.
Pintupi woman:	(angrily slapping my arm) *Kuunyi*. Poor thing. She should be outside *mungangka* [at night time] — with her friends. You should let her go.
Author:	She might have a baby.
Pintupi woman:	*Yuwa* [Yes]! Some girls having babies now — *Napanangka* nothing, *kuunyi* [Poor thing].
Author:	She has to study and work first, then have babies.
Pintupi woman:	(muttering) Cruel *nyuntu* [You are cruel].
Author:	*Wiya! Paluru whitefella* [No! She's a whitefella]. That's our way.
Pintupi woman:	Wrong way. She can't stay a young girl — no kids, grandkids. *Kuya, ngaltutjarra wiya* [Awful, no compassion].

A *kungkawara* (teenage girl), like my daughter, has little status in Pintupi society until she has children and gains the prestige of a *minyma*, with real power and influence coming only when she has her grandchildren. To marry children into strong families across the desert, to be able to travel widely and see relatives in many settlements who must help when they are visited in their own place, this is to be rich.

Family constellations are the cement of contemporary Pintupi life, so a society which aims at extending family, even to include whitefellas, while maintaining strong mutual obligations between members, now confronts one offering salvation through opportunities for individuals in education, training and work. This disagreement about what defines success in life, is one of the fundamental clashes between Pintupi lives and the assumptions of social policy aiming at equality.

SHARING AND CARING

> The qualities that feature so strongly in the Pintupi child's world — support, generosity, familiarity, and warmth — become precisely the qualities that ideally characterize relations among adult *walytja* ... [i]n moments of tranquillity ... Pintupi talk of themselves as 'all one family'. On occasions of dispute the others are not kin. Of course jealousy, envy, dislike, and greed are enduring parts of Pintupi life ... (Fred Myers 1986a, 111)

When a funding body asked Pintupi if they wanted community washing machines, the underlying assumption was that they would be used, and therefore also cared for, by everyone, because the collectivity of indigenous society has long been exalted as 'demonstrating the dependence of each on every other member' (for example, Stockton 1995, 175).

Pintupi, familiar with this representation of themselves and with the strings always attached to gifts, agreed that community ownership of the washing machines was fair. Located in open buildings, under 'community control', many of the new laundries quickly broke down, or were vandalised, as such unrestricted facilities would be in other Australian 'communities'. However, the free power available in the buildings was not overlooked by lucky people living nearby, and soon the useless machines were unplugged for extension cords, which snaked across the sand to run television sets sitting outside houses and shelters. In this way Pintupi managed, once again, to creatively use a resource delivered in the name of social justice, not in the way intended (that is, to improve cleanliness and therefore health) but to subvert attempts to 'teach' them to pay for services (electricity) previously delivered free.

Funding bodies insist on funding either settlements, as a whole, or versions of 'legitimate' groups within them, excluding and ignoring Pintupi polity, often wantonly scattering assets in their midst, believing that 'community' or institutional 'ownership' will ensure they are looked after. Then there is outrage when the lack of family ownership ensures that no one takes responsibility for them. Much higher standards of communal accountability are applied to Pintupi than to western society. Would doorless laundries in the middle of empty unlit paddocks be expected to survive long in an Australian suburb? Yet this is presumed to be feasible in a Pintupi settlement, because they are conceived by the wider Australian community to be a strongly collective society. Rather than questioning such preconceptions, government, and its bureaucracies, prefers to make incessant mistakes based on them, while Pintupi are endlessly exhorted to overcome their 'problems' and act as the community they are presumed to be. As Hirst points out:

> Socialism has collapsed in Russia and Europe, the drop-out communes have dissolved long since, every day shared households break up in disputes over depleted fridges and inflated phone bills, but the Aborigines, poor bastards, must be cooperative and share everything equally. Only on these terms will they receive funding. (1994, 14–15)

COMMUNITY OWNERSHIP

> They sustain the community not by legislation or subordination of individuals to an institution that represents them collectively, but rather by continually renegotiating their relatedness in consensus. (Fred Myers 1986a, 270)

Pintupi man:	(shaking the hand of the administrator, as is Pintupi custom when one is 'sorry' because of a death) Did you hear?
Administrator:	Yes I did. I was sorry to hear about that (death).
Pintupi man:	Can I have one Toyota to go to Papunya? For the funeral.
Administrator:	We need it for the community here — if someone gets sick.
Pintupi man:	Three Toyotas here.
Administrator:	Well yes, but the doctor needs one and then the health workers.
Pintupi man:	Can I take the runabout?
Administrator:	We might need that too.
Pintupi man:	What about — (name of Pintupi man)? He took one Toyota.
Administrator:	He shouldn't have.
Pintupi man:	Should be same law for everyone.
Administrator:	There is one rule but sometimes people break the rules.
Pintupi man:	Three cars sitting there, just sitting, sitting. Too greedy for those Toyotas you mob.

Administrator:	We're running a clinic here. The Toyotas are for health.
Pintupi man:	(angrily) Those Toyotas not private cars. Should have a meeting to talk about those Toyotas. That's (pointing) not your private car. That Toyota for everyone. You not helping Aboriginal people.

Myers' ethnography reveals that Pintupi 'are not communal' even though

> ... considerable social energy is devoted to the appearance of all being related, of being from "one camp" ... [However] [a]lthough in a sense they do stand as a group in contrast to other similar residential groups this corporate identity remains contingent rather than enduring. (1986a, 164, 257)

While there are certainly ways in which Pintupi display great community solidarity, such as in football competitions, they are not so in many of the ways policy assumes them to be. In particular, Pintupi want their settlements served by pan-community institutions, like clinics, that will treat each of them, but they do not place communal goals such as improved health status over individual and family aspirations.

Therefore, a health service must care equally for all but, contrary to the tacit western understanding of the phrase 'community ownership', it also means that individuals each feel they have personal ownership of any of the assets of the service that might usefully augment their lives. Attempting to minimise this pressure through invoking ideas of community benefit are '... without persuasive force, because individuals do not regard themselves as members of a joint undertaking to which they all have a responsibility' (Myers 1986a, 268). A community asset, which in a sense belongs to everyone, is constantly put under great pressure by individuals asserting their right to a turn, just as a family asset is placed under pressure from its individual members to ensure they get their fair access.

Providing resources under 'community control', which in Pintupi terms means everybody has a right to personally access them to fulfill their immediate needs, while insisting on full mainstream 'accountability', is one of the current means of attempting to fulfill western ideals on Pintupi settlements. It is of no account whatsoever that the ideals of 'community ownership' and 'accountability' directly contradict each other when applied to another culture. Such contradictions, born of profound cultural differences, are usually irrelevant to policy considerations.

BOSSES FOR PINTUPI

> Those who do not demonstrate feelings of relatedness with generosity are believed to be 'hard' or, as the Pintupi sometimes put it, 'like rocks'. Like rocks, they are without emotion, without recognition of shared identity, and perhaps not quite human. (Fred Myers 1986a, 115)

One of the most striking aspects of a Pintupi settlement is that white-fellas occupy most of the 'boss' roles in its western institutions. Their assumed power over indigenous people, through these roles, is often taken for granted by outsiders, yet Pintupi usually consider these administrators to be mere 'bosses for paper'.

If whitefella bosses are too directive they are called *ramarama* (mad) or 'cheeky', or told they are thinking they are 'big bosses'. Unlike 'paper bosses', 'big bosses' have legitimate power over people in certain ceremonial contexts, and can order others about. Pintupi workers may sometimes allow 'paper bosses' to tell them what to do, but they say they can work 'selves' (without direction).

In declaring whitefellas 'paper bosses', Pintupi are saying they have no inherent power over them. For Pintupi the context of power is personal; their view is that a boss must first develop a relationship with them, after which work is negotiated within that relationship. A boss who slashes his workers' pay merely because they have not attended to all their duties is considered to care very little for the relationship, and perhaps to be unworthy of being a boss for them at all. As Myers puts it, 'Hierarchy ... exposed as non-nurturant [is] rejected' (1986a, 268).

When I first came to Walungurru settlement, the Pintupi school staff patiently began to explain my obligations to them and made it very clear that, despite my title, they would not automatically grant me any authority over them. I had to earn it. Pintupi management embodies the key values of their society; it is essentially a nurturing relationship, embodying *kanyilpayi* or 'holding'. In practical terms this means giving generously to each individual, rather than withholding resources for a common good.

I was told not to treat my workers merely as instruments of production. They were, they insisted, 'not machines'. I must show compassion towards them, and they explained that, just as a school teacher 'holds' the children, so the school boss (Principal) 'holds' them and must help and look after them and their families. I was told that I must 'help Aboriginal people' and especially my new 'family', the school workers, since, as Myers explains, there are 'no limits' to the application of relatedness (1986b, 433).

When Pintupi died, I was instructed to be 'sorry', just as Pintupi insisted they would be if a member of my own family passed away. Those who just tell grieving workers to 'get back to your job' are *ngur-rpa* (ignorant) and should leave. Bosses who are *ninti* (knowledgeable) show compassion. If a worker, or one of their family members, has died they take food and blankets to the sorry camp, shake the hands of the people there, help the *walytja* of the deceased and attend the funeral. If Pintupi are 'too sorry' to work, bosses should still do the appropriate paperwork so that the institutions will continue to provide benefits for their families.

When I had stayed some time at Walungurru it became clear that my obligations had increased. Pintupi now told me that, as a result of their 'growing me up', I was no longer *ngurrpa* (ignorant) or *pina wiya* (unable to hear and therefore mad), or at least this should certainly be the case, given their patient instruction. Despite my insistence that, regardless of their best efforts, I remained somewhat ignorant they countered that, if nothing else, I must surely now know that 'business', travel, football, church, money, card games, hunting, cars and visiting *walytja* are among their preoccupations, and that mobility now takes in shopping trips to Alice Springs as well as frequent ceremonial travel across vast distances. Knowing what the real interests of Pintupi are, knowledgeable bosses, as they strongly suspected I must be, should allow Pintupi workers the autonomy to pursue them without penalty. In my recalcitrant clinging to western accountabilities I was a sad disappointment to them.

Writing about the Mardu, Tonkinson claims that community councillors are in a no-win situation as 'bosses' (1991, 168), but Pintupi have never accepted such a demeaning role for themselves. Influential men like Cameron Tjapaltjarri insist they are not bosses, managers or 'community carers', as presented in the stereotypes of indigenous leadership (for instance, Tregenza and Abbott 1995, 14). Yet in no way should the rejection of boss roles by Pintupi imply that they are dominated by the whitefellas who assume those positions.

PINTUPI AND WORK

> I have known many [Aborigines] who, intuiting something of the pressures behind the mask over our way of life, were repelled, especially by the disciplines of regular work and fixed hours, and by the social costs we bear. (W E H Stanner 1979, 54)

Pintupi have incorporated aspects of their encounter with the West in ways that serve and sustain them, and rejected those that do not. For example, work is often depicted as a source of salvation for indigenous people sitting idly in their camps, with nothing to do but talk to their relatives. According to Community Aid Abroad (1997, 3) 'all [indigenous Australians] want is the chance to work themselves out of poverty'. However, this hypothesis ignores the fact that Pintupi are primarily a social people, and spending time with relatives is the very essence of a fulfilling life.

Yuyuya Nampitjinpa and Mimala Napanga_ti, 2000.

When the workplace accommodates family life, as in the art industry where artists often sit in their camps painting, many labour tireless-
ly for long periods almost every day. Through these endeavours Pintupi
artists at Wa_lungurru sustain a global industry supplying urban westerners with their highly prized works. However, Pintupi whose options
are limited to performing work within the confines of inflexible western institutions unsympathetic to their paramount obligations to family often choose to remain unemployed.

At Papunya in the 1960s limited work was necessary to receive food
and, later, money, and many of the workers in settlement institutions
today reluctantly adopted some of the routines of western employment
at that time. In the 1970s unemployment benefits were proposed,
although some observers thought that there might be problems created when this 'sitdown' money was applied to a social order very different from the one in which it originated.

Dr H C 'Nugget' Coombs, then working in Central Australia,
believed 'sitdown' was irrational when there was so much work to be
performed in indigenous settlements, but equality arguments over-
came any concerns about inapplicability. In contrast to their Papunya
superintendents, the Canberra bosses, who supplied the 'sitdown
money', demanded nothing in return for their largesse and were rarely,
if ever, seen. With the system change Pintupi happily continued their
older traditions of daily life, most choosing to reject the now-optional

routines of employment in western institutions. Today, not all Pintupi are on 'sitdown', but a relationship with their employer based on a mere exchange of labour for money is antithetical to all of them.

The Pintupi tradition of work has always been to do what is necessary to sustain them physically and then move on to other fulfilling social activities. Their pattern of work included and, for many, still includes such activities as walking for hours in 40-degree heat while hunting and gathering prized foods and *mingkulpa* (native tobacco). Whitefellas consider this labour to be so daunting that they can rarely be persuaded to participate in these expeditions, preferring to rest in the shade of trees, waiting for the return of the hunters to share in their bounty. However, for Pintupi this activity is not considered work and is engaged in with an enthusiasm they never show for the relentless routines of prescribed activity that define western employment.

Like everything else, work finds meaning within relationships that sustain it. The concept of employment as a sustained, impersonal activity that overrides other considerations in people's lives is wholly alien and, where work is performed, it is completed between pressing social responsibilities, the neglect of which can result in physical punishment. The expectation that Pintupi pass up these duties to relatives, and the negotiating and fighting needed to redress grievances according to the code of Pintupi morality, in order to spend eight hours a day, five days a week in western employment they do not, and cannot, take seriously.

Their inevitable frequent absences create a dilemma for settlement bosses beyond the problem of achieving the outcomes for which they were employed. Using the rigorous accountabilities of western society in determining Pintupi pay inevitably leads to the untenable situation of employees, who engage in some limited work, often receiving less money in their fortnightly paypacket than those who have engaged in none and receive a reliable cheque from 'sitdown'. There is little incentive to take on a job if it means the possibility of less money, combined with the conflict inherent in trying to satisfy obligations to both societies.

As well, in a culture where immediacy is important, the meticulous processes of western bureaucracies mean that pay deductions occur well after an absence, creating a situation where workers might receive a full cheque when they have not worked and then nothing when they have. This apparently arbitrary allocation of their pay confirms to Pintupi their belief in the personal nature of the distribution of western resources, and leads to much resentment towards bosses who are seen to be unreasonably refusing to 'hold' their employees properly.

When the relationship is breached by such unconscionable behaviour, the worker is then liable to go on 'strike' until the boss finds some means of healing the rift so, rather than maximising work output, rigorous accounting can actually substantially reduce it. Ignoring absences and maintaining pay also has the same effect, as this confirms their belief they should be paid for the positions they hold, for who and what they *are*, rather than what they actually *do* in performing the work associated with the job. At Papunya in the early 60s it was reported that 'collection of pay is not seen to be earned by the performance of work, but by the mere fact of having one's name on the roll book' (quoted in Rowse 1998, 169).

It is a mistake to ever assume a commonality of meaning in even the most apparently simple transaction with Pintupi workers. Mediating the meanings of western employment is one of the most complex and problematic interactions between the two societies at the interface. The idea that Pintupi can be 'educated', or coerced, into the performance of western employment routines through the strict application of pay for work performed will always fail, because they already have their own explanations through which their loss of pay is interpreted.

Pintupi worker:	*Ngumula tjilpi* [boy who is old] (uninitiated adult male, therefore not a man – a derogatory term, but humorous when applied to a whitefella). You cheated me!
Author:	How did I cheat you?
Pintupi worker:	You gave me small pay.
Author:	I gave you more pay than you earned. You were away most of last month on business (traditional ceremonies).
Pintupi worker:	*Wiya* [No]! I'm the gardener.
Author:	Well you should do the work of a gardener.
Pintupi worker:	You can't rob me. I got big family, lotsa kids. I can't get half pay. You can't steal my pay.
Author:	You didn't work every day last week either.
Pintupi worker:	You talking wrong way. You bin sitting down here too long.
Author:	I live here.
Pintupi worker:	*Wiya* [No]. You whitefella. You don't live here. Go back to your country *mayutju mingarrtju* [hard boss].
Author:	If you want your pay you should do your job.
Pintupi worker:	*Wati ngayulu. Nyuntu ula* [I'm a man. You're just a boy].
Author:	If you work full time you'll get full pay. You were away last month. I still gave you something but I can't give you full pay for not working. My town bosses get angry.

Pintupi worker:	How many kids you got? You got no grown up kids? Nothing! You just got two kids, no grandkids, nothing – just one daughter and one son with that first wife. That one ran away. Can't find her (laughs). Son got kids yet? *Wiya* [No]! He just a youngfella. I got grandkids everyway. Not like you. *Yuwani kuwarr* [Give to me now]!
Author:	You didn't come to work every day.
Pintupi worker:	I was working here first, working long time. You came after me from somewhere, I don't know where. I saw you coming from that way (pointing east). You were travelling round. You saw a fire over here and you came, sat down here.
Author:	(exasperated) Yes, yes. I know you've been working a long time. So have I.
Pintupi worker:	(thoughtfully) You bin sitting down here too long. You might die here. I might bury you that way (indicating my backyard).
Author:	*Palya* [good]. You can look after my grave. You're the gardener.
Pintupi worker:	(laughs) *Tjinguru* [Maybe]. (Prolonged silence.)
Pintupi worker:	Lotsa kids, sons, and two daughters! (Prolonged silence.) (worker holds up a closed hand) *Kuya yalatji* [Bad way]. (Opening out the hand in a gesture of giving) *Palya yalatji* [Good way]. (Prolonged silence.)
Author:	Come and see me at home after work. I'll give you some flour.

The entrenched belief that Pintupi should be, and therefore are, keen to adopt routines of work to give meaning to what the West conceives as aimless lives, led to one of their settlements being given a CDEP (Community Development Employment Program). Part of the operation of this 'work for the dole' program aimed at indigenous clients is that recipient settlements receive a lump sum which covers the social security benefits due to its residents, plus an administrative fee. From this people who work are paid a small wage, as opposed to 'sit-down', while those who choose not to work get less than they would on unemployment benefits. The fact that most people chose to suffer the starvation hand-out, rather than work for a reasonable wage, was a source of a great deal of bureaucratic bewilderment and frustration.

Pintupi do not usually allow themselves the luxury of expressing to outsiders particular views they may have which sharply contradict western priorities. However, during discussions regarding a work creation project one woman, speaking from a wealth of experience in trying to balance work with extensive family duties, voiced the opinion to an incredulous government representative that, 'We tried work. We didn't like it'.

As she had discovered, in the clash of accountabilities inevitable in accepting a job, workers will usually satisfy no one and will risk damaging important relationships if they attempt to meet their western employer's expectations. Most Pintupi find it more sensible to avoid the conflict altogether, preferring to satisfy their family obligations unhindered, even if it means a more materially impoverished life.

Tjakamarra was school janitor for nearly 10 years, taken in 1993.

DECISION-MAKING

The Aborigines have *their why*, as well as *their how* ... (A P Elkin 1944, 28)

Pintupi stand in a relationship with government in which they defer to Canberra bosses and, in exchange, expect to be looked after by them. These bosses are believed to be sending money out into the desert, to 'hold' Pintupi in the familiar relationship entered into at first contact.

Welfare payments from government arriving regularly by plane may appear to fail to 'generate a sense of where the money comes from' as Alcorn contends (1994, 51), but they confirm Pintupi beliefs about this relationship.

If Pintupi do not like the way they are 'looked after' they may seek to increase their influence with bosses, or to find ones who will properly look after them. It is largely in seeking this power that they established their own settlements. Having accomplished this, they are conscious of their own responsibilities in their relationship with government, to defer politely to the schemes of their bosses, however bizarre they seem. However, this deference is usually in word rather than action because, unlike the days when the relationship with bosses was personal and immediate, Canberra bosses are now distant and consequently undemanding.

> It is not difficult to see that the Pintupi assimilated government actions and their relations with it to their own, indigenous political theory. In accord with their expectations, the Pintupi did — in fact — alter much of their behaviour in the presence of whites so as to show respect for the latter, as befits a 'boss'. (Myers 1980, 318)

Officials who ran Papunya found 'it ... so hard to consult with (the indigenous people) in any meaningful way. Proposals were put by the settlement staff, after which a request was made for the Aboriginals to agree, which they did with a chorus of yeses' (Davis et al. 1977, 107). In this tradition of deference to bosses Pintupi apply relentless pressure on local administrators to fulfil their own objectives but, in a face-to-face encounter with the *mayutju puḻka* (big bosses) who are *yungku-payi* (always giving), they politely acquiesce, even about issues they have been raging about prior to their arrival.

Administrator:	We want to talk with you (bureaucrat) about the housing problem here.
Bureaucrat:	Lots of communities have housing problems.
Administrator:	Well this mob has certainly been talking about housing. Do you mob (Pintupi) want to say something? (Long silence.) I can't talk for everyone.
Bureaucrat:	Your community's had its share of housing money. We gave you more than your share last year because we liked your program but we can't give that extra money every year. There are lots of other communities. At — (name of community) there are twenty families with no houses.
Administrator:	(to Pintupi) Any comment? Are there any people here without houses?

	(Silence.)
Pintupi 1:	(to bureaucrat) *Yuwa tjilpi* [Yes, old man]. (respectful term) We're happy for the houses here.
Pintupi 2:	*Yuwa. Waala palya* [Yes. Houses good].

In such a way Pintupi fulfil their part of the bargain, in return for which they expect continued patronage. That government bosses rarely meet their needs in a direct fashion does not appear to diminish these hopes or their status. However, the interactions are somewhat different once the government resources arrive in the settlement, where Pintupi are the majority society and their administrators mere 'bosses for paper'.

Pintupi man:	*Tuyuta yuwa* [Give me that Toyota].
Administrator:	You already got a car.
Pintupi man:	That car's broke. You understand. I have to go for my son — I worrying for him, might be sick.
Administrator:	At the last meeting you said, 'We can't take that Toyota. That Toyota for council use, not private. It's for council business. Can't have it running around all the time'.
Pintupi man:	(threateningly) Too hard. This not Papunya. You talking wrong way. Always saying no to Aboriginal people.
Administrator:	I'm just sticking to the rules we made at the meeting.
Pintupi man:	(menacingly) I asking you — the boss — I just asking. Asking you all the time. *Walypala putu kulinu* [The whitefella can't 'hear'/understand].
Administrator:	(after looking for support from other councillors in the office, who suddenly look very busy) Well! ... Why should I care if no one else does? This is supposed to be your Toyota, why am I the one being yelled at? You mob can be the ones to explain what happened next time that government mob come out from town. (angrily throwing keys at man) You'll have to bring it straight back and pay for the diesel.

As Myers explains, '... the most salient aspect of living in Pintupi communities is its affective basis, the reliance on emotional criteria rather than on rules as the framework of sociality' (1986a, 18). Thus a man may forcefully refuse to accept the view that group decisions are binding, despite having himself spoken strongly the day before at a community meeting, telling others that an institutional vehicle could not be used for private purposes. After the above conversation the man hotly denied to the incredulous administrator that he had 'changed his mind'. 'Decisions' at meetings are not permanent, they are often made for the benefit of the people at the meeting, in order to sustain the relationship among speakers present, to avoid antagonistic debates (Myers 1986a, 271). These decisions are not considered to be binding, or to constrain individual action.

Decisions made with great passion and intent in the past, in different circumstances, with different people, have no bearing whatsoever on those made in the here and now. The man did not 'change his mind' but, rather, the decision was re-made by changing circumstances, when the requests of relatives led him to demand the vehicle. This logic, and the force with which such demands are argued, so defies both western administrative imagination and the personal fortitude of most administrators that it often succeeds in its intent.

Western institutions on Pintupi settlements are not comfortable places to be, as evidenced by the generally rapid turnover of their whitefella administrators. Meanings are contested on a daily basis, and any western processes not defended vigorously are quickly overridden, with institutional rules detrimental to Pintupi cultural imperatives only maintained through the force of the traditions and relationships developed by the current administrator. They have no validity beyond this personal relationship, and never take root in a western institution beyond the continuity of any particular administrator. In this turbulent arena of highly contested western and indigenous values, such continuity is rare, and with each new administrator Pintupi have the chance to explain institutional traditions in ways that better suit their own preferences.

Reflecting on his time with the Warlpiri people of the Central Desert, Ted Egan says, 'Forty years later there is only one indication that I spent four years at Yuendumu flogging my guts out. Yuendumu has some fine footballers' (1997, 183). Egan returned to the Warlpiri settlement of Yuendumu and, to his dismay, found no trace of the enterprises he worked so hard to build there. For desert people those relationships with them (that, incidentally, sustained the enterprises he valued while he was there) are his achievements and, despite the intervening years, were still well remembered and prized.

Compromises between the cultural imperatives of the two societies are continually being forged in the local maelstrom of community politics. However, these hard-won understandings have no force with distant politicians, or the policy-makers of faceless Canberra bureaucracies and, while continually undermining it at the settlement level, they leave the wider political agenda unchallenged.

The author with Cameron Tjapaltjarri, 2000.

CHAPTER 3
MEASURING PINTUPI
SOCIETY

Not that we have ever been a people remarkable for an intelligent appraisal of other races and cultures. (W E H Stanner 1979, 50)

One of my first impressions of Walungurru was of what appeared to me to be a confusing and disturbing paradox. Pintupi revelled in using cars, televisions, refrigerators, air conditioners and video players and, like other Australians, many believe their lives are lacking or incomplete without them. If, as anthropologist Robert Tonkinson claims, Western Desert people have been forced into 'totally unprecedented dealings' with western society (1991, 159), in the case of Pintupi, at least, they have found aspects of the encounter very desirable indeed.

However, while Pintupi eagerly sought material goods, such as cars, they instantly discounted their material value whenever issues of relationship arose. For example, when an old woman passed away the priceless works of art she had painstakingly painted on the walls of the school were obliterated, while her personal effects were systematically pounded with rocks and then burned. On another occasion, a man publicly shot out the tyres of his car and then burned it in order to stop the incessant fighting over it by his relatives.

Although this behaviour initially seemed inexplicable to me, Hannerz makes clear (1990, 176) that the spread of western goods around the world does not mean that the globalisation of western knowledge and meaning follows along. The addition of new material goods to Pintupi lives has not led them to change the much higher value they place on *walytja* over possessions. They have not chosen to adopt western customs along with western goods. Therefore, however materially valuable, visible reminders of the deceased must be removed or obliterated lest they remind grieving relatives of their sorrow, while any object that creates too much conflict between relatives may be destroyed.

There is no cultural and developmental universal, except perhaps that there are many small-scale societies in the world assigning their own meanings to what we call 'modernisation'. Their endeavours, like those of the Pintupi, are usually ignored because, as Hannerz observes, the centre is self-absorbed and disregards the relative autonomy of the peripheries and the interplay between the global and the local (1992, 226).

A consequence of the resilience of Pintupi knowledge in the modern world is that it cannot be assumed that material prosperity can just be grafted from a western society onto their own. The ownership of desirable goods does not mean that, as individuals, Pintupi can possess, use, or look after them like other Australians. These aspects, like everything else, will depend on the network of relationships that sustain every aspect of their wellbeing.

Social justice policy aims to overcome the divisiveness of disadvantage in a single nation through creating equal outcomes in key areas such as material prosperity, health, education and employment. But Pintupi place primary value on their relationships; their interest lies in emotional wellbeing through the careful maintenance of family ties and obligations. Consequently, the connection between the resourcing of equality and the outcomes of that experimentation are infinitely more complex than policy allows.

MEASURING THE DIFFERENCE

If we can judge by the results, nothing seems to work — in education, in health, in economic development, in social progress ... [there is] the presumption that our measures and methods *should* work, and the presumption that there is something almost inexplicable in their failure or comparative failure. (W E H Stanner 1979, 342)

Measuring indigenous societies has always been a preoccupation of the West. In 1931, for instance, an Adelaide anthropological expedition took a lot of plaster casts, blood samples and body temperature readings of Pintupi and there have been many other countings, measurings and probings (Davis et al. 1977, 21). This obsession with statistics, along with the assumption that all societies are comparable, is one of the practices inherited from the assimilation policy.

Arguments based on such qualitative 'facts' are compelling, their force obvious, but their meaning is a matter of interpretation. Statistics have an aura of objectivity, as if they can provide a measure of the substance of a society but, as Begley argues, it is the political, cultural and social influences of the time that affect the questions science asks and what counts as data (1998, 81). What is chosen to be examined, and compared, is in no way objective or scientific but culturally embedded and inseparable from the social context in which the questions are formulated.

Comparing societies that are inherently very different to see what needs to be 'improved' in any of them in order to make them 'equal' indicates a profoundly conservative approach. It implies one way of living, a proposition rejected by many societies that seek to reap the material benefits of the West while firmly rejecting the idea that other people's lives are superior to their own and should be emulated at all costs (see, for example, Appadurai 1990, 1995; Hannerz 1990, 1992).

Despite this rejection, statistical analysis has long been used by politicians and policy-makers both to quantify perceived problems and to highlight their attempts to counter them. It was not so long ago that the policy focus was on the so-called 'half-caste problem' and the new science of census-taking, coupled with tools of statistical analysis, enabled the extent of this 'problem' to be demonstrated in the 1930s (Kidd 1997, 136–7). Once measured, and 'proven' by statistics, the problem then became an objective one, demanding action by authorities to 'breed out the colour'. The subsequent creation of the 'stolen generations' amply demonstrates that, as Alistair Mant puts it, wisdom is needed to see what to measure in the first place because '[o]nce the … measures are in place … the operatives are relieved, to some extent, of the need to exercise judgement' (1997, 55–6). Indeed, the purpose of measures can often be 'not to learn but to apportion responsibility and blame' (55).

However, statistical comparison is also used by advocates of indigenous groups, for whom it yields 'needs-based funding', even though this process channels funding in ways that allows no recognition of distinctive indigenous pathways of life which, inconveniently, do not conform to equality assumptions. For these societies, measuring mostly what is 'missing' or different about them, rather than celebrating their own achievements, will always be a dispiriting and demeaning process.

Choosing the 'achievements' of a western society as the yardstick against which Pintupi lives are measured, and judging their choices accordingly, creates a deficit model which sentences both societies to a fruitless and frustrating search for the right answers to what must inevitably be the wrong questions. Moreover, indigenous people are treated as an amorphous group with similar needs and aspirations, yet there is actually a diversity of societies and measurements become arbitrary when taken out of their cultural context and applied to very different social groups.

Statistical measures, which are in reality not objective but rather culturally loaded and, further, limited in their scope, can also create the impression that changes that register 'improvement' or 'progress' mean that people are happier: the opposite may be true.

And this can be the case even in those societies for which the measures have most relevance. In her Boyer Lectures, Eva Cox noted that many statistical indicators in areas such as mortality and morbidity show improvements for most Australians, yet the figures also report that people are feeling unhappier, that things are perceived as getting worse (1998, 158).

The application of statistics in policies for improving the wellbeing of people in those societies not involved in choosing the measures is even more problematic. The callous removal of their children from some indigenous people was once called progress, but actually created immense misery. According to the Northern Territory *Annual Report* of 1933, the children were to be provided the opportunity to be 'elevated to the white standard' (7); in other words, to achieve the same outcomes as non-indigenous children. As Rosalind Kidd puts it, '[t]he figures bespoke the problem: what should be done about the mixed-race group?' (1997, 137)

Mant notes that capacity for self-deception is limitless when guided by statistics (1997, 56), and measuring seems to preclude consideration of other possibilities, as if even the imagination of western society is shackled to the figures. Perhaps it is easier to proselytise than to acknowledge the virtues of another culture, however alien its forms. For instance, if longevity is the yardstick, does this mean that those societies where lifespans are longer are in some way more valuable?

These questions are very confronting as they probe near-sacred western tenets of what is valuable in human life. But if the West is so sure it measures the universal true values of life, then all its members should be willing to apply to themselves the standards they apply to Pintupi. Everyone should be prepared to make any required changes, including rejecting everything of value to wellbeing which conflicts with better outcomes, in order to 'catch up' to those groups that measure up best in areas of identified priority, such as health and education.

SHAPING EQUALITY

> Our intentions are now so benevolent that we find it difficult to see that they are fundamentally dictatorial. (W E H Stanner 1964, ix)

On the basis of decades of close association with many different indigenous peoples the 'working anthropologist', William Stanner, concluded that indigenous and European societies have 'two distinct logics of life' (1979, 324). Surely it is not inconceivable that radically different life plans will not produce identical outcomes in all areas, though it might seem perfectly natural, from the standpoint of western society, for indigenous groups to make the required 'lifestyle' changes for such a good cause.

At Papunya, Pintupi rejected the idea that they should do every-thing whitefellas do. Similarly, the statistical comparison approach is blind to indigenous choice, it makes no allowance for the possibility that statistical methods 'may reflect the priorities of ... bureaucrats, rather than those of Aboriginal people themselves' (Council for Aboriginal Reconciliation 1994a, 15). Tim Rowse comments:

> I do not wish to dispute that Aboriginal people should be allowed the choice to own property, to earn wages and enjoy the privileges of citi-zenship as most Australians have come to understand it. But the liberal critique of factors delaying that choice, and the model of Aboriginal potential it entailed, could also be culturally myopic. (1993, 36)

Both because of the importance assigned to the humanitarian val-ues of equality, tolerance and a sense of fairness, and also what Stanner calls 'our presupposition that our styles of life have a natural virtue' (1979, 44), groups like Pintupi are fully expected to want to share this self-evident good fortune. But in this endeavour lies the assumption, challenged forty years ago by Stanner (1979, 59), that indigenous peo-ple are '... lying somewhere along a uniform linear serial sequence with us', and that familiar and beneficial social change must follow programs designed to move them steadily along this line.

This assumption — that 'development' in official directions is infal-libly cost-neutral, that areas of change indicated by the method of direct comparison will always create more advantage than disadvantage — is not necessarily valid. For example, if all indigenous societies are measured by indicators which include business ownership, the per-centage of tertiary education graduates, professionals, the numbers of persons per house and, as Bucknall suggests, the number of indigenous pilots compared with that of the pilot population at large (1995, 42), then pressure is brought to bear on groups such as Pintupi to make a dramatic shift towards the western values these gauges are reflecting. In other words, they are being pressed to westernise.

While most Australians can shrug off, or ridicule, efforts to make them conform to external standards, Pintupi are in no position to do this: indigenous societies can rarely afford the luxury of outright oppo-sition to mainstream ideals. As a small minority within another minor-ity, Pintupi have not decided how 'progress', and therefore change, within their own society is to be measured, but they cannot ignore equality judgements. The fundamental direction of change is mediated by the dominant society, as it always has been; indigenous alternatives are limited to either accepting that model and making what they can of it, or missing out altogether, left financially high and dry by the west-ernisation agenda.

To expect ideals of equality to apply to societies which do not share the same meanings is incompatible with respecting cultural difference.

This was recognised under the assimilation policy, which openly aimed to eliminate differences seen as standing in the way of indigenous peoples living like other Australian citizens. Although the idea of assimilation has become anathema to contemporary thought, equality with western achievements still remains the premise of indigenous policy. As Rowse notes, '[p]eople are being asked to be self-determining within the social forms bequeathed by an era of "assimilation"' (1998, 10).

Statistical arguments are used by governments, and also by indigenous groups and their advocates, to channel funding but the inequity gap appears stubbornly resistant to their efforts. For example, the expenditure of an estimated $540 million on Western Australian indigenous education is reported to have entirely failed to lift outcomes and, according to the Aboriginal Affairs Minister, Senator John Herron, some $16,000 million expended during the thirteen years of the previous Labor government produced no significant results. Mick Dodson, the Aboriginal and Torres Strait Islander Social Justice Commissioner, commented that, even at a time of unprecedented political will to do so, 'valid attempts have not achieved the results one might have anticipated' (1994, 2), while according to the Council for Aboriginal Reconciliation even 'the special programs aimed at helping indigenous Australians to overcome their disadvantage have not been as successful as they might have been' (1994a, 19).

Some explanations for this lack of statistical improvement have centred on the legacy of dispossession, discrimination, cultural insensitivity and institutionalised ethnocentrism. The Council for Aboriginal Reconciliation argued that there is continuing discrimination, with non-indigenous cultural norms determining rules and practices for key institutions and government services, without considering that strong indigenous societies might have the capacity to negatively affect outcomes of equality at the interface (1994b, 22).

The Council also believed that a history of control and exclusion has had 'a deep and lasting spiritual and psychological impact [on indigenous Australians] … influenc[ing] the way they relate to the mainstream society and economy' (1994b, 19). The historical legacy is believed to affect family circumstances, as poverty is transmitted across generations (1994b, 21). Other explanations are also sought: Dodson, for example, cites underfunding and 'ponderous and complex' administrative structures and procedures, and 'certain perspectives … which undermine rather than promote the right of self determination' (Aboriginal and Torres Strait Islander Social Justice Commissioner 1994, 103).

Do these explanations really account for the gulf between programs specifically targeting inequality and the change that is actually incorporated into some indigenous lives? As Mary Edmunds noted on this issue some years ago, so much well-meaning work has been performed by so many agencies (both mainstream and indigenous) for 'so little apparent result' in improving indigenous living conditions (1989, 79).

Social justice policy is only the latest attempt by the dominant society to be seen to be addressing inequalities of outcome which cannot be ignored without sparking accusations of negligence on the world stage. But defining a relationship mainly in terms of what a strong indigenous society living on its own country lacks in comparison to other Australians is surely cultural blindness? By offering what is of value in the West to overcome the identified deficiencies, and caring far more that the gifts are used in ensuring Pintupi progress along official pathways, rather than enhancing the practice of their own lives, the possibility that the meanings of social justice are not the same in every culture is denied.

Western society gathers statistics with a connoisseur's enthusiasm and reverence to see if its goals are being achieved, but the things most valued by Pintupi, such as compassion, children's autonomy and 'holding', utterly defy this calibration. The dilemmas of this assumed comparability are felt by each society in the statistical equation. Both are subject to ceaseless criticism: governments because they cannot avoid ultimate responsibility for quantifiable outcomes in areas such as health and education, condemned for either not applying enough funding or for the 'wasted' billions which have not achieved equality, and Pintupi for not conforming to the lifeways necessary to produce the expected results.

CHAPTER 4
THE ASSUMPTIONS
OF SOCIAL JUSTICE

Surely, the deepest aspiration of Aborigines is to 'have a decent home, to see their adolescent daughters growing up in an environment that will enable them to live a civilised life'.
(Kim Beazley snr, 1950, quoted in Griffiths 1995, 73)

There are many fundamental assumptions woven throughout the fabric of contact history, though they are well disguised to each new generation. The prime assumption has always been that the centre is the reference point, indigenous people at the periphery have, or are, the problems, and ultimately they must do the changing. By examining such patterns of civilisation it may be possible to acknowledge the difficulties Pintupi have with policy, instead of always focussing on the problems policy finds with them.

Stanner observed that 'we deal with the present and future on the basis of what we believe the past to have been' (1979, 51). Contemporary indigenous policy has been created on the basis of a past where the complexity of race relationships is denied.

Rejecting the violence or paternalism of previous history as either horrendous mistakes or moral lapses ignores the enduring cultural differences to which early policies were a response. The identical process today is the celebration of equal outcomes as 'salvation', behind which is the continuing collision of the West with resilient indigenous cultures. To see that collision requires interrogating the taken-for-granted advantages of western society, in a particular contemporary indigenous cultural context.

EMOTIONAL PROSPERITY

The complexity [of indigenous social structure] is in the most striking contrast with the comparative simplicity ... [of] material culture ... We have, I think, to try to account for this contrast in some way. (W E H Stanner 1979, 47)

Many of the 'self-evident' ideals of material prosperity applied to Australian indigenous societies are embodied in policy launched in 1988 under the title, 'Foundations for the Future', and broadly termed 'social justice'. Articulated by the federal Labor government in *Social Justice for Indigenous Australians* (1991–92), and continued to the present, social justice has as its central objective the development of a more prosperous, just and fairer society for every Australian. These 'holistic' ideals are simply assumed to accommodate any problems of culture clash: social justice is assumed to be 'consistent with culture' (1991–92, 4).

Material improvement of indigenous lives is a major platform of this social justice policy and, like many of the tenets of the West, this is exalted as essential to indigenous lives: without it they will sink into apathetic despondency. If made sufficiently available with all its obvious benefits modelled often enough, social justice engineers believe it must surely catch on eventually. But as Parkin has argued, enquiries at the local level are very often subversive to assumed global meanings (1995, 144). For Pintupi, the possibilities of material improvement are constantly overridden by social considerations of *walytja*, an indigenous blueprint of a life which Stanner described as an 'intellectual and social achievement of a high order' (1979, 33).

The social justice agenda of prosperity requires that Pintupi take 'proper' care of their possessions. However, within extended Pintupi families each person who gains control of a possession must maximise its use while they retain control, which is always contested, and there is no incentive to take care of a resource on which there are so many demands. The lifespan of a vehicle is usually measured in weeks and if there is an attempt, real or imagined, to withhold it from *walytja* it may be vandalised, to shame the person who withheld it, or destroyed to reestablish relationships upset by the constant conflict. For example, vehicles under intense competing demands by relatives fighting over them may be publicly burned to end the fighting which disrupts harmony with kin.

Whereas using a car for hunting to the point of destruction is judged wasteful by western standards, for Pintupi it is not only wasteful but also stupid not to do so. Value is expressed through use, rather than hoarding, and it is only while a vehicle is being used that claims from others can be warded off. The owner of a vehicle which is not used is 'greedy' or 'jealous' for it, and even whitefellas, who may consider themselves to stand outside the kinship system, are considered shameless if they have a car or two parked in their yards on weekends while Pintupi sit restlessly in their camps. Protestations that a vehicle is solely for institutional use are regarded as feeble excuses for such overt greediness.

A claimant will call the owner of a desired possession by the relationship term that signifies mutual obligations, and indicate how his side has been kept, such as *yungunanta tala* (I gave you money). A request justly made in accordance with the kinship code may be repeated over and over since — unlike in western society — while there is no embarrassment in making even apparently outrageous demands, there is much shame in their denial. Eventually the owner of the possession will 'feel sorry' and lend it to the claimant. Such *ngaltutjarra* (compassion) is sometimes out of an awareness of the consequences of not helping, since to deny the rights of relatives is to deny relatedness and that invites violence. This may involve items of relatively moderate material value: for example, a man and his wife were stabbed by a relative after they refused to lend him their video player.

All denial is serious and deeply felt. Children may react to a minor rebuff by weeping in order to publicly shame a relative's antisocial behaviour. At one point parents, unable to deny their crying children, directed a store manager to stop ordering bicycles for the store because their children's incessant demands for them meant they could no longer afford basic food. At other times, because of their alarm at the decline of its store profits, community councils have directed that only whitefellas serve on cash registers because they, unlike Pintupi with their extensive obligations to *walytja*, are capable of being 'hard' in denying requests. This was despite both the availability of Pintupi workers well trained for the job and the reluctance of whitefellas to perform the work.

While the consequences of denial seem disproportionate to outsiders, the values of sharing between *walytja* are fundamental to Pintupi society and they cement relationships, both through the act of sharing and also in their remembered history. For example, my 'relatives', who I took hunting in my car and who showed me country, frequently recount and relive our shared history in that vehicle, both acknowledging the strengthening of our relationships through these trips and reasserting their established rights to travel in my car.

Walytja provide Pintupi with absolute proof of the meaningfulness of their lives, in which emotional prosperity is created through sharing with a plethora of relatives and growing up successive generations. There is a great sense of purpose and place for all in a society where everyone, except perhaps the deranged succeeds, with the responsibility for their success placed on those relatives who 'hold' them. Pintupi all have a vast network of relatives, whose rightful demand for material support cannot be denied outright. On the other hand, to be successful capitalism requires the conservation of acquired goods, with future income being used for further material accumulation. This accumulation is best achieved within the western model of a small, acquisitive, preferably nuclear family.

Pintupi maintain that only whitefellas can deny *kuru lingku* (face to face), although few whitefellas living on their settlements would agree we find it all that easy. Just as western society views Pintupi as perversely profligate with their material resources, whitefellas are seen by Pintupi as fundamentally irresponsible in valuing individual material accumulation over obligations to their relatives, circumscribing the claims they allow on themselves by restricting the concept of family to just a few close relatives with limited mutual obligations.

A Pintupi man was utterly astonished when I told him that my son, living in Adelaide, had asked me to give him my car but I had declined to part with it. He looked puzzled before saying, 'He's your son', as if reminding me of the relationship would stir my sense of obligation. I explained that I needed my car and could not afford to buy another one, but that was clearly irrelevant in this dereliction of my duty. Suddenly his frown lifted as he understood it as a normal feature of an alien culture, of which he had some knowledge. 'Ah!' he proclaimed, 'Whitefellas don't do that!'

Family accountability for and to others is irrespective of age: Pintupi cannot dismiss their responsibility for *walytja* merely because they are now adults, neither can they avoid them because of their own old age or ill health. Responsibilities grow larger throughout life because existing relationships do not wane as new ones are formed. For example, a Pintupi woman is no less a daughter because she marries, her responsibilities to her mother(s) are undiminished, and she may spend as much time at a mother's camp as her husband's.

The maintenance of *walytja,* and the emotional prosperity it represents, requires relatives to unreservedly share. Nampitjinpa, probably in her mid-forties, is one of the youngest of the 'last contact' generation. Amongst her close *walytja* she now has two brothers, three grown-up daughters and a son, fourteen grandchildren and seven nephews and nieces. In Pintupi society, grandmothers do much of the child rearing, and Nampitjinpa takes on most of the day-to-day care of several of her grandchildren. While Nampitjinpa's *walytja* have responsibilities to her, they can also demand any money she earns, any food she has, or her television set. Any disharmony with *walytja* is traumatic, so reluctance on Nampitjinpa's part is usually overcome through repeated begging or demands.

Within *walytja* there are many demands since 'dependency' has value, because '... being a relative requires regularly demonstrating the relationship' (Myers 1986a, 163). As Laughren explains, kin relations are seen as much more important 'than the idea of ... relying on your own resources. People rely on their kin well before they rely on themselves ...' (in Barnett et al. 1995, 102), a way of looking at relationships that also affects how Pintupi see their interactions with western society. Demanding from relatives, regardless of need, such as asking for money when you have your own, may look fraudulent, but it is a way of testing the relationship, of reaffirming its unconditional value.

Moreover, *walytja* is a regional, not a settlement, concept. For example, if a man dies his wife and children are left penniless and without any household goods. Publicly, at least, they uncomplainingly see all his money, his vehicle and any other possessions, such as the family fridge and television, given away to a distant group of potential sons-in-law in other settlements. Giving to these particular recipients, who belong to the group of potential husbands for the dead man's daughters, is an investment in Pintupi society that operates on a regional basis. But the deceased's family is not left indigent. Just as they are bound by a code where they must give away all their possessions, other *walytja* are then obligated to help them. The wife and children will, in their turn, make demands on the generosity of those relatives who must protect and support them.

However, this generosity operates only at the level of *walytja*. Because Pintupi have to share with many others, irrespective of their own needs or wishes, requests from those not considered *walytja* are frequently rejected. That those outside *walytja* are hungry does not compel Pintupi to give them anything, as long as they are prepared to risk denying relatedness, which is why it would be shameful not to hide their own food while expressing compassion for their predicament.

Caring and sharing, lauded as a cohesive feature of indigenous life, and a fundamental assumption in much government policy, is certainly a pivotal practice of Pintupi, but its social context is *walytja* not some abstract ideal of 'community'. Of course, *walytja* itself is not some pre-determined set of relatives and it can, at times of tranquillity, encompass an ideal of Pintupi as 'all one family' (Myers 1986a, 111). This managing of relatedness is fundamental to Pintupi society where:

> ... relations are the source of most valuables in Pintupi life, including food, a spouse, rights in ceremony and protection ... [a] network involv[ing] persons who do not consider themselves to be related ... [in which] one cannot afford to reject or ignore ties with some neighbours to concentrate only on a few other relations. (Myers 1986a, 163)

Their flexibility of relatedness is confusing for outsiders who anticipate some settled social order, however alien, with which they can come to terms in their interactions with indigenous people. They find no reliably cohesive communities or networks within them, in which they could begin the exercise of western-style accountability.

The social justice ideal of material equality, confidently proclaimed as compatible with indigenous self-determination, is actually being constantly overridden by the resilient cultural difference in what Pintupi consider responsible behaviour. When this happens, the lack of accountability is seen by mainstream bureaucracies to lie on the indigenous side. However, while the values of shared identity and *walytja* create obvious difficulties for material prosperity, this is an outcome that represents a different logic of responsibility, not a lack of it.

The apparently arbitrary intractability of Pintupi in not accepting a western interpretation of an appropriate balance between equality and their own lifeway, which naturally favours the considerations of policy over *walytja*, is seen as a frustrating hindrance in an inevitable process of change. Such a view is reinforced by the undoubted interest of groups like Pintupi in western goods. Trigger claims that, for the Doomadgee people, the 'treadmill of consumption (of western goods), with its experienced immediacy of material needs' has 'enmeshed Aboriginal people', and is merely 'resignation to what are thought to be the inevitable conditions of life' (1992, 223). By contrast, Pintupi interest in western things has a vibrant life of its own and is balanced by shared use within families, rapid disposal of those goods, and a resilient rejection of the western ideology of 'appropriate' use.

So video players, television sets and many other symbols of prosperity are highly sought after and frequently carried around the settlement as they pass between *walytja*. Used according to the values of kinship, which Pintupi describe as 'holding right way', they are of necessity disposable items, bought, used to destruction by a range of kin, then thrown away. Thus, any surplus in Pintupi society is exploited to reinforce relatedness with *walytja*, rather than to improve living standards, and any mainstream ideal of increasing material prosperity is undermined in favour of their own imperative to create social capital. Despite the dominant society's indignation at this subversion Pintupi are not at all unique in this process of indigenisation of western values and products, which is elaborated by the anthropologist Arjun Appadurai (1990) in his studies of other indigenous societies. Signe Howell similarly notes:

> ... just as we in the industrialised West take what we want from other cultural practices and make them compatible with our own, so in many cases do members of other cultures take what they want from western traditions and inventions ... (1995, 176)

A PINTUPI ECONOMY

> There are many hints in the present-day behaviour of Aborigines, e.g. the ways in which they still like to divide their disposable income, which ought to be telling us that we have not grasped even their distributive system and values, and that their theory of provenance of wealth is not ours ... Aboriginal economy was deeply principled. (W E H Stanner 1979, 371)

In 1962 Barry Christophers advocated that indigenous people be allowed more access to money because, 'If Aborigines were allowed to handle money they would learn how to use it intelligently ... you cannot teach a person to swim without taking him near water' (in Rowse 1998, 114). Certainly, Pintupi did learn quickly how to use their money intelligently, to the frustrated bewilderment of the dominant society, with its immense faith in the objective rationality of its own system.

In accordance with the values of their own society, Pintupi dispose of money as quickly as possible. A man who won a major art prize was broke a few days later and he and his relatives, who had all benefited, were well satisfied with his sagacious use of a windfall. Whitefella attempts to characterise this alternative economic system as mere short-sighted profligacy are received with bewilderment, and some amusement, by Pintupi.

It is difficult for outsiders to comprehend that an economic system that does not deliver an opportunity for material prosperity could be worth maintaining. However, in *The Sustaining Ideals of Australian Aboriginal Societies*, Strehlow argued that the indigenous system of Central Australia has none of the inequality, and consequent resentment between different sections, of western society (1966, 6). Rather than securing the subordination or domination of one group or class by another, their system operates to achieve efficient means of co-ordination between all groups, so that each group can achieve its ends more fully.

Pintupi society, which developed in an environment disposed towards feast and famine, with little point to material accumulation, has always excelled at consuming surplus by dispersing it via the kinship network. This tradition is continued with respect to resources provided by the dominant society, much of which arrives under the mantle of social justice. On receiving her superannuation payment of more than $40,000, Mimala purchased a fleet of cars for her extended family. When the money was exhausted she remarked that she did not have enough left to buy a car for herself, but there was no regret. Satisfying kin brings immense joy, while selfishly spending money on yourself, or hoarding it, produces bitter conflict.

Cowlishaw states that at the indigenous community of Bulman, Arnhem Land, 'Private ownership and varied incomes mean that it is the educated and employed men and women who have access to more resources, and other kin must rely on them' (1999, 267). But for the resilient and innovative Pintupi economy, differing incomes offer no difficulty.

> For the Pintupi, to own something is to have the right to be asked about it. The norms of kinship and compassion force one to grant the request, but one should be asked ... what do the Pintupi seek to gain as value here, and what do they lose? ... what they seek is ... to maintain personal autonomy

... [to have] others recognize one's rights; recognition achieved, what else is to be gained by forbidding access? (Myers 1986a, 99)

Everyone is 'broke' most of the time and, far from reliance on relatives being a problem, it is the life-blood of both the family and economic system. Reciprocal claims on relatives ensure everyone can always survive emotionally and economically, with both a surplus and shortfall of money useful in reinforcing relatedness between *walytja*, creating social capital and ensuring economic equality.

Because the Pintupi economy is antithetical to much that western society holds sacred, the dominant society mistakenly assumes that the absence of a Pintupi impetus towards material accumulation is indicative of a deep malaise. This then leads to a misinterpretation of legitimate economic mechanisms within their society as evidence for this preconception of wretchedness.

For example, aspects like endemic gambling are seen as mindless pursuits born of grinding poverty and despair, a product of what Hunter calls, 'the topography of poverty, broken fleetingly by the dreams of a big win ...' (1993, 252). Typically, a person will receive a welfare cheque, buy food and then gamble the remainder, which is not what is surplus to subsistence needs for the pay period, as Hunter contends (1993, 251), but is actually what cannot be immediately used.

But this gambling is not an aberration created through poverty. It operates as a legitimate means of accumulating enough cash to buy larger items, such as vehicles, in a society where saving is precluded by economic obligations to relatives. A win allows a major purchase, a loss reinforces access to the money or goods of other relatives, with neither outcome creating despair in the gambler. Through gambling Pintupi society is able to maintain its own imperatives while also acquiring desirable western goods.

Pintupi maintain important traditions in the face of immense pressure to westernise but this is not to argue that their society is either static, or its values uncontested. Contemporary lifeways provide increased opportunities to minimise responsibilities to relatives. There can be no shame in denial if one has nothing, even if one's own money has actually been secreted away. Those who receive wages may have a proportion of their money channelled into bank accounts in Alice Springs, which cannot be accessed without going to town, since that device withholds the money from distant relatives, while leaving the wage-earners 'poor' and entitled to make their own claims. The argument that 'my money's in town, I can't get it' is a valid reason to ask a relative for help, while banking also justifies a trip to town when money has accumulated.

Another response to the difficulties of conserving a fortnightly wage is for workers to prefer to be paid on a daily basis, through a small advance from their employer. A small wage can be held onto for food, while a fortnightly pay cannot possibly be kept by the individual who receives it. This mechanism allows the gradual use of money as a kind of saving that ensures individuals, or their closer *walytja,* are able to spend it for their own purposes.

It seems unlikely that the strength of kinship will, in the near future, allow more western outcomes through a societal succumbing to the pressure to hoard assets individually. Money may be saved but, while longer-term accumulation of money may allow control over how it is expended, its ultimate use still triggers the demands of relatives that are potentially too shameful to deny. If money builds up sufficiently in bank accounts, relatives may just drag the hoarder off to town to get a share of it, or they may stake out the popular banks just in case a relative decides to make a withdrawal. When the savings are finally spent there is no less pressure on the purchases; if a car is bought relatives are just as demanding when it appears on the settlement.

Even if these imperatives of the Pintupi economy are ignored, there is still no simple connection between increased income and equal outcomes in terms of prosperity. For example, more money means more vehicles on settlements, which means more travel and more of the temporary 'unhealthy' and unprosperous conditions of life, such as houses overflowing with visiting relatives and more trips to town to buy grog.

It is in the arena of material equality that the engagement between the two societies generates most heat, because both are powerfully motivated and there is much at stake. In a clash where both have a lot to lose, the creation of material prosperity, which is so vital to the dominant society's plan for Pintupi, demands changes which they can only make by abandoning core values.

A SYMBOL OF PROSPERITY

> The atmosphere is one of anarchy and purposes obscurely crossed. We picture ourselves as trying to bridge the gap by goodwill, material help and general solicitude, and are rather baffled by the fact that there seems no firm place for the other pylon of the bridge, only ground which is shifting and uncertain. (W E H Stanner 1979, 43)

The reputation of the government is always foremost in any formulation of indigenous policy: the last blueprint was obviously wrong but the latest is self-evidently right, not just logically but morally. While conjuring the illusion of a clear break with a discredited past by embarking on an internationally approved human rights agenda, it is easy to forget that every previous policy directed at Pintupi was also pursued on the highest contemporary ethical plane. At the time of their enactment policies always seem to be both fair and viable.

The policy of assimilation, like that of social justice, was closely associated with ideas about equality (Peterson 1998, 154), but it was never assumed that indigenous people would immediately embrace it. Even into the early 70s at Papunya, the government could still acknowledge that it was actually imposing health and education programs for 'humanitarian reasons ...', recognising that this course of action would be 'at the expense of self-determination in some instances' (Davis et al. 1977, 105).

Such overt imposition of equality, in an era of self-determination, is now anathema. With an eye to its present reputation, policy now aims to address inequality and the need for 'cultural maintenance' simultaneously and, far from seeing these goals as potentially incompatible, both are to be achieved by indigenous people exercising 'their right to self-determination ...' (*Report of the Aboriginal Education Policy Task Force* 1988, 2). A lack of real self-determination is still seen as undermining achievement in improving indigenous living conditions (for instance, Bennett 1999, 148). This is why material prosperity is promoted as the means to a healthy life, without in any way considering indigenous concepts of wellbeing and how these affect the health status choices people make. As a result, the outputs of social justice health programs are subject to far more complex variables than are conceded by their architects.

Because most health statistics refuse to budge despite a plethora of health programs, Pintupi are often seen as acting irrationally even though, according to social justice rhetoric, maintaining their own cultural imperatives is desirable. After all, they are merely choosing the balance between western values and their own in a way which suits their lifeways, a process the *National Aboriginal and Torres Strait Islander Education Policy* calls balancing 'participation in mainstream economic and social life with their desire to maintain Aboriginal cultural values and lifestyles' (1989, 9).

However, Pintupi self-determination creates a huge and resilient 'problem', one which is rarely acknowledged, since it exposes the gap between the official policy direction for Pintupi and their own path. It leaves both the architects of national policy and their agencies at the interface baffled and frustrated, because, despite all their efforts to improve outcomes by providing western material resources, the values underpinning the so-called appropriate use of these resources are so little internalised that the anticipated narrowing of statistical gaps does not occur.

It was widely thought that a major obstacle to improving nutrition and, therefore, health outcomes was that until the early 1990s few Pintupi households had refrigerators. It was assumed that this was why, instead of using a welfare or salary cheque to invest in a supply of food that would last a fortnight, people were purchasing for just a single meal or two and then disposing of the rest of their money. Over the next decade, as incomes increased and more Pintupi had houses, fridges became commonplace. However, this change in fortunes has not influenced spending patterns because the obstacle to purchasing more food was not lack of storage, but the demands of relatives. Anyone who keeps food in such an ostentatious storage place as a refrigerator cannot expect to withhold it from their many needy relatives, who do nothing wrong by simply going in and taking it. Any serious protest by the owner, as with any attempt to prioritise the material over relationships, creates a public outpouring of protest to shame the hoarder. In such a way Pintupi pursue their ideal of emotional prosperity over non-indigenous ideas of a healthy life.

Equity measures, such as providing new houses in Pintupi settlements, allow government attempts at redressing poverty to be highlighted even though, against all expectations, overall health statistics may not improve. This is partly because the provision of new houses is seen as a visible manifestation of concern, while maintenance of those houses once built is usually ignored or underfunded. When symbols of social justice, such as houses, are provided there is an anticipation of equal outcomes in that area, and of grateful Pintupi repaying the government by living in the houses like the exemplary members of Australian society they are expected to become. Yet, what bureaucracies see as a small price to pay for government 'generosity', is actually an extremely difficult and complex expectation to fulfil.

Pintupi values are of far more immediate, personal and social consequence than the concept of 'improved health'. These values include allowing children to have a high degree of personal autonomy, considered by parents and grandparents to be both their right and a prerequisite for growing up to become a good Pintupi citizen. They also include providing support to family by providing shelter to numerous relatives who visit, or come to stay for an indefinite period.

Because Pintupi must take in their relatives, including those who have authority over them — such as an uncle or older sister or brother — the condition of their house is contingent on the actions of others who they are not in a position to control. As well, Pintupi residence at any one place has always been, and still is, essentially temporary. Few live in the same house for years on end because where they live depends on complex and very fluid social factors, many of which have to do with high levels of accountability to family members. For example, marriage partners may separate for a time, having been obliged to fight each other when relatives they are individually required to defend fall into dispute. Many other circumstances, such as deaths of relatives, which necessitate moving temporarily to 'sorry' camps and possibly abandoning a house altogether, are quite outside the jurisdiction of the individual.

A focus on wellbeing through the satisfaction of cultural imperatives which overrides any desire Pintupi might have to improve health through living in houses in the same way as Westerners. Along with many other Pintupi, Cameron Tjapaltjarri and his family may leave their house and camp en masse in the bush at the coldest time of the year so they can have ready access to firewood, because their tradition is to travel to a resource rather than to bring it home. Living outside at this time is no obstacle, most sleep outside their houses anyway. They have an outdoor culture and feel sorry for whitefellas, who miss so much life by being constantly shut up in houses, alone or only with our immediate family.

Pintupi do not hesitate to leave their houses to go to live in materially wretched and insanitary 'sorry' camps when a relative dies, sometimes for weeks at a time, even though there may be no facilities, not even a tap. A woman whose husband has gone away does not refuse to move in with other relatives because her house is likely to be vandalised while it is unoccupied. Nor do Pintupi, who are making up after a fight, decline to live together because of the consideration that twenty people will be sharing a single toilet. No Pintupi has ever been known to refuse to participate in ceremonial life on the grounds that spending a few weeks in hand-hewn bush shelters with no facilities is unhealthy. This blatant disregard for equality of outcomes has allowed ceremonial life to flourish, as has the 'inequitable' use of settlement resources, often given over to one group to sustain travelling ceremonies.

All Pintupi have relatives in other settlements and the congestion of living with them may objectively pose health risks, but it is in no way seen as a problem. Mimala told me that she was 'broke' because she had a lot of relatives visiting and they had eaten all her food, but there was no hint of complaint, though perhaps an expectation that, as her older 'brother', I would help her restock her larder. The idea that too many relatives crowded together could somehow be a health problem is beyond comprehension. Pintupi wellbeing soars when they are surrounded by *walytja*, no matter what living conditions result. Myers observed that, 'to be among kin, to be shown affection and concern and to show it: these are what should make one happy' (1986a, 111).

Pintupi never complain that they have no space to themselves, because being with *walytja* is so critical to personal wellbeing. Privacy is not expressed in external, physical conditions, like the western idea of 'personal space', but is valued as something internal as, for example, the right to be silent irrespective of the wishes of others. Thus, Pintupi see no problem in being without personal living space, while maintaining the right to keep their own counsel to an extent that can seem rude to whitefellas, such as when a direct question is answered by a distant stare.

Pintupi express concern about the emotional wellbeing of those rare individuals who spend time sitting by themselves, while to mourn for a deceased relative by oneself is considered to be highly dangerous. Separation from kin has connotations of unbearable isolation, or *watjilpa* (loneliness), feelings which may be associated with self-destructive impulses. Pintupi who are not known to drink alcohol may do so in a strange place because they had no *walytja*, 'I was by myself'.

The primacy of *walytja* means that Pintupi will not live as expected in their new houses. A family usually lives in the largest single room of a house where all relatives can be together. Children of all ages, often in large numbers, demand the freedom of behaviour that is their right and essential in the formation of the Pintupi self. At times an abundance of relatives is welcomed to the house for extended stays to renew contact, even though they produce severe overcrowding and subsequent damage. Such visits put enormous pressure on the facilities of some houses, while elsewhere others will be left empty, and vulnerable to vandalism, because a death is associated with them, or an entire family is off travelling.

Houses on Pintupi settlements are either overflowing with people, creating unhygienic conditions, or completely empty and the target of vandalism. They have not, as yet, despite the best intentions of policymakers, been an effective health measure.

ASSUMPTIONS OF FAIRNESS

> Where is this thing called communitas, this organised social group of people who share government, who have something like lore, law, custom, folkways and history in common? (Colin Tatz 1990, 246)

Although contemporary policy proceeds in more subtle ways, through 'consultation', incentives and outright bribery, rather than force and coercion, Pintupi are still being told how best to live their lives, and there is endless frustration in mainstream bureaucracies at their propensity to prefer their own mode of living. When Pintupi vote with their feet by refusing to tread preordained pathways they are still seen to be defying rationality itself, because of the power of those myths which still portray the dominant society as the harbinger of 'civilisation', now called equality with western lives.

The objective of a fairer society for every Australian, as expressed in *Social Justice for Indigenous Australians* (1991–92), is commendable when kept to the context of the contribution of the dominant society to all the disparate groups under its umbrella. But this goal becomes more problematic when tied to expectations that treating each group fairly will lead to equal outcomes for all. When this does not happen there is a great temptation for the mainstream to engage in social engineering using the resources supplied under the auspices of policies aimed at a fairer society, or to withdraw the resources which have been 'misused'.

While western society is, itself, a long way from achieving its stated ideal of a fair society — with visible and growing gulfs of economic opportunity and outcome between many groups — it remains assured in its self-appointed position as the arbiter of equitable use of resources. Pintupi have created and sustained an eminently equitable society, but through a system that is not conducive to equality of outcome with non-indigenous society, and which is consequently considered illegitimate.

Pintupi 'fairness' cannot easily be represented to the rest of the nation. Their society disallows mainstream forms of democratic decision-making about contentious issues, with its system of advocates, opposition and vote-gathering to make the 'right' decision. They rely on a consensus model, in which one view may be seen to prevail, while those who remain silent reserve the right to ignore any decisions made, and in which it is also perfectly acceptable not to attend the meeting at all, while maintaining the right to criticise those who reached a decision without the dissenters. In the end, such decisions are not considered binding on anyone anyway, not even on those who made them, as they would be in western society. As Myers explains, '"Democratic representation" is a cultural construct that is not first nature to all people' (1982, 101).

Because the dominant society predicates so much of its policy and resourcing on its own ideal of community 'sharing and caring', a concept then grafted onto the real polity of indigenous settlements, Pintupi fairness is considered both aberrant and unacceptable. The impression is of chaos marked by individual excess and public remonstration, as Pintupi assert their own values through apparently unruly negotiation, with individuals grabbing as big a share as possible for themselves and their relatives at the expense of the so-called community.

At a community meeting a vocal critic of the monopolising of resources by men launched into a tirade of protest on behalf of the women, only to desist in her argument as soon as she was reassured that her own son would be a beneficiary of any spoils. This, she agreed, was fair. However, rather than accept that an equitable, though profoundly different, system exists with its own rigorously enforced mechanism of checks and balances, the dominant society continues to believe that, 'the moral superiority of many western moral and legal principles can hardly be denied' (Partington 1996, 133). It is on this assumption that much social justice funding is given, even though groups approved and identified by officialdom, towards which funding is directed because of this assumption, are consistently overridden by *walytja*.

Many social justice programs both expect and require Pintupi to reject *walytja* in favour of the community but this is *kuntangka* (shameful) and, therefore, unjust in their terms. Equitable distribution of benefits, for the purpose of producing statistical results equal with the West in such areas as health and education is fully expected to happen through community control of institutions and their resources. Indeed, dramatic improvement in health is boldly claimed to be a matter, not of individuals or family constellations, but of whole communities determining all aspects of their lives (*National Aboriginal Health Strategy* 1989, xiii–xviii).

Like many of the ideals relentlessly applied to the Pintupi, 'community control' achieves its western aims with enormous difficulty. 'Fairness' manifested as community control makes the official function of an institution difficult in a society where accountability to *walytja* is far stronger than to any community service. As Myers explains, Pintupi 'maintain such communal institutions without renouncing their individual autonomy ...' (1986a, 276). Thus, settlement institutions must care equally for all; but a Pintupi interpretation of 'community ownership' is each individual having a personal stake in institutional assets, which leads individuals and their families to feel they should have access to the resources, at any time, according to their own immediate needs.

How can western institutions under community control be 'fair' when they expect relationships between Pintupi to be overridden, especially when Pintupi have been told they actually own them? Bureaucracies do not accept for a moment that particular groups chosen by Pintupi should be able to prioritise their access to resources ahead of the groups they (the bureaucrats) have chosen, such as the sick, women, children, the old, or outstation residents. But how is it possible for a person to tell *walytja* they cannot borrow a clinic vehicle to go to a funeral because it might be needed the next day if someone is sick? Such a precedent for its use would mean the institution to which it belongs will rarely have a vehicle, as everyone else in the settlement demands their own equitable use of it. Yet this western principle of prioritising institutional over individual need is expected to be maintained in a society where the failure to respond compassionately to the demands of *walytja* defies logic and fully justifies violence.

The idea that community should have priority over the felt needs of individuals and their families as a way of structuring societal institutions seems natural to most Australians. For Pintupi the exact opposite view of institutions is what appears right and just. Pejorative expressions, such as 'illegitimate', 'selfish' or 'corrupt', are assigned because of the passionate western belief that Pintupi are wrongheaded in their view; or excuses are made for the community through the scapegoating of individuals to avoid acknowledging the cultural difference. With equally passionate certainty Pintupi accuse whitefellas of 'holding wrong way', of being 'too hard' and 'greedy', when they or their relatives are denied.

Because a western form of community control of institutions is actually an accountability alien to the practice of Pintupi lives, it is rarely possible for them to override local demands in its favour. Of course, whitefellas are extremely disappointed, even outraged, when this does not happen because they want community ownership in their own image and confidently expect Pintupi to renounce their own *walytja* to achieve this. However, it is not surprising that Pintupi, having been told they own a resource, are also extremely disappointed and outraged when they are thwarted in their attempts to express their ownership in ways that seem just and equitable to them. It is hardly astounding that this attempt to wed divergent traditions produces frequent wildfires of conflict.

'Pintupi fairness' is an ethic that runs counter to many of the aspirations other Australians hold for indigenous people, especially in the arena of material equality; and in the gulf of misunderstanding it is Pintupi who have the most to lose. What they cannot represent is given no value, and the outward manifestations of their resilient cultural differences put them at great risk of being misunderstood in ways that have dire consequences for their access to resources. While Pintupi seek to maintain, and extend, their own world they have no option but to be acutely aware of the constraints and opportunities of a western version of equality.

A WESTERN UTOPIA

> All we have to do is instruct them in the manifest virtues of our style of life and, without undue strain, they will follow. This is a fantasy that perishes upon a single fact. They have to 'unlearn' being Aborigines, in mind, body and estate. (W E H Stanner 1979, 59)

Pintupi are constantly subjected to well-meaning suggestions from whitefellas about how to improve their society. Establishing fixed rights to property above the value of shared identity, which means constantly negotiating ownership, would allow material goods to be cared for by a single family. Excluding distant relatives and not moving from the site of a death would mean less overcrowding, and houses might last longer and be less insanitary. Staying in one place, rather than pursuing a life marked by frequent travel to see relatives, might allow more money to be spent on improving material living conditions. Treating surplus as what is left over at the end of a pay period, rather than when payday shopping is finished, could cut down on gambling, described by Ernest Hunter as a 'major drain on resources and energy' (1993, 251). Saving money would mean that Pintupi would not live a feast-and-famine existence where money is, by other standards, 'wasted' because of the need to dispose of it as quickly as possible.

Yet what is ignored in such earnest and relentless suggestions to Pintupi about how they can redeem their society through 'lifestyle' improvements is that the traditions to be disposed of are the very sustenance of their lives. It is ironic that these well-intentioned attempts to make Pintupi society more materially prosperous are often upset by the very aspects of their lives that lie at the core of their well-being.

> ... but the white man, they found, had little faith in anything but himself and worried about everything. Not less confused were they by our competitive way of life with its greed, selfishness, and amassing of wealth ... (Duguid 1963, 184)

Many of the 'improvements' required of Pintupi in the name of social justice rely on the denial of *walytja,* but such denial is shameful, unjust and sure to lead to violent upheaval. It is also unjust for Pintupi parents to deny the expressed needs of their children if they have the money to fulfil those needs, an especially risky enterprise when relatives are nearby. For example, parents with money dare not deny their children sugary 'cool drinks' on the grounds that habitually drinking them may have negative health consequences in the future. The resultant tantrum and conflict is a much more immediate negative consequence brought on by the denial than the possibility of distant disease.

In a multitude of other social ways the pervasive, but theoretical, possibilities of a prosperous, equitable and 'just' future are subsumed to the immediacy of needs and demands deeply felt and forcefully expressed. Western outcomes simply do not furnish the basis on which one can legitimately refuse or exclude another (Myers 1986a, 265), and social justice ideals will always seem unjust to Pintupi if they rely on immediate breaches of kinship obligations, in order to achieve distant 'improvements'. Because of this clash of values, the changes sought in the name of equality are not unequivocally positive, even if the costs are harder for western society to understand than the possibilities of apparent gains.

The potential results of western ideals are invariably portrayed as positive. However if, for example, shame no longer operated as a barrier to individual prosperity, that change would also be at the cost of undermining an important sanction which operates to control all manner of aberrant behaviour. If the traditional Pintupi consideration that relatives are of far more importance than material possessions (Myers 1986a, 111) were challenged by the increasingly desirable goods being dangled before them, no one can predict what the real consequences would be.

The present dynamic between the two societies is far from immutable and Pintupi are subject to competing pressures. *Walytja* is still the overwhelming preoccupation of Pintupi, with relatives making incessant demands on each other, as is their right, and also reciprocating, as is their obligation. But Pintupi are also exposed to images of the western material prosperity that they are constantly told they must, and can, easily have; they are never told of the potential costs. For most other Australians there is no choice and, therefore, no loss in terms of their own lives, so it is assumed there is none for Pintupi.

Pintupi are continually testing and changing their own 'rules' about such things as deserting houses after a death, without showing any inclination to revise core values about the primacy of *walytja*, which are too integral to wellbeing to show flexibility. Family is an aspect of indigenous life Stanner called a 'one possibility thing' (1979, 35); to try to have material prosperity at the cost of this might be a poor trade. The dilemma is that, although western affluence is obviously desirable, it is unjust and therefore a cause of conflict, whereas *walytja* is the reason for living, irrespective of whether relatives bring joy or pain.

A critical question for rising generations is whether a desire for material prosperity can overwhelm a society that places supreme value on justice through relationships satisfied. Writing about the indigenous people he knew in a previous era Stanner asked whether they would 'invest in their old tradition rather than in our utopia?' (1979, 397). Because the changes the dominant society seeks in Pintupi society do not necessarily produce the lives held out to them, a further question is whether, should they ever seriously pursue 'utopia', they will reap its benefits, or be left bereft of the advantages of either society.

Playing cards, 2000.

The inability of mainstream bureaucracies to tackle inequity often leaves them feeling tricked or misled by Pintupi, who seem to metamorphose before their eyes from caring, sharing members of community groups to greedy individuals fighting to misuse resources for their own and their relatives' benefit. However, such conjuring is merely the price of modern Pintupi lives at the interface, manipulating a system they did not devise but which, they are constantly told, is highly supportive of their own endeavours.

Despite the current rhetoric of self-determination, western ideals for indigenous people have never really changed, because achieving homogeneity has long defined the pattern of civilisation. Although confronted by persistent failures, changing another culture has always seemed so much easier than questioning the relevance of western lifeways to them.

However, ignoring resilient cultural variation does not make it disappear, no matter what the dominant society might hope, and the clash at the interface is as vigorous as ever. Compulsion is apparently gone, the 'four-by-two' days (when some settlement superintendents took to recalcitrant indigenous residents with lengths of construction timber) are long over. But policy is still formulated on the basis of the desirability of movement towards equality and, under cover of denunciation and denial of past policy, the identical expectations of culture change underpin these current policies bearing new names.

FAMILY
PHOTOGRAPHS
Photographer: Mimala
Napangaṯi, 2000.

Shimona Napaltjarri,
Stephanie Napaltjarri,
Tinella Nakamarra,
three of Mimala's
granddaughters, with
Lorna Nangala, one of
Mimala's daughters, in
Mimala's house.

Tinella Nakamarra
with her favourite
dogs.

Tinella Nakamarra, and
Andreana Nakamarra,
two of Mimala's grand-
daughters.

Joey West Tjupurrula, John West Tjupurrula and Rosita Napurrula, two uncles and an auntie.

Joseph Tjupurrula Jackson, Mimala's son, with the two Nakamarras.

Eric Tjapangati and Jake Tjapaltjarri, a brother and uncle of Mimala.

CHAPTER 5
INTERVENTION

At times I wonder if there may not be a large file marked
'Facts we would rather not know about'.
(W E H Stanner 1979, 46)

Going Forward, a submission to the federal government from the
Council for Aboriginal Reconciliation, sums up many of the ideals that
underpin contemporary policies of social justice and justify intervention (1995, 65). These are:

there should be maximum control of the programs and processes
by indigenous people;
all funds must be equitably applied;
all funds should be applied in a culturally appropriate fashion.

As with many such policies applied to Pintupi, they are expected to
be fully accountable for them. However, if they must have maximum
control of programs and processes, then surely they cannot also be
expected to apply the funds in a manner considered equitable by the
mainstream? The strength of Pintupi society, past, present and for the
foreseeable future, lies in a distribution of resources which, in many
ways, is far more just than would be tolerated in much of western society, but it is situated within a family rather than a communal system.
Moreover, because Pintupi are not communal in the ways demanded
by policy, invoking community control where States and Territories do
not meet their performance indicators cannot produce the sponta-
neous health and educational revolution alluded to in much of the
social justice literature (for example, *Going Forward* 1995, 67).

To the contrary, if all funds must be equitably applied according to a mainstream model, this is something outsiders are going to have to ensure. The primacy of *walytja* as the basis for Pintupi society means a western-style equitable distribution of resources cannot possibly be a process of re-establishing the strength of indigenous society as O'Donoghue (1992, 2) believes. Indigenous people are invariably called 'strong' when, and only when, they seem to be embracing western ideals, but such judgement posits a wholly premature assumption of the westernisation of their cultures. If 'proper' accountability is prioritised over Pintupi management, then that choice should be acknowledged, rather than putting in programs with antithetical messages, the failure of which is then blamed on Pintupi recipients rather than the on architects of policy.

Applying funds in a culturally appropriate way does not automatically redress statistical disadvantage. In many cases redressing disadvantage is not culturally appropriate at all. For example, if welfare dependency, considered evidence of crippling inequality, is to be eradicated then, in the case of Pintupi, Tickner was wrong to say their own cultural explanations are being valued (1992, 1). Moving away from welfare actually means overriding cultural considerations of being 'held' or 'looked after' by government. Although the Australian Reconciliation Convention believes that reconciliation demands removal of dependency (1997, 3), Pintupi could never feel reconciled with a government that seeks to cast them adrift.

Perhaps it is inevitable that indigenous policy will remain blind to Pintupi precepts, but just as they are no longer blamed for the failures of the assimilationist policy of the past, they should not be blamed for those of the present. However, as continued denial of the contradictions between western ideals and Pintupi lives through social justice remains far more expedient and politically acceptable than actually admitting that hard compromises need to be made, this is most unlikely to happen.

CREATING EQUALITY

Intervention [at Papunya] brought satisfaction when human problems seemed intractable even if it suggests that management may have lost interest in or despaired of any worthwhile achievement in human terms. (Jeremy Long 1970, 181)

A consequence of policy aiming at equality is that indigenous people are represented as a damaged, but potentially exemplary, culture, in constant need of outside expertise to attempt the necessary repairs. One of the ways governments and their agencies try to effect those repairs is by direct intervention.

The unrelenting demands of statistical equality create a rising tide of frustration, failure and waste. To the implementers of social justice policies the apparently irrational obstinacy on the part of Pintupi, in not travelling along the preordained equality path, calls for the linking of program funding to a guarantee of mainstream outcomes, or at least a movement towards them. Direct intervention, like much of indigenous policy, often reappears from a vilified history, rejuvenated behind new disguises but promising, once again, to finally win through. Intervention in Pintupi society never requires much justification at the time, but always a great deal afterwards. This is because the present, as opposed to past, influences of policy on indigenous society are rarely conceived as anything but positive.

In the 1960s the superintendent at Papunya had sweeping powers: for instance, if a tap was left on the water supply to the whole area was cut off for a time (Bardon 1991, 15). Indigenous children were often excluded from the white residential area as well as the central area of the settlement (Davis et al. 1977, 36). The superintendent imposed and enforced a sunset curfew, violation of which could lead to food being withheld.

In the early years Pintupi were rounded up for a medical examination every day, and their eating was supervised in an effort to ensure they ate the lethal, institutional food considered to be good for them. Mothers of babies aged over six weeks were required to present them so they could be fed baby food, and if they failed to do this, the mothers themselves were denied food. Schoolteachers ran down, caught, and held captive the children in school, where they supervised their toilet, fed, washed, deloused and clothed them. There were even attempts to completely quarantine the recalcitrant Pintupi from the rest of the settlement with a fence, to prevent the civilising benefits of assimilation being subverted by these wild blackfellas. A participant of the day recalled that these wooden fence posts were very much appreciated by Pintupi families on cold nights, each morning there were fewer of them, until finally there were none at all (pers. comm.).

Currently, there are interventionist programs that repeatedly treat scabies and trachoma, nutritional programs that monitor and feed underweight children, old people's feeding programs and playgroups to care for the very young. Experiments elsewhere in the Western Desert have implemented very high levels of intervention such as teams that frequently clean and maintain houses, provide toilet paper and generally ensure that they are kept to a standard compatible with western ideas of house dwelling (Alcorn 1994, 48).

As with other areas of interaction with Pintupi, intervention provides advantages as well as disadvantages for both societies. This has always been the case. Feeding programs at Papunya were a powerful attraction for Pintupi who appreciated the food, though they rejected the concurrent attempts to train them as 'useful black citizens, through the teaching of European table manners in order to make them more acceptable in the wider community' (Davis et al. 1977, 140). The barbed-wire fences at Papunya shielded *walytja* from the dilemma of a collective responsibility for 'communal' property, in which they are now expected to place the sanctity of material goods over their responsibility to nurture the autonomy of children.

Today the same measure is often called for again by Pintupi, who are less sensitive than most whitefellas to the politically unsound implications of barbed wire fences, and much more aware of their practical advantages on settlements where large groups of children roam happily, but sometimes destructively. Such physical symbols of paternalism and interference, criticised by most observers, such as Tregenza and Abbott (1995, 17), can sometimes belie real benefits to Pintupi in living their lives on their own terms.

Intervention can be frustrating and wasteful when attempting to fix the 'problems' of a people who have their own coherent society. It also has the potential to create the very problems it sets out to redress. Some forms create crossed purposes with other programs, while others have been exploited by Pintupi to distribute benefits according to their own values, rather than those of the program. Other types of intervention defeat local initiatives the dominant society views as small, but inadequate, moves towards success, by attempting to manipulate them further and faster in favour of western outcomes.

A FEEDING PROGRAM

> There is a plane of wishful policy and a plane of actuality, and only myth closes the gap between them. Strangely enough it is not always easy to see the gap. (W E H Stanner 1979, 7)

Those seen as the most vulnerable of Pintupi are targeted by intervention programs aiming to boost the health of young children and to ensure they survive. One of these initiatives is feeding programs for underweight children who fail to thrive, introduced in order to reduce infant mortality rates that have long been highlighted by social justice policy (for example, *Social Justice for Indigenous Australians* 1993–94, 11).

These programs are welcomed by Pintupi since they provide free food for children, confirming their view that government should 'look after them', feeding their children just as they were themselves fed at the ration station of Haasts Bluff and in the communal kitchen at Papunya. Such a view is reinforced by the agency of whitefellas, who run the program as the representatives of government.

Were Pintupi to hand out the food themselves they would have no choice but to feed the children of their own relatives, whether or not they needed the food, but the whitefellas who perform this work stand outside the kinship system and are expected to be fair to everyone.

Their role is to 'help Pintupi' and that means giving equally to all, not just those who are skinny. In the view of Pintupi, ensuring equal access for all is precisely what they are employed for.

A few years ago a feeding program was begun in Walungurru and its operation followed a familiar course. Initially many children come begging for food and most are refused, since the aim is to feed only the small group identified as undernourished. Soon there is disquiet directed at the 'hard' whitefellas because, by not giving freely to all the children, they have undermined their authority and, along with it, their very rationale for being in the settlement 'to help' people.

The denial of a child's request for food, when the food is clearly visible and being given freely to others, is shameful in Pintupi society and the rejected children cry loudly and harass their parents to intervene on their behalf. The mothers politely but insistently complain to the exasperated whitefellas, exhorting them over and over again to feel sorry for their children and give them food, but to no avail. There is little common ground between the parents and the whitefellas, who see the dilemma of the distraught parents less than a bunch of spoilt, undisciplined children upsetting their program.

With their repeated pleas for compassion rudely ignored and the children now screaming in protest at the perceived betrayal, the parents become angry. They drag their protesting children away while muttering that the whitefellas are 'too hard' and are 'no help' (because they are not helping *them*) and that whitefellas who do not help should leave. Some also fail to understand why they should spend their own 'private money' feeding their children when other families do not have to.

The whitefellas who run the feeding program become concerned, and indignant at the rising dissent at what is viewed as arbitrary favouritism, and see the solution in collecting money from the parents of the children they are feeding. They announce that those parents whose children are fed will have to pay for the meals and they take the lack of dissent to this proposition as agreement. On 'sitdown' (unemployment benefit) and pension days, they wait in the settlement store to ambush parents who cash their welfare cheques. However, the parents refuse to hand over their money, and the attempt to make Pintupi pay for a service previously provided free fails, merely alienating more parents. The whitefellas have fed the children for free before, they have established that tradition and, having shown that it is their responsibility, they cannot now demand payment.

Like many health problems, failure to thrive is seen by Pintupi as caused by far more than a mere lack of food. Perhaps the child was too quiet (and did not demand food) because it was kept in hospital too long, and was consequently not smoked by the old women after birth. Skinny children may be covered with a protective layer of fat and then encouraged to touch a *kuturu Tjukurrpa* (sacred stick) while the old women sing to invoke the *Tjukurrpa tina* (big Dreaming) that can cure them. The *tulku Tjukurrpa* (sacred songs) make children fat as well as cure disease.

Parents may welcome a free nutrition program but they do not acknowledge any responsibility to pay for extra feeding when they have already provided as much food as their children have demanded, thereby fulfilling their own obligations. As Myers explains, 'Children are granted an autonomy of desire', they are expected to assert themselves to gain their needs (1986a, 110). Therefore, if children are skinny because they have not demanded sufficient food, there is no further parental responsibility, an outlook that once admirably selected survivors for their life in the desert.

This lack of common meanings is ubiquitous, ensuring that the best-intentioned intervention efforts are liable to be undermined in a clash of values that confounds many a government intervention. The consequent failure to achieve the forecast results leaves the whitefellas trying to implement programs at the interface, and the bureaucracies that employ them, extremely disillusioned.

A WOMEN'S VEHICLE

> It is our fault as theoreticians, and their calamity as [indigenous] people, that we are not bright enough to find words for [indigenous] principles. (W E H Stanner 1979, 371)

In their time, all policies directed at indigenous people are claimed to embody moral and legal principles of the highest order. However, this is only because the indigenous principles they inevitably contradict are completely ignored.

A four-wheel drive truck was given to Pintupi women under a federal women's initiative program which aimed to empower them as a group, to improve their status and redress their 'double disadvantage' of gender and race (*Social Justice for Indigenous Australians* 1992–93, 50). The vehicle was expected to provide a focus for creating women's group allegiances in their own settlement, while allowing them to network with women elsewhere.

This sudden channelling of government resources fuelled the expansion of women's interests. These were strengthened by the role of whitefellas who supported what they saw as the women's interests against the men who, Pintupi women indignantly explained, were always greedy for anything they had.

Newly acquired settlement resources are often used for their intended purposes initially, perhaps out of deference to the government bosses who provide them, or because there is not yet a precedent for any other use. This interlude lasts only until 'ownership' of the resource can be established and claims are quickly staked, since each and every time a resource is used determines rights to it. As Myers explains, obligations and responsibilities are established through practice, 'once is a precedent, twice a tradition' (1980, 320).

The women's truck was used for travel to 'sorry business' after the death of a relative of one of the women in a distant settlement, and to bring home a granddaughter of another woman who 'held' the truck. Although the whitefellas had been wary of this 'private' usage, the women who asked for the truck pointed out that it was, after all, not the whitefella's personal property. The husband of one of the Pintupi women did the driving, thus establishing precedents for both 'private' use and male drivers. This was not lost on other men or relatives.

Similar claims on the vehicle were soon made, there was much 'sorry business' to attend to and children in far-flung settlements to collect, and the precedents for using it rapidly expanded. Soon the truck was demanded merely on the grounds that 'a woman is going too' or 'an old woman might need a lift home'. Pintupi began to refer to the vehicle as the 'sorry truck' because it was constantly travelling to 'sorry business' in other settlements.

In this climate of 'chaotic' use, the whitefellas decided that strong rules were needed to exclude those they believed should have no access to the vehicle. Decisions along these lines were forcefully endorsed by Pintupi women when they met as an exclusive group and they seemed binding enough at the time, but outside the meetings the rules were instantly discarded. The rules were summed up by one woman as 'not helping anyone', and shameful edicts were quickly reversed or ignored in the face of demands from *walytja*. Ultimately, Pintupi could only make decisions based on relationships, not the official purposes based on a collective of women. Distant relatives could be put off (though not ignored, since they might still, in anger at the rejection, sabotage the truck), but close *walytja* could not be refused.

One of the whitefellas, who many women now insisted was the 'boss' for the truck with its shameful rules, complained bitterly that she felt little support. If she withheld the keys there was little public back-up from the women, though they privately exhorted her to maintain the rules when their own family was not involved. Enforcing the rules led to accusations of her being 'cheeky' and above herself, of 'holding wrong way', sometimes by the very women she thought she was defending.

In the periods between 'private' use, the truck was used vigorously by the women, as are all resources that are tenuous, and those 'owned' outside the kinship system are the most tenuous of all. A youth who had been left behind on a trip retaliated by smashing the truck windscreen when it returned, and the women soothed the youth's feelings of rejection by explaining that the whitefella 'boss' of the truck was deaf. She had not listened to them when they told her to stop, although the 'boss' herself denied there had been any such requests. On the contrary, the women had been insistent he not be picked up.

Men then took the truck on travelling ceremonies. This was a request that was impossible for the women or the whitefella 'boss' to refuse, particularly since the women in the group whose husbands wanted the truck opposed her. On its return the 'boss' was roundly criticised by the women, who claimed she should not have given in to the men. The funding body was called in to retrieve the truck for the women, who were still angry at the damage the men had caused, damage for which both men and women now refused to pay. Exasperated, the whitefella disclaimed her 'boss' status on the grounds that the women as a group were not fully supporting her role. Some women muttered that she was now 'not helping', a severe criticism in their society.

The status of the vehicle, as owned by any individual or group, now became nebulous and a series of public fights over its use erupted until it was vandalised during a fight and removed to the settlement garage. Some Pintupi said it should be burned. A vehicle that had been fiercely fought over was suddenly ignored, with many Pintupi expressing satisfaction that it had been immobilised since that stopped the incessant fighting.

Later, when the women needed a vehicle to attend a cultural festival, they reasserted their claim and demanded that it be repaired – though not by them, since they had not caused the damage. Once repaired it was taken over by the *walytja* of one of the women who had previously 'held' it, and who claimed its use on the basis that she had personally paid for a new tyre for it. Circulating from one far-flung relative to another, it travelled relentlessly in the desert, rarely showing up in its home settlement, since that might jeopardise its 'ownership'. When it did return it was the subject of heated argument, occasionally being taken by a different relative who similarly travelled extensively. In a short time the ferocious use of the vehicle took its inevitable toll. Its badly battered body was sold to a community institution which fixed it up and then, once it was mobile again, this institution became embroiled in arguments as to the price paid for it, accused of stealing a valuable resource from the women.

In such a way, a material resource offered in the quest for 'social justice' for a particular group is appropriated by Pintupi society, rather than changing it in the way intended. Targeting of disadvantage based on alien common-interest groups reinforces a view of government as an unfathomable and unpredictable boss, but since it provides opportunities for Pintupi to meet their own agenda they do not argue. While their options have been restricted to seizing these varied, apparently arbitrary, opportunities as they come along, they do not jeopardise their own enduring relationships with *walytja* in the process.

Like the women who negotiated relatedness around a new truck, Pintupi stress a flexibility of shared identity in which they are not confined to particular, fixed groups. In creating common-interest groups, Pintupi may emphasise connections between members based on generation, gender, skin groups, affiliation to country, or even residence in one place. The concept of 'one countryman' epitomises the negotiability of this shared identity. According to Myers this refers to 'a widely extended set of persons with whom one might reside and cooperate ... people from one country should help each other and ... claims to be "countrymen" thereby open up access to resources and labour' (1986a, 91).

Everyone is potentially related to everyone else as all Pintupi are *kutju ngurrara pini* (one countryman), but individuals choose which particular social relations to sustain. These groupings are never fixed. A person may create distance from another by saying they come from different places, but the next day argue that there is a powerful connection between them based on a relative who has an association with that place. As Myers explains:

> [O]n the one hand, individuals do not identify entirely with or subordinate their autonomy to the band they are currently living with; on the other hand, they must sustain the possibility of entering into productive relations with others not included in the current residential group. (1986a, 291)

The ability of Pintupi to form common-interest networks, in order to tap the ephemeral resources of the desert by invoking relatedness, is now of immense value to them in dealing with a larger society which only acknowledges the legitimacy of the particular groups it defines, rather than *walytja*, when distributing resources. In this way, Pintupi are able to tap the mainstream version of a 'fair' society in any of the manifestations demanded of them, without undermining the fundamental groupings of their own society.

The fact that the cohesion of these dominant-society-defined groups breaks down quickly in the face of kinship obligations once a resource is actually on the settlement, in no way diminishes the importance of the relationships at the time they are formed. For example, groupings based on gender are important and the women would never accept the cynical explanation that they are merely opportunistic. However, this process is seen as corrupt by bureaucracy, because it does not fit western notions of accountability to apply for a resource under the auspices of a grouping whose aims have approval, only to find it being used by others for different purposes.

While Pintupi accept, and expect, that decisions will become meaningless in changed circumstances with different participants, mainstream bureaucracies call into question the 'integrity' of the original decision. But Pintupi see themselves as ultimately accountable to one another, rather than to external bodies and their ideals. In the midst of the turmoil between the values of the women as a group and those of *walytja*, one woman sought to intervene in the conflict between the two systems by promoting herself as custodian of the women's vehicle. In order to lay claim to it, she declared, 'I've got no sons'.

Despite relentless training, encouragement and exhortation to 'say no to the men', to have rules such as 'no men in the women's truck' and to paint women's designs on the truck to deter men's use, those rules could never be enforced by the women themselves. This was not merely an expression of unequal gender relations, but because being shamelessly 'hard' towards their own relatives was not something the Pintupi women aspired to. Only an outsider would behave in a way so lacking in compassion. So, for Pintupi, the 'boss' role of the whitefella was not a transitional arrangement to be superseded when they were 'empowered', or 'trained', to perform this role for themselves.

Only through the long-term 'holding' of the vehicle by the women, as an exclusive group, looking after it by themselves without outside help, would the dominant society consider a real step towards gender empowerment and equality had been achieved. That, however, would create socially damaging conflict, and probably violence, both between the women and other groups and, even more importantly, between themselves and their own *walytja*, an outcome they could not countenance. The failure of yet another program of intervention was attributed to the intransigence of the recipients, without any consideration of the dilemmas, inherent in its aims, it created in an indigenous society.

A CRAFT BUSINESS

> It is the very nature of mainstream life to be unknowingly provincial and self-centred (while ascribing such traits only to others, who are outside the mainstream) ... (Joshua Fishman 1991, 65)

Sometimes attempts to graft equality onto Pintupi society destroy what is already working successfully in quite different terms from the ones that are considered legitimate by the dominant society.

An art and craft program, run by Pintupi women for their own benefit, operated on and off for years with an adult educator organising materials. It provided an opportunity for the women to print fabric for their own use and, importantly for the women, they did not classify it as work because there was no boss and therefore no compulsion. They felt no constraints and remained free agents who could participate as they chose, making items of clothing for themselves and their *walytja*, occasionally selling or exchanging an item. Their personal autonomy was, for these older women, an especially important prerequisite of their involvement because, as Myers explains, the Pintupi life cycle is seen as a continuous progression towards autonomy (1986a, 240).

At the time it was government policy to achieve equal outcomes in the self-employment of indigenous groups in business by the year 2000 through the Aboriginal Employment Development Policy (*Social Justice for Indigenous Australians* 1991, 22–24). Like most indigenous policies this was broadly developed for all indigenous people and then applied, without reflection, to particular societies like the Pintupi.

To field officers, keen to apply this federal policy and to develop economic self-reliance, breaking the pattern of what is viewed as debilitating dependency, the art and craft program appeared to have great potential. It was obviously an embryonic business enterprise, only in need of support through training in commercial screenprinting and some small business management to put it on a sound financial footing. The women would do the work, running and operating the business for themselves, and profits would be used to buy materials, with any surplus going back to the women.

The officers were excited at this prospect. The women would seize this opportunity to become self-reliant, empowering themselves as a group and setting an example for others in the settlement. An enthusiastic field worker stated: 'This enterprise could be the start — the first Pintupi business. Who knows! In a few years ...'

With this heady vision in mind, a training program was immediately provided and the women welcomed it. No expense would be spared to ensure the success of this 'business'. The women were provided with an instructor and materials, and they were paid for a month's training during which time they printed silk scarves and clothes. All the materials were paid for by the funding body and the women finished the course well satisfied with the scarves and the training wage.

The field officer started looking for markets for the printed materials the women would now be making. But when the training finished and the instructor wanted the women to continue making articles for their own use and for sale in the settlement as a first step towards fulfilling the self-sufficiency aims of the program, they asked if the wage would continue. When they were told it would not, they replied that they were not going to work unpaid, and many of them complained that they had already worked for nothing 'for years' before the government stepped in.

It was many years before the original program started again and in this time the mere mention of it made the women angry. Meanwhile, the training body had moved on to other ventures, optimistic still, leaving behind the Pintupi women's craft enterprise as one of many inexplicable failures, brought about through the apparently arbitrary refusal of Pintupi to help themselves.

The failure was not unpredictable. Making materials for others was work because it implied constraints by bosses, even though the women were the beneficiaries, and they considered they should be well paid for their loss of autonomy. Even though the women had enjoyed, and benefited from, the training program they now felt cheated by a government that had demonstrated that it should pay them but now wanted them to work for nothing once again. One woman questioned the original program before the government had stepped in, and claimed, 'It was like jail'.

The assumption that Pintupi would strive towards collective self-reliance by grasping a generous opportunity to be trained led to the project backfiring. The women's major consideration was not the printing group, but individual autonomy and the possibility of helping their own *walytja*. The program created 'dependency' in women who previously had made some clothes for themselves and their *walytja*, but were then shown by the payment of a wage that they had been tricked into doing it for nothing. They demanded continuation of the payment they had received in the training program, which had been demonstrated by government to be their right, and rather than being the start of something big the training program killed off the project that had originally spawned it.

The enthusiasm to encourage indigenous people to become like other Australians entails societies like the Pintupi being constantly monitored by agencies, ever ready to step in and assist any movement in the official directions. Yet, because the motivation of Pintupi is usually misunderstood, these interventions have the potential to create the unintended consequence of killing off the very efforts they aim to strengthen.

MEDICAL INTERVENTION

> ... our sense of wellbeing must be in the linkages, in the bonds we have within families, amongst friends, workmates, neighbours, communities and the broader social system. As basically social beings, the capacity we have to live and work in groups is intrinsic to our quality of life. (Eva Cox 1998, 161)

Success in terms of social justice is defined as statistically identifiable movement towards equal outcomes in areas comparable with other Australians. This ensures that high value is placed on programs that promise dramatic breakthroughs, regardless of their real chances of success, or even of a proven history of failure.

By the early 1970s, officials at Papunya were forced to admit that their decade-long environmental strategy of improving Pintupi health through provision of nutrition, housing and sanitation had not worked. The realisation that Pintupi had themselves 'slowed' what was seen as the 'normal acculturation process' prompted calls for even greater intervention (Davis et al. 1977, 116).

To provide new cures, Tatz called for fundamental research into indigenous health, to find a remedy for *otitis media* (producing suppurating ears) respiratory infections and virus infections (1964, 139). Despite Stanner's warning in 1972 that problems of ill-health in indigenous populations would not be solved simply by the provision of better health services, the next strategy was one of medical intervention — a massive new hospital. This was to be a showcase facility which served to address national and international concern at high indigenous infant mortality rates.

If Pintupi could not be induced to change the way they lived, perhaps their health could be improved by intensive medical intervention to eliminate much disease. Sick people, especially the young, were to be periodically kept in a sanitary environment, away from their obviously unhealthy lives. While infant mortality rates were improved at this time, the health results were not dramatic enough, and the focus then returned to education and prevention.

Two decades on, the wheel has turned full circle, coming back to medical intervention. Alcorn reports that the Menzies School of Health believes that the rejection of medicine during the early 90s in favour of primary health care, concentrating on health promotion, education and improving living environments, has gone too far (1994, 49). Medical intervention is again in favour, accompanied by the argument that it was never really tried because it was underfunded in the past (48).

Medical approaches are clearly of high value to Pintupi and they are already well used. According to the Pintubi Homelands Health Service (PHHS), from 1993 to 1994 a third of the 60 children under five years of age resident at Walungurru were evacuated by air for serious illness, staying an average of nineteen days, but some for three months or more, in Alice Springs Hospital, (PHHS 1994, 16). Of these 60 infants, 92% were evacuated and admitted to hospital at some stage, a rate almost identical to that a decade before (PHHS 1985, 16). Thus, only a very small percentage of Pintupi children get through the first few years without needing hospitalisation, much of it involving lengthy stays.

Medical intervention saves many young Pintupi lives and has, at least for now, contradicted the conventional wisdom that the cause of the increased life expectancy of the young has less to do with the technology of modern medicine than old-fashioned stratagems such as improved personal hygiene (for example, Maddox 1998, 336). This achievement of modern medicine has come about mainly because it *is* possible to intervene in the lives of infants in the dramatic fashion required to produce results. Pintupi families largely cooperate in these intervention programs. For instance, there is high compliance with the vaccination of infants, because there is an acceptance of the curative power of injections. Similarly parents are happy to allow programs such as one in which health teams regularly treat their children for scabies, reducing its incidence and possibly the complication of kidney disease in later life; or another aimed at the treatment of the active trachoma infecting at least one-third of school-aged Pintupi children.

The decline in infant mortality, produced through frequent rounds of treatment and prolonged hospitalisation to put on weight as well as to treat illness, has helped to favour medical intervention again. But, despite its obvious and commendable success with children, there is no counter-part for the ills of adults. This is at least part of the explanation for the reversal of Third World trends, where those who manage to survive an uncertain childhood can expect a relatively long life. In Pintupi settlements childhood is largely survivable, but middle age increasingly is not.

'Lifestyle' diseases among the middle aged are showing a dramatic increase. Cases of chronic hypertension leaped threefold from 1983 to 1997, diabetes increased sixfold (PHHS 1996–97, 13), while kidney disease is increasing by more than 20 per cent a year. This is just the start. According to a Walungurru doctor, problems such as hyperten-sion, end stage renal disease and heart disease will be viewed as 'just beginning in the nineties' (pers. comm.).

Many of the ways of managing chronic illness, in order to delay death, are difficult enough to apply in urban society, and almost impos-sible in a Pintupi settlement. Frequent self-monitoring, with appropri-ately timed and dosed medication, is a burden of vigilance and fastidiousness antithetical to Pintupi lifeways, so the outcome of chron-ic disease is almost always catastrophic. Patient transfers to city hospi-tals, already running at a high rate, are virtually irrelevant to the course of most chronic disease, and dramatic lifestyle change is not easy for individuals in Pintupi society. As one diabetic explained patiently, after yet another lecture about an appropriate diet, 'We eat with our families at different camps. We can't eat something different'.

While this may seem a rather trivial obstacle to overcome in order to achieve better health, it is these links between *walytja*, sustained by such shared activities, which are critical to a Pintupi sense of wellbeing. As Colin Mathers (1998, 146–7) points out, the world health com-munity is beginning to acknowledge a definition of health that incor-porates concepts of physical, mental, social and spiritual wellbeing. In this new understanding good health status is much more than just the absence of disease.

Physical health is an aspect of, but not synonymous with, total well-being. Even in western society, which places an extremely high value on physical wellbeing, many individuals engage in practices which improve their overall sense of wellbeing, even though they are injuri-ous to their health. While a sense of wellbeing may be experienced despite poor health status, it is hard to see how a society whose sense of wellbeing has been undermined could improve its health outcomes.

The growing rate of suicide in some of those indigenous settlements that have a longer and more intrusive contact history than Pintupi is one manifestation of this incompatibility.

Band-Aid medicine endlessly treats but never cures, at least for long, because the underlying conditions and causes of disease are not changed. It is described by Griffiths as 'a cynical reflection on the unpalatable fact that outback nurses and doctors treated Aborigines for a variety of diseases, only to see them return again and again with the same symptoms' (1995, 197). Band-Aid medicine is usually viewed as a kind of salvage operation redeeming lost souls from otherwise destitute lives, only to lose them again. Yet, it is the style of care that all clinics in Pintupi settlements end up performing, because this is what Pintupi demand of them, and are willing to accept.

Moving away from being Band-Aid institutions, effective in their context, in order to try to create dramatic change in Pintupi lives is not only frustrating but also insulting to a people who have their own system of health understandings which furnish their wellbeing and for which they often sacrifice western-type health status. Though relentlessly maligned, Band-Aid medicine *can* provide efficient primary health care in a form that is appropriate in the context of a cross-cultural setting in which the people the clinic serves are well-satisfied with the integrity of their own health belief system, which is not based on a western scientific model.

The condemnation of Band Aid medicine is a symptom of what Mathers calls a 'lopsidedness' where 'health care' focuses only on dealing with disease and trying to prevent death, while ignoring the 'positive constructs of physical, social and spiritual wellbeing' (1998, 150). Yet the obvious limits to dramatically changing the health status of a people who do not consider themselves unhealthy, and who have not yet been convinced to sacrifice their own cultural understandings — let alone their practices — for the vague promise of equal outcomes, is not a feature of the rhetoric or analysis of indigenous policy debate.

Fifteen years ago, a Walungurru doctor lamented, 'We run an efficient Bandaid-style clinic, and yet we cannot say with any conviction that the fundamental health problems here are any closer to being solved' (Pintubi Homelands Health Service 1985, 28). That such work is often successful in local terms, even though it offers no miracles, rarely comforts medical staff, who are bombarded with the external criteria against which to measure their endeavours, and their personal and professional success. As so often happens with western institutions on Pintupi settlements, the real constraints on their work are overlooked.

The Aboriginal and Torres Strait Islander Social Justice Commissioner has said that just 'because some people have different outlooks and perceptions, there is no reason to think that they do not have health rights equal to others' (1994, 175). However, if the outcomes of their access are not equal this is not, invariably, an artefact of 'abuse of human rights', as the Commissioner (1993, 6) believes. Far from health and education systems being 'punitive' because they do not achieve equal outcomes, as he later contends (1995, 17), in the case of Pintupi they would have to become punitive in the extreme to achieve anything like that goal. Moreover, it needs to be considered that if Pintupi were persuaded to pursue a western model of 'health' at the expense of their own feelings of wellbeing the costs may be severe.

The 'last contact' Pintupi often outlive their children, the original settlement-born generation, producing a dramatic structural change in the population. Thus far, Pintupi health statistics have benefited from the longevity of those men and women who 'walked the country', where only the strongest survived to adulthood, but this is a historical 'one-off', now being swamped by the early deaths of settlement-born and-bred generations.

It is obvious that a medical approach cannot create health equality in Pintupi society, but at present high public relations value is placed on the cost of indigenous health 'fixes'. Increased health expenditure has been a matter of reassurance, but static or declining results under this regime put such spending at risk when it does not fulfill the high expectations.

In the end, the equality approach ensures that the outcomes of expanded intervention will never be commensurate with expectations and efforts. Consequently policy-makers and their agencies and indigenous clients are sentenced to an endless roundabout of failed solutions and recycled answers in pursuit of the unattainable, while small achievements are overlooked and lost in the scramble.

LAW

I saw a dying community:
Dying spiritually — There is very little of the Aboriginal soul ... no Aboriginal power or structures. (*Between Two Worlds*, Report of a World Council of Churches Team Visit to Aboriginal Communities in Australia 1991, 47)

Sometimes intervention in Pintupi society is promoted as an unequivocal improvement because it is seen as eliminating something that is abhorrent to international sensibilities. Like many aspects of indigenous policy, the West's version of 'justice' is assumed to be a universal, applicable to any social order, when it has really evolved within a particular tradition. Pintupi justice is not expressed in a formal structure of power, such as a council or law court or even mythologised elders, but is regulated in a system maintained by everyone, in which all are accountable, both in observing and upholding it. As with everything else in their society, Pintupi justice works through relationships: justice is relationships satisfied.

Violence as punishment, that potent and persistent expression of Pintupi justice, can be contrasted with the stereotype of a brutal and anachronistic force described by Amnesty International as a violation of international human rights (Sheehan 1998, 14). Like so many aspects of Pintupi lifeways, violence is no aberration in a social order unable to come to terms with modern life: it is an ancient sanction with contemporary relevance for modern Pintupi.

In a confusion of mixed messages from the mainstream, Pintupi face accusations of either not controlling their own society, or going too far in using violence to exercise authority. Often the same outsiders who exhort them to act on problems like petrol-sniffing recoil in horror when they do. Yet in a society made up largely of young people raised to prize individual freedom of action, a lack of powerful constraints and incentives to shared identity is a recipe for chaos. It is precisely the decline of ritual, lawful violence that breeds the uncontrolled variety reviled by both societies. When lawful violence is not allowed in favour of taking the path that least offends mainstream Australia's sensibilities, that society should not be shocked when, as Tatz observes, indigenous Australians merely 'sit and watch disinterestedly, such hitherto punishable behaviours [rape and incest]' (1990, 18).

While it is often assumed by westerners that indigenous people need to overcome violence in order to build a just society, violence as punishment is actually one of the few sanctions that make any sense in Pintupi society. However, far from being difficult to eradicate (as it is often portrayed) these forms of punishment are actually very difficult for Pintupi to maintain because they have not delegated them to others; offenders are not conveniently carted off to jails through largely anonymous forces. There is no Pintupi 'police force' to administer their own law, so everyone must make decisions for themselves and act accordingly. Every individual is a lawyer, judge and policeman judged in turn by everyone else. All Pintupi must take responsibility, not only for their own actions and those of their *walytja*, but also for inflicting just punishment on others.

Violence as law, with the involvement of dozens of people from different family groups, is often portrayed in press reports as merely riotous behaviour, something in need of control from the outside, if necessary, for a well-ordered society to be possible. In fact, it is highly structured and not at all uncontrolled. Even in a heated response to murder, spearing and beating with clubs is not orgiastic but controlled by opposing *walytja,* who ensure both that justice is done and also that it is 'finished' forever at the time of punishment.

Those who are punished must be forgiven, and must forgive their punishers, because they are still living together in the same small society. Pintupi speak in astonishment about whitefellas who can publicly shake hands after an argument to signify that their fight is over, only to take up their differences again the very next day. Pintupi see public resolutions as finishing a fight between individuals and different *walytja,* who must co-exist and may, in the future, need each other. The marks of punishment are worn proudly by the one who took the payback without flinching and invited more of the same. This invitation is not just to show strength but to make sure that more was offered than was required so there can be no excuse for further revenge. As one man put it, 'When we see those scars [from spear wounds] we're happy'.

Western ideals are ill-fitted to Pintupi law, which applies to people rather than property, and does not allow for the concept of an accident for which no one can be blamed. This focus has produced a very different law. Even the passengers in a car in which a person has died are jointly held responsible, and must be punished for failing to warn the driver. A passenger who was injured in a vehicle accident in which the driver was killed refused to be evacuated to Alice Springs hospital because he wanted to 'tell the right story to relatives'. To not do so would have made him look even more guilty and invited greater punishment. When a man was killed in a drunken fight, not only was his attacker punished, but also those who had bought the grog because they were deemed to have contributed to his death, both by buying the alcohol and not acting quickly enough to save the injured man.

On the other hand, there is no 'hard law' when it comes to material goods. Young children can playfully damage property with impunity, and petrol-sniffing youths sometimes cut swathes of destruction through settlement infrastructure. As long as no one is hurt little is done, much to the astonishment and frustrated anger of whitefellas living on the settlement. As well, what is considered vandalism by western society can be a form of justice for Pintupi. The destruction of property is considered perfectly just if it resolves conflict between people, and the costs to material goods weigh very lightly in the human equation. For example, the complete destruction of a new video player by people fighting over it may be a perfectly satisfactory outcome for Pintupi, because the cause of the fight is removed and harmony between the protagonists reinstated. As Myers shows, 'burning the truck' does not contradict the ideal of Pintupi to invest in people rather than things and at times, such as after a death, may be essential to it (1991, 64).

This focus of Pintupi law on people, rather than possessions, does not serve the interests of western institutions in their settlements well. The resultant lack of Pintupi support for their preoccupation with the preservation of property threatens to choke off the flow of resources from wary government bureaucracies. To counter this many Pintupi look to law enforcement by outsiders.

However, like so much grafted onto Pintupi society, the benefits of western law to a people practising their own customary law do not come cost-free. Pintupi deal with breaches of their law by physical punishment meted out swiftly by their fellows, the aim of which is to satisfy aggrieved relatives. Whitefella law is abstract, slow, cumbersome and often turns to sanctions that contradict important tenets of Pintupi society, and are therefore contested. For example, a man was forbidden by the courts to return to the settlement he had offended in. Many months later, when he was arrested for doing so, his relatives angrily claimed he had been 'sent to jail for visiting his mother'.

A law that places the value of material goods above relationships sanctions shameful behaviour, even if it is maintained by outsiders. It is illegal in whitefella law to vandalise another person's vehicle, just because it is linked to fighting, or to beat a man who lives in the house of a dead relative, no matter that these actions break Pintupi law, or how shameful not punishing would be. As a Pintupi woman explained to me:

> If he goes back to that house all the people will go there *kuturutjarra* [with clubs]. The people will say 'What are you doing here? You shouldn't be here'. If he doesn't leave we'll hit him like this [demonstrating blows across head].

Both laws have merit in their context, but they are rarely additive and most often contradictory. Police officers can be important authority figures for youth and, as an authority external to Pintupi society, they can be a valuable constraint on crimes against property and whitefellas. On the other hand mainstream law enforcement has the potential to undermine customary punishment, both because this is often against the laws of the wider society and because if someone else is willing to bear the responsibility of punishment relatives are relieved of the duty of carrying it out themselves. Some Pintupi are reluctant, punishing not because they want to but because it is shameful not to do so. A woman who was obliged to punish was ridiculed for merely telling the person off. People said 'That's wrong. That's not our way', and the shame forced her to punish properly. There would be 'too much talk' if she failed to fulfil her duty.

Given that Pintupi must carry out their own punishment, it is not surprising that the intervention of western justice provides the opportunity for a denial of responsibility on the grounds that the police should do it. A man may fail to fulfil his duty because 'I don't want to go to jail' or because 'we have whitefella law'. However, if customary law is not applied because of this, while the western legal system assumes it will be and either invokes 'community solutions' to a non-communal society or applies meaningless sanctions, there may be a shifting of responsibilities between the two and, ultimately, no law at all.

'CULTURALLY APPROPRIATE' INTERVENTION

> After all, we have not developed accounting procedures that will evaluate, except in terms of money, the necessary social and psychological changes. (quoted in Davis et al. 1977, 101)

Many outsiders visiting Pintupi settlements have declared over the years that a society that cannot even stop its own children engaging in petrol-sniffing is surely in terminal decay. For those making that judgement the failure of their own western societies to control drug abuse is rarely a consideration. Moreover, there is usually a high degree of misplaced confidence from them that intervention programs in indigenous societies will be more successful than those instituted in their own.

From the 1980s, enlightened programs of intervention aimed to understand the recipient culture and work within it to control petrol-sniffing. The Healthy Aboriginal Life Team (HALT) was to work hand-in-hand with families because — the culturally-sensitive reasoning went — they are the only valid authority system in indigenous society. HALT aimed to identify, and prop up, disintegrating family structures, to use the 'right' relatives in the kinship system to care for and control the petrol-sniffers.

HALT was promoted as a positive system of support with families helping their own, and this struck an immediate response with indigenous audiences, who felt that at last a program of intervention understood them. Implicitly, petrol-sniffing children were seen by these teams as neglected, and this also struck a chord in Pintupi settlements where children and teenagers are rarely blamed for their own actions, their families being held accountable by others for their behaviour.

However, petrol-sniffing among Pintupi often gains momentum, not because of some catastrophic breakdown in a family system in desperate need of outside intervention to re-establish itself, but because of its continuing strength. The same 'neglectful' relatives who are assumed 'not to care' for the sniffers are ever willing to launch themselves into a frenzied public defence of their worst excesses, on a daily basis if necessary. The sight of exhausted relatives storming into community meetings and loudly protesting, to the point of physical violence if necessary, in order to defend their petrol-sniffing children from the slightest innuendo of wrongdoing, is not uncommon. In doing so Pintupi are 'holding' their families in the prescribed manner and, while they are concerned about petrol sniffing, they cannot stop giving unconditional support in order to control their children.

Petrol-sniffing is not at all condoned, and parents often despair for their sniffing children, but ultimately Pintupi youth have the personal autonomy to engage in it, no matter what the consequences. While this autonomy is considered by many outsiders to be a central problem in petrol-sniffing, many children of the West, subject to far more constraints on their personal freedom, also indulge in a great deal of drug use in their teenage years. *Walytja* is a system with a primary focus on total support and, through it, the cultivation of self-worth so that, unlike many of their drug-taking contemporaries in non-indigenous society, petrol-sniffers are still treated as valued members of their families. Their social rights are undiminished and, probably because of this, the vast majority remain socially responsible members of their own society, no matter how destructive they might appear to outsiders.

The HALT program eventually foundered, but since it was a fine-sounding idea, apparently 'culturally appropriate' and well promoted by its non-indigenous founders, it continued to receive substantial funding for many years. However, its assets were rarely used for the benefit of substance abusers, but were assimilated to the values of *walytja,* as might be expected in an indigenous-controlled program. While funding bodies complained about this 'misuse', perhaps it was just as well, because intervention that legitimises and provides benefits to common-interest groups can be problematic when applied to self-destructive ones.

OUTCOMES OF INTERVENTION

> There are a number of doors through none of which the Aborigines seem to want to go, but through which different European interests are trying to pull them. And each door is marked: this way to our version of a full life. I do not know every Aboriginal in Australia, but those I do know show plainly that they want to combine Aboriginal and European things in a manner of their own choice. It is this strong preference which underlies the struggle ... (W E H Stanner 1979, 53–4)

Each generation of policy-makers, aiming at the same thing but calling it something completely different, believes they will be the ones to lead Pintupi onto the 'right' path. And each new generation believes that only the methods and policies of the past were mistaken. Currently one error is seen to have been because 'they imposed decisions without regard to the real needs and aspirations of the people themselves' (*Social Justice for Indigenous Australians* 1993–94, 1); but the faith the West feels in its own ability to recognise the 'real needs' of indigenous societies has not changed.

The real purpose of much intervention is westernisation but, as Long (1964, 80) noted at Papunya, the more services provided to support this process, the greater the population of whitefellas needed to deliver them. This actually created more social distance between the two societies, resulting in fewer opportunities for acculturation, an equation that still holds true. Further, while policy rhetoric stresses self-sufficiency through indigenous involvement in western-style enterprises, intervention programs confirm to Pintupi that government is responsible for delivering equal outcomes, reassuring them that they are being looked after by government. This is irrespective of the stated aims of the programs, or their lack of success in achieving movement towards mainstream outcomes.

Given that the 'problems' in Pintupi society are always oversimplified, it is not surprising that intervention is so keenly implemented, imbued with all the faith the western world places in the self-evident superiority of its own ways. The real limits of programs and the implications of cultural differences are always ignored and this seems equally true of programs like HALT — which attempted to create change by tapping into the real structure of indigenous society — as of those that ignore it.

One of the difficulties with intervention is that its meanings are rarely shared with those of Pintupi. For example, there is nothing intrinsically wrong with a very high level of intervention to create the appearance that Pintupi are living like whitefellas, as long as they are not blamed for not eventually doing this for themselves. Yet it is the clear understanding and expectation of governments in providing these services that Pintupi will adopt the strategies for living according to the introduced model.

The assistance of whitefellas in attempting to keep Pintupi settlements clean, and otherwise conjuring the appearance of community 'caring and sharing' is not provided on the basis that it will continue for ever. Intervention by health teams to repeatedly treat preventable health problems, such as scabies, are not designed to go on indefinitely, but rather are supposed to show Pintupi what is possible, to educate them into better ways by demonstrating the benefits of preventive hygiene. This assistance models change that the wider society believes all indigenous Australians must adopt for themselves and, if they do not, then the conclusion is usually that they, rather than the providers, have squandered valuable resources. However, Pintupi may consider that the tradition of obligation by government has expanded through these programs, creating more responsibilities towards them rather than fewer. This lack of shared meanings regarding intervention is a source of much of the bewilderment and conflict at the interface.

Equal outcomes weigh more heavily with non-indigenous Australians than the maintenance of the chosen lifeway of another people, and the possibility of negative effects are rarely considered because the benefits are believed to far outweigh them. A new facility or service in a Pintupi settlement becomes a monument of visible, positive change, no matter what its future consequences. The benefits are thought to be unambiguous because social justice programs provide Pintupi with the basic ingredients for an improved life according to western values, with better housing, increased income, proper education and improved health care.

These 'indicators' provide a familiar, concrete reality in which indigenous people are seen to be proceeding along a fixed route, differing from western society only in their degree of disadvantage, although nearly thirty years ago, Rowley cautioned against what he termed the 'illusion of inevitable progress' (1971, 358). Grafting change, as if a version of 'progress', like a technology, can be transplanted to another society, rarely produces gains that match expectations, and there can be unexpected costs to the process.

Having been encouraged to pay lip service to all the contradictory ideals, Pintupi seize the opportunities on offer and look to continued experimentation to maintain, or increase, their access to the things they find of value in their own lives. Their reluctance either to change in the ways demanded by social justice policy or to challenge the expectation that they do so, comes partly from their understanding of their relationship with the wider Australian community, but also from a realistic assessment that they are not seen as capable of directing their own lives in meaningful ways. And while Pintupi may consider policy to be irrelevant as long as they can achieve some of their own goals, the current process certainly reveals something of the deeper level of interaction between the two societies, in which recognition of cultural variation is excluded if it threatens western tenets of what constitutes a worthwhile life.

None of this is visible to the vast majority of Australians, living far from the heart of Pintupi country, but statistics of entrenched disadvantage cannot indefinitely win their hearts and minds, as they are repeatedly struck by the failure of programs aimed at redressing this disadvantage. The right of an indigenous people to statistical equality with other Australians has, for some considerable time, enjoyed powerful emotive and political appeal. Whether it is sustainable in the long term remains to be seen. Some time ago Stanner was worried by this same question, which seems especially relevant now:

> What troubles me is an attitude of mind that could come to prevail amongst white Australians ... that we are saddled with the responsibility for problems not really of our making ... to argue that every new generation of white Australians accept a liability to compensate every new generation of Aborigines is simply not an argument from a domain of the real world. (1979, ix)

CHAPTER 6
DIRECTING 'PROGRESS'
IN PINTUPI SOCIETY

Where we have gone most seriously wrong is … to imagine that the way to change this kind of [Aboriginal] continuity is by rational demonstration. (W E H Stanner 1979, 59)

Contemporary indigenous policy purports to break with the past because it no longer overtly controls, or blatantly oppresses, groups like the Pintupi. However, the dominant society still exerts power by defining discourses of change, deciding what is, and is not, 'progress' in indigenous society. It does this with reference only to its own precepts, although it pays lip-service to consultation, in a process where one of the many possible ways of representing the world is given primacy over the others (Mehan 1989, 137).

Foucault contends that the production of discourse is controlled for the purpose of warding off alternatives (in Young 1986, 48, 49). For example, in deciding that 'progress' for Pintupi is statistical equality with other Australians, indigenous policy becomes limited to attempting to replicate western outcomes, which will be the only ones that count. The dominant society will never feel comfortable with Pintupi choosing to be different, if their choices produce inequality.

However, just because the dominant society defines 'progress', does not mean indigenous Australians are not involved in affirming the importance of equality goals. Indigenous groups who more closely share meanings with the dominant society may themselves contribute to public policy, as long as the views they express remain within the parameters of western tenets. These groups, able to benefit most from ideals of social justice as equality of outcomes, promote them on behalf of themselves and others, including Pintupi, for whom the short-term material benefits can also be very meaningful, no matter how incompatible their long-term aims are.

It is because of this process that the inevitable failure to achieve these equal outcomes on Pintupi settlements is interpreted by the dominant society as proof of a progressive loss of self-esteem, persistent cultural malaise and inevitable social disintegration, demanding ever more concerted equality efforts. There is nothing new in this. As Rowse (1998, 80) notes, 'advocates of assimilation held that Aboriginal society had crumbled, or was now crumbling, into fragments'. Tatz also sees a 'violence wave' marked by drunkenness and the destruction of property (1990, 258), fuelling the perspective that indigenous Australian society has virtually collapsed since the 1980s, and must now be resurrected.

Because cultural choices leading to inequality are not permissible, lying outside the discourse of progress, they lead to redoubled efforts to redress inequality. For example, a decision made by all Pintupi at Walungurra in 1990 to spend part of their development monies on transport was overruled on the grounds that they should first 'clean up' their settlement, and a federal government official suggested to them that a bulldozer would be appropriate for the job, to level their settlement and start again.

Pintupi are labelled as being in need of equity programs even when, or because, they make eloquent cultural choices in shaping their own destinies. Because these choices are subsumed by the discourse of progress, resilient cultural difference poses no challenge whatsoever to policy preconceptions and ideals. If Pintupi decision-making produces unwelcome outcomes, for instance, if a service considered vital by the wider community decides not to spend its funding on its official function, government cannot stand by without intervening. It usually tries either to change the decision, or rescues the decision-makers from consequences which seem to other Australians devastating, denying the validity of the self-determination that produced this embarrassing outcome.

This 'progress' as equality is not at all a calculated subversion of another culture but, once again, proceeds from the very best of intentions. Equal outcomes policy that is benevolent, high-minded and apparently supported by groups of indigenous Australians is blind, and because it is blind it is reinforced, rather than challenged, by its own failures. There are two possible reactions to the continual failure to achieve 'progress' in Pintupi settlements: the first is to question precepts of progress and the other is to use failure as further evidence to invoke and reinforce them. It is this latter response which is the norm.

In this paradox, the failure to achieve policy goals for indigenous Australians continually reinforces faith in those goals. At Papunya, during the 1960s, the persistent failure to assimilate Pintupi through a series of training and work programs led to very little reconsideration of assimilation as a policy. For a decade the obstacle was believed to be the scale and type of training, justifying repeated expansion of these programs. By the 1970s, some forty different types of training schemes had been trialled at Papunya, all with similar failure in expected outcomes (Davis et al. 1977).

My own reaction to the failure of my empowerment mission at Walungurru was, for some time, to dramatically intensify my efforts. After all, I reassured myself, although it was frustrating, the reluctance of a dispirited society like that of the Pintupi to seize self-management should not be unexpected. Pintupi were, I theorised, victims of what the Council for Aboriginal Reconciliation calls a 'hegemony of inequality', which 'permeates cultures, institutions and structures within society and which is often perpetuated by unconscious habits of thought by indigenous and non-indigenous people alike' (1993, 41).

Similarly, the refusal of Pintupi women to publicly deny their own family members access to their 'women's vehicle' did not lead to a re-examination of simplistic assumptions about Pintupi social relationships, but reinforced the view that gender disadvantage was even more profound than previously thought. The reluctance of families to exert overt control over their petrol-sniffing children reinforced the premise of the HALT program that more support was needed to 'empower' the families to take charge of their children, while the failure of the women's craft project was viewed by bureaucrats as a problem of training, not of any fundamental misconception on their part.

That all such efforts are equally foredoomed in their over-ambitious aims, because they could only succeed in the long term if they fundamentally changed a valued lifeway, is never a consideration. Neither is the possibility that, in the unlikely event programs actually succeed in changing that lifeway in the dramatic fashion that would be necessary, the outcomes may actually be less, rather than more, equal outcomes. Because there is so little appreciation of Pintupi lifeways, many Australians believe that only ever managing to marginally improve physical conditions is the worst of all possible outcomes, but this is not necessarily the case. The much proclaimed 'failure' of present programs could be the least of the dominant society's worries, as it saves both societies from the likely consequences of success in making fundamental changes to Pintupi society.

Far from entertaining doubts about the positive transformative power of its attempts to reform another society, the persistent 'road blocks' the dominant society encounters incite a passionate belief in the necessity for change, with the process grinding itself deeper and deeper into the task of making the solutions to the 'problems' work. Failure has always been seen as a challenge to provide better answers, rather than a fundamental change in the questions, and there is never a shortage of refurbished solutions.

This ensures that programs spiral endlessly around a succession of failed 'solutions' and 'breakthroughs', periodically recycled in slightly different form. Despite forty years of largely unsuccessful attempts, current efforts, through social justice policy, show there is no lessening of the conviction that Pintupi need to be saved.

FITTING PINTUPI TO THE POLICY

It is perfectly natural in the face of untreated strangeness to impose complete transformations on other cultures, receiving those other cultures not as they are but as, for the benefit of the receiver, they ought to be. (Edward Said 1979, 67)

Under the assimilation policy governments demanded that virtually everything about indigenous people change, without looking too closely at how this would affect the societies they were so keen to manipulate. No one thought that this would be possible without creating massive social transformation in the indigenous societies they were 'helping'. Under current policy it is assumed that the same differences will be voluntarily eliminated by indigenous Australians themselves, while at the same time those involved deny that this is orchestrating cultural change.

It is only possible to believe this proposition by way of a mental backflip, in which there is a useful flexibility in defining indigenous culture. In interpreting culture to fit the equal outcomes model, cultural epiphenomena — that is, those elements which do not conform to the model — are seen as disposable handicaps, usually assigned to the category of problems of contact. 'Lifestyle change' or 'acculturation' (Pollard 1992, 133), are the current terms for the anticipated positive results of pressures and incentives for Pintupi to westernise: that is to say, a more aesthetic and acceptable-sounding goal than the negatively perceived and historically discredited 'assimilation'. The anticipated cooperation of indigenous people in their 'acculturation' is the real difference between these policies.

Indigenous groups, especially the 'last contact people', have many, often deeply contradictory, images and ideals projected onto them by western society. Moreover, as Nicholas Thomas observes, there is a constant lurching between 'attitudes that can at no time be reconciled' (1999, 33). While encouraging immense change to suit the demands of equality. Pintupi must also remain 'traditional' people who deeply respect and continue the practices of their past. Especially valued by the West are those aspects Pintupi themselves are in the process of discarding as 'cultural epiphemonena'.

In the much-lamented 'breakdown' of traditions, such as the cessation of some ceremonies, the lack of common meanings in what is considered integral to Pintupi culture, as opposed to cultural epiphenoma, is made visible. For example, prior to contact, Pintupi maintained their universe through increase ceremonies, part of the spiritual basis for the creation of life. In explanation of this process Cameron Tjapaltjarri says that after the songs associated with the *Papa Tjukurrpa* (Dog Dreaming) were sung, dogs would later appear in a material form. He goes on to explain that government has now taken over from such ceremonies, in exchange for Pintupi agreeing to live in one place, and it is believed to have a responsibility to provide for them in place of the ceremonies that are no longer performed.

One of the last of these ceremonies was at Balgo in the late 1970s, where it was performed to improve wages, because at that time Pintupi in the Territory were receiving unemployment benefits while their relatives at the Balgo mission were still on mission 'pocket money'. Pintupi have happily done away with some areas of ceremonial life, such as increase ceremonies, and because these are tangible — and, therefore, potent — symbols of the continuing strength of an indigenous society, this is viewed with dismay by the dominant society as indications of cultural disintegration.

However, while increase ceremonies are no longer performed, 'increase thinking' continues as strongly as ever. Recently it was suggested that the flow of money into the settlement had slowed because the singing had stopped at the church. At the same time, some Pintupi also speculate that 'increase business' must surely exist in Australian society generally, though it is, of course, highly secret and not revealed to them. My friend Tjupurrula cited the Canberra Mint as likely evidence for this proposition and asked me to procure for him a money printing press on a trip to Canberra. His assumption was that as a whitefella representative of government I would have access to important whitefella 'increase business'. My amusement at the idea that Walungurru might acquire its own mint was accepted as a polite refusal of his request, much as Pintupi decline to reveal their own ceremonial life to whitefellas.

The strength of this way of thinking about material accumulation is viewed in the West with as much dismay as the loss of its outward forms. Whereas the performance of ceremonies is considered an innocuous, and exotically attractive, expression of indigenous cultural maintenance, the deeper meanings associated with these ceremonies are seen to stand in the way of Pintupi equality. The maintenance of indigenous theories of wealth creation means that exhortations from western society about the value of adopting its own traditions will fall on deaf ears.

Pintupi are not simultaneously either as traditional or western as is demanded of them, but other Australians are not expected to be shackled by their 'authentic' culture. While the basic societal tenets of the West stem from ancient cultural traditions, most Australians do not revere any of those associated forms of expression which no longer have a meaning in the modern context. Few speak the ancient forms of the languages of their ancestors, or perform ceremonies that no longer have currency in the contemporary world, or bother to learn old technologies such as spinning and weaving. Western youth are teaching their elders to use the internet, rather than sitting at their feet learning Morse code, and there would be an outcry if time better spent on educating them for a profitable role in the present was wasted on such pursuits. This does not stop the wider community exhorting indigenous groups to do the equivalent.

Howell observes that moralistic preoccupation with cultural authenticity is most noticeable in considerations of non-western forms of life (1995, 165). He argues that the West encourages the expansion of its own knowledge, regardless of its source, and does not assume such acquisitions to be inherently destructive of western culture; however, it deplores such processes in other societies, to which much higher standards of cultural purity are applied (178). Therefore, attempts to legitimate and define what is of value by narrowing the creativity of Pintupi and proscribing innovation, as if outsiders are arbiters of what is traditionally correct, are considered eminently justifiable rather than hypocritical.

For example, the generally recognised ability of, and need for, languages to evolve to remain viable, is often deplored as undermining, or corrupting, living indigenous languages. Young speakers of them are even sometimes described as having a deficient language, incapable of expressing all necessary meanings, merely because it is not the same as that of their ancestors. While there is a place for the preservation of old forms of languages and the cultural knowledge they express, the expectation that they will then be resurrected as the standard for contemporary speakers is unrealistic. After all, no one expects Middle English to become a modern-day means of communication.

Outsiders are indeed implacably rigorous when applying their ideals of cultural authenticity to indigenous people, whom they vigorously attempt to educate away from innovation. Pintupi dancers are sometimes criticised when they abandon hand-grinding ochre and opt for bright acrylic paints to decorate their bodies. Spectators care little for the religious significance of the marks, because they do not understand them, but condemn the practice as corrupt because Pintupi have creatively used an artefact from western society to satisfy their artistry.

Pintupi art is promoted as expressing traditional 'timeless' values, while being consumerised to fit the international art market: so initially artists were given only the colours considered 'traditional' by western buyers, to avoid offending their sensibilities with a sudden anarchic burst of colour. A meaningless design in colours of ochre is often accorded more value by outsiders than a colourful representation of an important Dreaming story, because this is a convenient means of comprehending, and therefore defining, traditional.

Pintupi are subject to incessant complaints that they are not really living in their houses like westerners, or using their vehicles 'properly', or spending (and saving) their money appropriately. At the same time they are fully expected to accept complaints that they are losing their 'authentic' culture and language, and to appreciate the efforts of outsiders in helping them to maintain these things, as if their identity, language or society is going to collapse without non-indigenous assistance. Because it is still assumed that the majority society is directing progress to its own design (and, therefore, changing or preserving indigenous society rather than adapting its own institutions), Pintupi are expected to take these criticisms very seriously.

It has always been clear who has been changing, maintaining or resurrecting whom. This is demonstrated in the comparisons between the two societies, where statistics that run the other way are ignored, including those aspects of Pintupi society which indicate better 'health' and wealth in western terms. Contributions to GDP by indigenous societies, including Pintupi, through large-scale production of paintings for the international art market, and a burgeoning cultural tourist market, are rarely considered. In the area of health, Pintupi children, unlike many of their contemporaries in western society, do not have to be subjected to long-term drug therapy in order to conform to cultural expectations of appropriate childhood behaviour, and youth suicide is completely unknown, as is any suicide outside jail. Abuse of children by their parents is extremely rare but an increasing problem in the West, with more than 45,000 cases reported in Australia each year.

The reverse scenario, the notion that Pintupi could help other Australians solve these problems or prevent the 'cultural disintegration' of western society is obviously absurd, though the dominant society's endeavours to change or save Pintupi society are taken very seriously indeed. Its exhortations to Pintupi for cultural salvation in past traditions, coupled with attempts to direct what is seen as long-overdue 'progress' towards mainstream outcomes, are just as irrelevant to them. The difference is that the Pintupi are not in a position to say so.

At Papunya it was reported that the requests of the indigenous people to the government were far simpler than the expectations of government of them (Davis et al. 1977, 108). Their requests for transport and money were refused, because giving Pintupi what they want on their own terms has never been seen as a potential means to bring about the changes demanded of them. This has important implications for what Pintupi self-determination can be.

Within current policy it is accepted on faith that Pintupi can hold onto important aspects of their own culture (as defined by others), while enjoying all the benefits that most other Australians have. This is convenient because no one needs to either tell Pintupi the unpalatable fact that they cannot have everything, or to look at the many contradictory faces of change, which in practice is rarely free of costs. Governments do not want to admit this, because it means accepting any negative effect on another people as not just something that happened in the bad old days, while Pintupi are naturally reluctant to give up the material equality dream offered them. As the recipients, rather than architects of social justice policy, they do not accept the responsibility for either its outcomes or evaluation.

Under social justice policies both societies are following the same imperative: to maximise material benefits while minimising negative effects. But what is valued by each society, and what is rejected, remains a fundamental difference that sends each on divergent journeys.

A CULTURE LIVE AND KICKING

> Grieving for the vanishing 'Other' is, after all, in some ways easier than confronting it live and kicking. (Ulf Hannerz 1991, 109)

Pintupi choices, and their insistence upon making them at every opportunity, mean that while Canberra alludes to a self-assured, managed direction of change through the refrain of health, housing and education, the actual process is one where very little is controlled. The failure to regulate the direction of change, such as to make Pintupi hoard their money, or take more responsibility for the infrastructure in their settlements, is usually viewed as evidence of intransigence. Conversely, most changes Pintupi, and other indigenous groups, have made in response to contact are reviled and many in western society rail against their inability to stay the same.

To fit the official discourses of social justice, Pintupi would have to accept 'appropriate' technology, such as hand-powered washers and wood-chip water heaters, while listening to endless equality pronouncements. They would need to adopt tidy western domesticity and work habits, then spend their 'free' time maintaining ceremonies and transmitting the old Dreamtime stories, while rejecting the rightful claims of relatives, especially children. They would have to speak Standard English during office hours, and old Pintupi at other times, while ruthlessly monitoring that dialect for incursions from other languages.

One of the problems with this cut-and-paste approach to fitting the pieces of indigenous culture into the official model of how it should be is that elements are not easily extracted from the whole to fit its requirements. A few disparate parts are separated out and joined with large blocks of western culture to create a new, jigsaw-puzzle society which conforms with social justice ideals, but Pintupi do not either see or live their lives as a static collection of pieces.

It is often the most inconvenient parts of Pintupi society that seem immutable. Cowlishaw believes that 'the place where Aborigines are remains a space of difference, but one where robust "racial" difference is being inexorably squeezed out while a malleable, tractable difference is encouraged' (1999, 296). Certainly, both societies want the 'other' to be far more malleable, but there is very little evidence that either is achieving this aim.

The Pintupi ideal of their relationship with government is meaningless beyond their settlements, while they themselves are unlikely to distinguish between aspects of their culture which are denigrated and parts that meet with official approval, except in their utility for obtaining resources. Yet, in an age of supposed self-determination, there seems no good reason why a western view of what is worth redeeming in their culture (and what must be eradicated) should mean anything to them.

Therefore, whether or not it suits the dominant society's aspirations for them, families are choosing to watch 'action' videos, rather than sitting dutifully around their campfires recounting Dreamtime stories, and people no longer travel around the country cleaning out rockholes. Ceremonial life has contracted its focus to journeys between settlements and is flourishing, but in a limited repertoire more in keeping with the practicalities of modern Pintupi lifeways. Old language continues to change, as living languages do, despite all efforts to fossilise it. Traditional bush shelters are rarely seen, although clever shelters made from iron and plastic, viewed by outsiders as eyesores and an affront to our common humanity, dot the settlements. While many promote tales of precontact times and now decontextualised Dreamtime stories as the only valid representations of indigenous culture, 'singalong' music creates a dynamic new context for vernacular literacy, as well as providing opportunities for elaborating the tradition of travelling ceremonies.

The autonomy of children and the 'abuse' of possessions are still resilient parts of the real, living culture and just because the dominant society deems them unacceptable, this does not mean they are an anomaly or an aberration. There is a burgeoning youthful population with relatively few middle aged adults, and the value of personal autonomy can be easily transmitted and learned in settlements, given free rein when children insist on being left behind with their friends while their parents go off hunting. The freedom of youths, and the resultant damage to settlement hardware, is far from in decline, despite all the earnest exhortations from outsiders.

Conversely, the transmission to the next generation of many of the revered 'authentic' aspects of culture, held by the middle-aged and the old, has become far more tenuous because it is no longer necessary for children to accompany groups when they are travelling around country.

Indeed, the high value the younger generation places on their relationships with peers means they often do not want to leave the settlement, unless they have friends at the destination to which they would be travelling.

In order to enhance the fulfilment of their own engagement with the contemporary world, Pintupi are quite comfortable with appropriating elements from western society, incorporating them within their own systems of meaning. As my daughter planned to leave Walungurru to embark on university studies, my younger 'sister', Mimala, insisted she become the godmother of her soon-to-be-born grand-daughter, the child of one of my daughter's friends. After a church ceremony the baby's relatives carefully explained that to be a godmother involved a full range of responsibilities, as well as substantial rights, for my daughter in the baby's upbringing.

My daughter was then often given the baby to care for while she was in the settlement. As Myers describes this process, '[a]ll the people who "look after" a child are held to share rights and duties for him or her … Pintupi acknowledge their shared identity by emphasizing that many people "grow up" a child' (1986a, 213). The ceremony and name may have been adopted from the dominant society, but the concept of what the relationship entailed was much closer to ideas of *walytja* than the responsibilities of a godmother in western society.

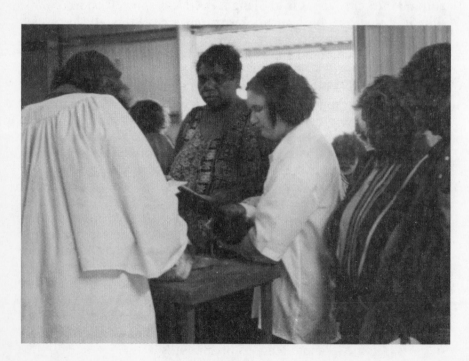

Making godmothers at Walungurru Church, 2000.

In contrast with this innovative, incorporative nature of Pintupi society, the contemporary 'blackfella domain' is usually described as being undermined or even destroyed by contact with the West (see, for example, Trigger 1992, 221). Hannerz (1991) explains that such a scenario posits that homogenisation results mainly from the centre–to–periphery flow of material culture, where the loss of local culture shows itself most distinctively at the margins. Yet, contrary to the opinion of the Council for Aboriginal Reconciliation (1994c, 49), western resources are now used to sustain and invigorate, rather than undermine, Pintupi cultural expression. Pintupi eagerly employ vehicles, money and faxed purchase orders, not only to expand social and ceremonial life, with 'sorry business' and men's business, together with singalong and football flourishing, but also to ensure participation by cutting off fuel supplies so the odd recalcitrants cannot escape their responsibilities.

Rather than suffer the much-lamented erosion of culture under the impact of 'modernisation', Pintupi have used new technologies to enhance their lives. As Piers Vitebsky states, modernisation, or globalisation, does not necessarily produce an abandonment of indigenous culture, but can lead to its reassertion (1995, 184). This interest in experimenting with, and commandeering, western resources, rather than actually using them to gain statistical equality, helps explain why putting more resources into Pintupi settlements has not lifted outcomes.

However, it is hard to know the effect the pressure to conform to western ideals is having on their society while the control of resources is still in the hands of the middle-aged. This is because the possibilities of change available to each generation of Pintupi depend not just on what they would like to do as individuals, but on the generation that 'holds' them. For example, a generation of Pintupi, who might themselves allow controlled mining on their land, will still say no for the sake of the grandfathers, 'We can't do that. The old people would cry'. So what seemed forbidden can abruptly be endorsed with enthusiasm with the demise of an older generation. Pressure for innovation builds up, but finds expression only when the older generation passes. Change can then happen very quickly.

Restraints of shame and compassion are still highly relevant for the grandchildren of the people who walked to Haasts Bluff and Papunya. Only when the young adults of today themselves become powerful in politics will the real outcomes of current attempts at social engineering be known. However, expecting that they will move neatly along predetermined social justice pathways is to be blind to the resilience of the core values of their society.

CHAPTER 7
THE 'TWO WAY' SOLUTION

The trouble is that our motives are mixed. We are concerned with our own
reputation as much as, if not a little more than, the Aboriginals' position.
(W E H Stanner 1979, 54)

Because of the entrenched belief in both the inherent fragility of
indigenous culture in contact with the West, and their willingness to
'acculturate', failure of policy reinforces the need for new answers
rather than questions. However, first, a great deal of energy is spent
disowning and disguising that failure. This is not too difficult because,
as Stanner pointed out, 'failure, in the nature of things, does not
become visible for a long time' (1979, 17). The Healthy Aboriginal
Life Team program ran for years on the basis of a need to do *something*
about substance abuse, combined with a somewhat plausible and well
publicised approach to redressing it. Similarly, 'success' in matters as
important as 'civilising' at Papunya could not be impeded by the
inconvenient and embarrassing reality that Pintupi were not willing to
cooperate. The predicted outcomes, therefore, had to be orchestrated.

As Colin Tatz discovered, assimilation was reduced to a facade of
statistical 'success' (1964, 64): officials statistically 'proved' the
achievements of the assimilationist schemes by the numbers of indigenous people pumped through training programs or 'registered for
courses', though later it appeared that little progress had actually been
made. This, of course, is another weakness of the equality approach; if
programs are based on statistical differences, this means success is susceptible to being equated merely with apparent — that is, numerical —
improvement, and as Mant explains, '… statistics are bound to "prove"
that there has been an "improvement"' (1997, 56).

Those who actually have to implement indigenous policy at the settlement level have always needed to disguise its failures, as well as those contradictions of policy that ensure failure. Officials at Papunya were told to create economic self-sufficiency, but were confronted with horrific mortality rates so, while they trained, they also provided food, clothing and medical care in order to keep most of the people alive. Both assimilation and welfare programs at Papunya were claimed to be successful but, as Tatz (1964) observed, they were clearly contradictory. You do not really achieve economic self-sufficiency by creating what looks like total dependency. On one hand, the appearance of assimilation was statistically manipulated and, on the other, welfare ameliorated the worst of the effects of contact.

To the annoyance of officials at Papunya, Tatz (who was researching a thesis at the settlement) contended that the 'incompatible aims' of the assimilation policy 'are not seen as such' (1964, 271). In the view of the officials, Tatz was a rank outsider who had little understanding of the local realities, but his real offence, of course, was not that he saw the blindingly obvious but that he publicly stated it. Privately, the officials agreed with Tatz, they knew that the various precepts of the assimilation policy could only be seen to be successful if they were propped up with a pot-pourri of programs with hopelessly crossed purposes.

The much-promoted assimilation of Pintupi was far more difficult than governments could publicly allow and, although the process was undermined by welfare measures, no one could countenance the catastrophic results of withdrawing them. Far from this contradiction being a kind of aberration, or problem unique to Papunya, Tatz had actually articulated the historic relationship between indigenous policy and its application, described in various ways down the years as the gap between 'rhetoric and reality'.

The 'crossed purposes' of policy, described by Tatz at Papunya, have been essential throughout contact history, although they have generally only been accepted as such when enough time has elapsed to remove the sting from this acknowledgment. The actual purposes alter a little under successive policies, although not to the extent implied by the condemnation to which earlier aims were later subjected. Although Tatz argued that the 'agents of policy' need only see the futility of pursuing what were obviously contradictory programs in order to rectify them (1964, 272), such 'blindness' is actually essential, disguising all the incompatible aims which must remain invisible so that policy seems plausible to its western audience. This is because the western precepts that underlie the incompatible aims applied to indigenous people are considered to be far more important than any contradictions that subsequently come to light in their execution.

In other words, it is far more important to have the 'right' policies than ones that achieve anything, and in this respect indigenous policy has been consistently successful. The attempt to expand the Pintupi women's craft industry by training the women to run their own business was certainly 'right' for its western audience, even if it destroyed the self-sufficiency the women already had. The HALT program was 'right' for its audience of the day in offering a culturally-sensitive approach to petrol-sniffing, even if it had little impact on substance abuse. The forced removal of children from their families was 'right' for an audience which believed they were being offered a brighter future by a magnanimous government.

As Tatz observed later, 'the gulfs between policies and their practice ... the contradictory ideas and ideals were and are still in vogue and operation' (1990, 249). The crossed purposes of social justice policy are currently hidden by denying its agenda of westernisation. Under the assimilation policy it was widely admitted within Australian society that indigenous people needed to forsake the integrity of their own ways for the benefits on offer, though the human cost of this loss was downplayed. Current indigenous policy claims not to tell Pintupi what is best for them, but still expects that they will choose the self-evident benefits of a 'better' way of life. Underlying this assumption is the belief that this choice will entail no costs to them — they will be able to have it all.

The crossed purposes of policy are now legitimated with their own name: 'two way'. Indigenous groups like the Pintupi can have their own way, with all its benefits, while also having those of other Australians. Again, implicit in this 'two way' is the denial that groups like the Pintupi have to undergo dramatic change to arrive at the equitable destination promoted by the dominant society. Once this 'two way' is accepted, then there is a further breathtaking step: equal outcomes are declared not just to be compatible with indigenous lives, but actually ensure their retention, according to *A Chance for the Future* (Commonwealth of Aust. 1989, 7).

HAVING IT BOTH WAYS

> Like all men, he too [the indigenous person] pays the price of his insights and solutions. (W E H Stanner 1979, 35)

'Two way' is the contemporary disguise of the pressure applied to indigenous societies to westernise. In the 'two way' model, indigenous Australians are represented as being able to have all western benefits as well as their own and because, as an ideal, this is a goal shared by both societies it is called 'self-determination'. This is the current way of representing the social changes decreed essential and, therefore, portrayed as part of a benevolent process of change. 'Two way' is right for its wider Australian audience, but it makes little sense when applied to Pintupi.

Myers identified a form of political correctness, where anthropologists counter criticism that they denigrate indigenous societies through their portrayals by ensuring they demonstrate how western values are satisfied (or even exemplified) in them (1985, 117). In other words, indigenous Australians are represented as the same as other Australians and, therefore, easily able to be made equal materially, while also having so much more, through their greater communality and spirituality. The politics of these representations do not allow that there are things that they may *not* be able to have, that there are costs to being what they are, just as there are costs for people in the West in their own forms of cultural expression.

The idea that Pintupi can simply add western perspectives to their lives in order to be 'two way' is an attractive proposition in the dominant society, where few contemplate the reverse scenario. Those who do usually end up regretting the attempt. Westerners cannot simply graft onto their own materialist tradition the concepts of spirituality and relatedness which underlie Pintupi society. Consequently they feel uncomfortable in the hurly-burly of their adopted *walytja*, where the ceaseless demands of relatives soon become an onerous and untenable imposition. Other whitefellas generally treat them with a contempt similar to that directed by Pintupi society towards any of their own who attempt to sacrifice cultural responsibilities in order to gain western benefits. Rarely does the experiment last long. The sacrifices and costs associated with their attempt at 'two ways' can never be compensated for by anything more than a half-hearted acceptance by another culture, the forms of which they can only attempt to emulate feebly and the benefits of which do not accrue to them.

'Two ways' asks what Pintupi would like to have from western society, rather than whether they will bear the costs of the acquisition, implying there is no sacrifice in choosing a different lifeway. For example, in 'two way' theory there is no conflict between indigenous lives and western employment, but it does not explain how Pintupi will find time for the commitments intrinsic to both. Pintupi are expected to be able to take over the western policing of their own settlements, but no one asks if they are willing to suffer the condemnation from non-relatives when someone is hurt because they did not act, or the rage of their own relatives when they lock up one of their own.

This is not merely an academic question. At a meeting to discuss a fight which arose when a Pintupi worker tried to restrain some drunks, and was rounded on by them and assaulted, one of the old men insisted the worker had acted 'wrong way'. He was not condoning the drunken behaviour but asserting that Pintupi should not play such a divisive role. Some family members, such as brothers, may restrain each other to prevent injury, and uncles may discipline their nieces and nephews, but Pintupi cannot simply boss each other around, like whitefellas do, without due regard to their proper relationships. In the view of Pintupi, attempts to do so cause far more serious offence than public drunkenness.

Exploiting 'two way' theory allows contradictory goals to seem attainable. For example, 'proper' (western democratic) operation of indigenous community councils, including the advocacy of opposing positions and majority rule, which Williams condemns as 'unworkable and unAboriginal' (1985, 17), can be promoted alongside policies supporting indigenous traditions and the kinship basis of their society. *Walytja* is thus expected to stay strong while relatives act in ways that reject their kinship ties. The Aboriginal and Torres Strait Islander Commission (ATSIC), for instance, urges people not to vote for their family members, but for people who will get the job done though, as the Council for Aboriginal Reconciliation admits, 'Such an advertisement could produce conflict for those who have responsibility to assist their family or group where possible' (1994a, 34). Mixed messages like this continue to assail settlements even though, as Williams comments, 'The "hows" of Aboriginal decision-making are not, after all, invisible or even mysterious' (1985, 40).

Much current reconciliation theory also embraces the palatable idea of 'two way', couched not just in terms of overriding concern for indigenous inequality, but also a belief that their culture 'should be recognised as an integral and distinctive part of the nation's life and heritage' (*Social Justice for Indigenous Australians* 1991–92). Like so many attempts to define progress in indigenous societies, reconciliation is right for its western audience, its contradictions invisible behind a veil of taken-for-granted ideals. According to this theory of reconciliation, all will be well between the societies once every indigenous group achieves equality, while also retaining all of their own cultural imperatives. How such a mind-boggling proposition of incompatible aims is to be implemented is not elaborated by its enthusiastic architects.

In an attempt to promote the possibility of such benevolent equality, which presumes no costs to Pintupi lifeways, a plethora of 'two way' programs have been spawned at all facets of the interface. 'Two way' school offers an especially attractive prospect: an image of Pintupi children 'retaining their own culture' while seamlessly adding to it an equitable western education. This is a massive shift from the 1960s when Papunya teachers were reminded that 'the progress of any (western) education is necessarily limited by the pace of social change' (Davis et al. 1977, 17). Schools are now expected to pursue equal educational outcomes, while *also* 'maintaining' indigenous culture.

'TWO WAY' SCHOOLING

> A common assertion has been that integration is to be a two-way process, but this does not mean that each group is equally influential. A basic parochialism, combined with ethnocentrism, has limited the expression of this view to lip-service. (J Wilson 1964, 152)

The idea of schools in indigenous settlements being able to create outcomes for their students equal with the mainstream, while simultaneously promoting and supporting the transmission and maintenance of their traditional culture, has been extremely popular. This notion of culturally sensitive, 'two way' schools generating mainstream-like results sounds attractive at a national level, where it is in harmony with the agenda of social justice (for example, Keeffe 1992, 129–132). However, like so many well-meaning and fine-sounding plans hatched by majority societies for indigenous people, there are fundamental problems with its implementation at the local level.

As Barnett et al. point out, remote desert schools are not a primary source of socialisation into indigenous family and settlement life (1995, 95). This is because school caters to people based on their residence in a single population centre, while Pintupi structures draw on kin resident in numerous settlements. By cutting right across the kinship structure at the heart of Pintupi society and dealing instead with the western administrative unit of 'community', school immediately declares itself as foreign to the culture into which it has been implanted. To ignore the real basis of Pintupi social organisation, while attempting to facilitate cultural maintenance, means that school has the potential to reduce a living culture to the decontextualised subject of indigenous studies: surely a destructive rather than constructive role in cultural transmission?

Schools attempting to fit the 'two way' agenda often teach western knowledge, and then its indigenous equivalent, aptly described by Cowlishaw as 'a plethora of phantoms and stereotypes' (1999, 299). In this process bits of 'traditional' knowledge are plucked out of context and grafted onto a western school curriculum, which is sometimes then depicted as being 'Aboriginal'. For example, Pintupi knowledge of the seasons is often displayed as a calendar, remarkably like the regular and predictable chart used to show the European seasons, even though the desert seasons are actually highly irregular and very unpredictable. Hoogenraad and Robertson comment that such charts suffer the problem of force-fitting indigenous knowledge into the parameters of another system (1997, 35). No wonder an indigenous teacher, who had undergone years of training, recoiled in horror at the suggestion she produce 'another Aboriginal calendar'.

As Cooke notes, it is only those aspects that can be pruned and manipulated to fit western concepts that find a place in school (1988, 4), and this consequently reflects a distorted and often outdated vision of its students' culture. Because of the disparate nature of the two societies these areas are very limited and consequently schools tend to recycle them over and over again. As well as the ever-popular Aboriginal calendar, another area thought to be suitable for this pruning is the indigenous health system, elements of which, such as Pintupi bush tucker and medicine, are usually incorporated because they have equivalents in western concepts of health. However, these surgically removed segments in no way represent a Pintupi understanding of health and sickness. This remains part of a totally different system of knowledge, what Stanner referred to as the religious tradition (1979, 123), a system fundamentally at odds with an institution whose primary educational agenda is the transmission of western, scientific thought.

However 'two way' they may aspire to be, western schools can only play an essentially symbolic role in their incorporation of indigenous cultural forms, for example, by facilitating the performance of occasional social ceremonies that are open to everyone. This limited engagement can then be used to suggest to outsiders that they are effectively 'two way' in 'maintaining' and 'transmitting' their students' culture. Such activities, which are valuable in their own right as a relaxed exchange between school and other settlement members, are subsequently promoted as so much more, a 'sign of hope', an attempt to 'recover old traditions and the spirituality inherent in them' (World Council of Churches 1991, 50). As James Clifford explains, 'what we see as different about the "Other" is defined (only) in terms of traditional pasts, inherited structures that either resist or yield to the new but cannot produce it' (1998, 5).

Those who promote this notion of school replicating (or resurrecting) indigenous culture do not seem aware that the inference that groups like Pintupi are incapable of making, and implementing, competent decisions about the transmission of their own culture, without considerable help from outsiders, could be offensive. Not only is this idea insulting, the emphasis put on 'traditional', as opposed to contemporary, cultural concepts and their maintenance by most 'two way' schools limits any dialogue between the two societies to those aspects of indigenous culture deemed authentic by the dominant society. This emphasis makes those aspects of the students' contemporary culture which do not fit the 'authentic' model unwelcome in the school. Moreover, for this controlled interaction of 'whitefellas keeping the culture strong', Pintupi generally expect payment because they are transmitting aspects of 'traditional', often pre-contact, culture they no longer automatically pass on, because they are not considered to have contemporary relevance.

One area of education where western society's preoccupation with indigenous cultural authenticity has been problematic is in the area of language. Using, and teaching literacy in, the students' contemporary first language is a valuable means of making schools more attractive, and relevant, to students who speak a living indigenous language. This facilitates the improvement of both their attendance and literacy attainments. However, its benefit is undermined when, rather than acknowledging and incorporating their real contemporary language, schools choose to promote rigorously a resurrected 'traditional' language within the school.

As well as being counter-productive in the struggle to improve attendance and outcomes, schools which attempt to adopt the role of guardian of 'authentic' language or culture may actually be endangering those very aims. Rather than convincing indigenous groups that schools are capable of transmitting their language and culture, it would be better if they were honest about their limitations. However 'two way' they might aspire to be, schools will never be able to force modern generations of indigenous children to shift to a more 'authentic' form of language, or to adopt cultural rites with no contemporary context in settlement life. They would do better to advise indigenous families who want to preserve old forms of language to use these regularly with children in the camps, because this is the only real chance they have of keeping them viable community languages.

The second aim of 'two way' schools — the creation of outcomes for indigenous students equal to those of their mainstream contemporaries — is just as problematic. School is often assumed to be such a powerful instrument of change in indigenous settlements that it can overcome the lack of out-of-school societal reinforcement of its western knowledge whereas in reality, as Fishman demonstrates, school is actually highly dependent on that arena for its own effectiveness (1991, 374). The need for school knowledge to have an important contemporary use in a society, or at least to be treated as valuable, before its transmission to students is effective, is not unique to indigenous societies. Fishman argues that elements of schooling in western society such as algebra, encounter the same problem if acquisition for retention is taught before there is any societal use for them (371).

Like all societies, the knowledge Pintupi want to acquire in, and out of, school is that which is useful in enhancing the lives they presently live. For example, English may be the national language of Australia, but it is not a Pintupi settlement language, and consequently is not transmitted by families. Each new generation must start from scratch, learning what is essentially a foreign language. Given this lack of local context, it is hardly surprising that schools struggle for improved results in areas such as English literacy and oracy: to expect them to produce outcomes on a par with their non-indigenous contemporaries, who speak English as a first language and live in a society where literacy is necessary for everyday survival, is unrealistic.

This need for context and utility is probably why literacy appears to have declined in Western Desert settlements since the advent of rad-phones, and then telephones, together with increased incomes and therefore greater mobility. Before these changes, people did have a functional need for literacy, writing to relatives in far-flung settlements was, at that time, the only way to stay in touch with them. Many of the older, often literate generation, responded by learning to read and write through bible studies, with the help of missionaries and the prim-itive curriculum materials which are scorned today. Their teachers were able to capitalise on an obvious utility rather than the far more ambi-tious, and abstract, goal of equal outcomes.

The idea of 'two ways' is problematic even in the deeper under-standings implicit in western educational institutions. At the funda-mental level of how knowledge is valued and transmitted, Western Desert schools and their students are both resolutely 'one way'. Pintupi students evaluate the western content of school through their own cul-tural precepts and, although they are always being told western knowl-edge is important, this is not self-evident, and whitefellas themselves certainly do not seem to treat it as valuable. Pintupi schools must encourage the interest and attendance of a student body who, unlike their mainstream counterparts, are not compelled to attend. The means schools employ in their endeavours to attract students are open-ness, accessibility, such as picking up reluctant students every morning, and assorted attempts at bribery, including paying senior students to attend.

This cajoling of Pintupi students to learn contrasts sharply with the attitudes of their own society, in which valuable knowledge is not at all freely available, and the younger generation are never paid or begged to acquire it. Pintupi knowledge that is designated as important, and therefore worth learning is withheld by its custodians until the young show themselves to be ready for it. It is this process of custodians hold-ing back, then gradually providing access to, knowledge, within the context of their relationship with the neophyte, which demonstrates its worth and powerfully motivates the young to demand it.

In contrast, the western 'gift of education' is not valued, precisely because it is a gift, usually offered by a near-stranger who has no sig-nificant relationship to the student. As such, school knowledge pro-claims itself of little worth to its Pintupi students. It is amazing how powerfully motivated to acquire knowledge, however esoteric it might seem to them, Pintupi children can become when they develop a good relationship with their whitefella teacher. When this relationship is sev-ered, as it frequently is through the high teacher turnover on settle-ments, students soon make clear, through their absences, how irrelevant they find the knowledge a western education offers them.

The reality that equal outcomes in western education actually requires what Bucknall calls 'radically changed perspectives' (1995, 43) is rarely acknowledged. This is because, in 'two way' theory such outcomes are assumed to be just added on to indigenous lifeways. But western education is integral to the society from which it evolved and its outcomes, far from being additive to indigenous society, require sacrifices for their achievement.

Despite this, proponents of 'two way' schooling never think to ask indigenous families if they are prepared to allow the level of discipline needed to produce equal outcomes, or even if they are willing to override the autonomy they ascribe to their children to make them go to school. According to Keeffe 'two way' schooling 'reconciles the apparent conflict between being Aboriginal and being equal'(1992, 119), but can it make Pintupi parents willing to sacrifice their societal imperatives, such as their own and their children's autonomy, in order to strive for success in mainstream education?

When confronted with the reality of the constraints imposed by the demands of western education, especially on teenagers, Pintupi parents are aghast. Just as many in the wider society recoil in horror at what they see as the rampant freedom of indigenous youth, Pintupi find the strictures placed on whitefella children in the name of education cruel and unnatural. My daughter was frequently described by our Pintupi 'relatives' as suffering unbearable oppression; they often challenged our prioritising of educational outcomes over nurturing and extending family.

The belief that adding prosperity produces equal material outcomes may displace the question as to what are the social imperatives of wealth for Pintupi. In a similar fashion, current theories about indigenous education preclude consideration of what western educational outcomes are essential to, and therefore valued by, Pintupi in pursuing their contemporary lives. This is the question indigenous parents are answering when, to everyone's surprise, they say they are happy with school (Barnett et al. 1995, 34), even though their schools have what Keeffe describes as 'the lowest rates of success in Australian education' (1992, 11). Their reply is arrogantly dismissed, with no acknowledgment of their ability to make competent judgements about their own children's welfare, on the basis that the parents are too uneducated themselves to judge the success, or otherwise, of their children's education (Barnett et al. 1995, 34).

Certainly, this relative lack of engagement with, and consequent attainment in, western education may make Pintupi vulnerable at some time in the future. Perhaps, as Peterson argues, indigenous people cannot remain economically passive in the long term (1998, 12), and there may be a time in the future when groups like the Pintupi are greatly disadvantaged, in their own terms, by their lack of achievement in western education. However, in the paramount context of the present, this is not obvious. Indeed, because there is little meaning in, and few social rewards for, high levels of achievement in mainstream education Pintupi are far from demoralised by their minimal literacy skills and simple spoken English as Keeffe (1992, 11) assumes they should be.

Because of their unequal attainment in school, Pintupi are usually considered by their non-indigenous judges to be grossly uneducated. Yet Pintupi, using their own measures of intellect, are also amazed at the intractable ignorance and obtuseness of the representatives of western culture with whom they come into contact. In contrast with their own multilingualism, most whitefellas know only one language, and seem incapable of picking up another. As for the inability of even long-term resident whitefellas, including myself, to grasp much beyond the simplest levels of their repeatedly explained Pintupi relationship system, not even toddlers are considered to be so backward and unteachable.

The idea that Pintupi will achieve equal outcomes, while having their own pre-contact and contemporary culture rigorously maintained within their schools, is very seductive, but the differences between the two cultures are far too great to allow anything but 'two way' tokenism to operate. Schools on Pintupi settlements are, at their most fruitful, a tenuous but effective accommodation to powerful and competing cultural pressures and constraints, rather than sites where joint ownership which fully satisfies the societal imperatives of both sides is possible. To set such an unattainable goal as the measure of Western Desert schools precludes appreciation of the real achievements that are possible at the interface.

TWO WAY MEDICINE

> Exhortation, social engineering and education simply do not produce social change in any predetermined direction: the process is far too complicated for that. (Charles Rowley 1971, 352)

Very soon after first contact, indigenous people at Papunya accepted pills and injections. This ready adoption of the accoutrements of western medicine by Pintupi has led many observers to assume that they are giving up on unscientific 'traditional' cures and this change must produce dramatic movement towards health outcomes equal with other Australians. However, this is not the case, because it is only some aspects of western medicine that have been assimilated into Pintupi lives and belief systems.

When the dominant society sees two discrete systems of medicine, one spiritual and the other scientific, it assumes that the obvious advantages of a scientific approach must vanquish the other. However, Pintupi are open to exploiting the advantages of both, adopting aspects of western medicine for their own reasons and on their own terms, without ever relinquishing the spiritual basis of their own health understandings. Pintupi use western medicine, not because they accept its precepts, but because it sometimes works against the diseases they believe whitefellas gave them.

A minor illness, such as an upset stomach, may be attributed to bad meat, but serious sickness is subject to a range of Pintupi interpretations. It may be caused by a stick, or stone, lodged inside the body, which must be withdrawn by a *ngangkari* (traditional healer). These embedded objects are the result of being ensorcelled by others, and even babies can be afflicted in this way. It is also possible to become ill by losing one's *kurrunpa* (spirit), by sleeping on one's back, thereby allowing the spirit to escape through the navel. Sorcery where *kurrunpa kutjanu* (the spirit was cooked) produces potentially lethal illness, as does eating one's totem, which is the origin of one's spirit, or touching, or even being near, a sacred object without the protection of fat smeared on the body. The latter can also cause madness.

While women now have their children in hospital, they still 'smoke' the new-born baby afterwards, protecting it from sickness and ensuring a 'cheeky' child. The basic causes of illness, and its treatment, largely remain unchanged. Tjakamarra often explained to me that his health problems were caused by a variety of objects embedded in his body, and that bouts of illness affecting numerous people were due to the absence of a *ngangkari* in the settlement at that time. Tjakamarra's own quest for healing was to find the 'right' *ngangkari*, the one with the power to make him well and who, he explained, probably lived to the west of Walungurru, where whitefellas are fewer and the healing power remains.

Pintupi seek out the white sister or doctor for treatment usually only after seeing the *ngangkari*, who alone has the power to cure the fundamental causes of illness. Cameron Tjapaltjarri once explained to me that, although he had been ill for several weeks, he was unable to seek help at the clinic because there was no *ngangkari* available in the settlement at that time. Every illness presented to the clinic must receive medical treatment, and patients may become upset if told there is no appropriate therapy from a scientific standpoint. A *takata kapi* (doctor water) was ridiculed as ineffectual because he gave sick people water instead of using the power of the needle.

Despite the dominant society's faith in the unfailingly positive effects of western medicine for them, its technology can create unintended problems for Pintupi. Their society copes well with sudden death (which has always been common) through a vast outpouring of grief shared with other relatives, but a life sustained technologically can create casualties among traumatised relatives as they literally worry themselves to death. The idea that doctors confer with relatives to discuss turning off a life-support system is horrific, because relatives can never be party to the death of their own and would have to be severely punished if they were. In these circumstances, the continuation of the relative's life vastly outweighs any other considerations, such as its quality.

It is in the many ways that western medicine does not work for Pintupi that their rejection of its precepts and 'two way' misconception becomes visible. In their own tradition, they seek medical cures in the form of 'special tablets', while disdaining prevention and often treatment as well, if it is protracted rather than instant. In the case of some illness, Pintupi cures are deemed to be able to work only if they have *not* previously been treated by western medicine, while the healing spirit of the *ngangkari* can be driven away by too much contact with whitefellas. Once a person has been in 'Ward 1' (a psychiatric ward of Alice Springs Hospital), Pintupi say they can no longer be helped by their own doctors.

Although the adoption of aspects of western medicine as a controlled colonisation of western life might be seen as 'two way' theory in practice, it certainly does not achieve the espoused goal of melding equal outcomes with Pintupi lifeways. That Pintupi take their illnesses to the clinic for treatment does not mean there is any agreement with their whitefella doctor about its cause, or how it could be prevented in the future. Neither does the fact that a *ngangkari* works through the clinic for payment implies no adoption of its beliefs or goals. If, for example, Pintupi believe, in the face of western health education, that a sickness is caused by a stick embedded internally through sorcery, or that an outbreak of systemic infections result from the absence of a traditional doctor, rather than contact with the effluvia from an overflowing toilet, it seems unlikely that they will devote much time to sanitising their environment.

Customs that appear to outsiders to be of little value, and which the dominant society believes should easily melt away in the face of the scientific evidence of their negative health effects, remain inexplicably entrenched. However, Pintupi place primary value on relatedness and conceptualise health in terms of social harmony. Because of this a mother cannot refuse her young daughter *mingkulpa* (chewing tobacco) when she demands it; although the mother may tell the child quite forcefully that she is too young, she will invariably hand it over. Subsequently, the *mingkulpa* will be passed from mouth to mouth because the value of shared identity is far higher than the health advantage of selfishly hoarding it on the grounds that infectious disease may be passed on with the *mingkulpa*. It is hard for the dominant society to concede that the values this sharing represents for Pintupi are very important, but *mingkulpa* use is increasingly common among young girls and is rarely disapproved of. For Pintupi there are felt costs to changing such customs as sharing *mingkulpa* or living in close proximity with mangy dog packs, though these may seem like simple and obvious changes for the better.

Mathers states that 'the measurement of the positive constructs of physical, mental, social and spiritual wellbeing is generally not seen as an aspect of health-sector activity' (1999, 150). The fact that Pintupi could escape the depression and despair of the better-resourced settlement of Papunya, to find 'health' through high individual and group self-esteem on their materially impoverished Kungkayunti outstation in 1975 (Morice 1976), has always been problematic for other Australians; so too is their use of resources to maintain existing lifestyles rather than to treat disease. That a people could be 'dirtier but healthier' is a woolly and unquantifiable notion that holds little sway in an era when hard statistics record each shift in the progress, or lack of it, towards equal outcomes.

Nevertheless, as Parkin shows, for all the advantages of western medicine, many people around the world do not find their need for emotional stability and cognitive reassurance well served by it (1995, 149). When Pintupi choose their own lifeways over those apparently more conducive to achieving parity with the health statistics of western societies, they are not just embarking on a prolonged binge of irrational behaviour. This is why the goal of equality is so problematic. If indigenous health problems really were merely the result of what Partington describes as 'their own fecklessness' (1996, 123), how much simpler and more effective the remedies would be.

However, Pintupi are — inconveniently for policy — not a passive, dispirited people but vigorous participants busily interpreting and refashioning earnest western endeavours to simultaneously change and fossilise their culture. Despite the misconception that their adopting western resources means they will come to live more like other Australians, they really use western goods to enhance the lives they already enjoy, including those aspects that preclude equal outcomes. This exercising of their prerogative to neither westernise nor stay resolutely the same is the cause of a great deal of misunderstanding at the interface.

Pintupi will use aspects of western medicine, while retaining their own explanations and, therefore, many of the 'unhealthy' customs of their lives; a completely unsatisfactory arrangement in the view of mainstream society, but just one of the many processes of indigenizaton common on Pintupi settlements . The arguments used to channel resources into settlements are almost entirely about movement towards equal outcomes, even though Pintupi continuously undermine this goal by diverting these resources to extend and enhance their own life plan. The resulting lack of 'progress' along official pathways may look like a conservative reluctance to accept change, but creatively experimenting with the possibilities thrown up by equity efforts is actually a consummate Pintupi pursuit.

Above Traditional dancing at Waḻungurru School, 2000.

Below Clinton Tjampitjinpa in front of a painting by Indigenous teachers on old Waḻungurru school building, 1994.

CHAPTER 8
THE WELL OF INSPIRATION

Consider the many challenges to survival, which they [Aborigines] have overcome, any one
of which, for all we know, may have affected their society more severely than we have ...
I can see no reason why we should suppose that their well of inspiration has run dry.
(W E H Stanner 1979, 358)

Instead of recognising that Pintupi actually maintain their own contemporary lifeways in the face of unrelenting pressure from the dominant society to be both statistically 'equal' and 'traditional', they are
often viewed as powerless, 'losing' their culture and generally not measuring up in any way against the policy yardsticks applied to them.
Having failed to see that there is more than one measure, governments
are both inspired and doomed to re-enact equity policy with increasing
vigour.

This zealotry of the state in projecting its own ideals onto indigenous people, to manipulate them into developmental models and make
them equal cannot be dismissed as merely negative, intrusive or
oppressive (for example, Tonkinson 1991, 181; Cowlishaw 1999, 38).
Its domination of the discourse can also be harnessed and used by
indigenous groups. The response of Pintupi to the Australian state is
not so much based on 'marginalised and muted' resistance, indepen-
dence and sovereignty as Keeffe believes (1992, 92), but draws instead
on their creativity and a knowledge of the well-known habitual patterns
of mainstream society.

As this historic opportunity for Pintupi ingenuity arose, another
closed off. At first contact Pintupi were confronted by a society that
drew them from the desert and offered, but also hoarded tantalisingly
in store, exciting goods on implacable terms. They responded by trying to strike upon a mutually respectful relationship. With remarkable

success, considering the times, the last-contact generation charmed and exhorted their bemused whitefella relatives to behave properly and share more of the desirable new goods with them. They were obviously rich beyond imagining and it was unthinkable that they would not share. This process continues today:

Pintupi man: *Tjangala* [skin-name]! *Ngalyarra* [Come here].
Whitefella: (suspiciously) What is it?
Pintupi man: *Malanypa ngayuku, ilta* [You're my little brother, true]?
Whitefella: (reluctantly) *Yuwa* [Yes].
Pintupi man: *Tjapilkitjananta. Kulini* [I want to ask you for something. Do you understand me]?

Long-term resident whitefellas in Pintupi settlements, like myself, who have been taught some of their language and shown some of their country, dances and bush food, are deemed to have obligations to those who taught them.

Pintupi man: *Ngayulu nintinu ngurra ngayuku* [I showed you my country].
Author: *Ngayuku Tuyutangka* [In my Toyota].
Pintupi man: *Nganana nyuntu tinanu ngaangka* [We grew you up here].
Pintupi man 2:   *Ngayulu nintinu kulintjaku* [I taught you to listen to my language].
Author: *Ngayulu nintirringu kuulangka* [I learned at school].
Pintupi man 2:   (emphatically) *Wiya! Ngayulunanta nintinu* [No! I taught you]!
Author: (reluctantly) *Yuwa, yuwa* [Yes, yes].
Pintupi man: *Kipara nyarratja, wanma wiya, ila. Yarralaka kukaku Tuyutangka!* [Bush turkey that way, not far, close up. Let's go for meat in your Toyota]!

Making claims in this way, using a traditional framework, is only powerful within Pintupi settlements, it cannot reach beyond them to influence government and its bureaucracies. Conversely, 'equality' claim-making is powerful at a national level, but has little force within settlements. From the beginnings of their first tenuous contact up to the present, Pintupi have found it immensely difficult to get their own needs met in ways that either meet with the approval of, or make sense to, other Australians. It is also the dilemma of government, relentlessly pressured to create equality of outcomes in indigenous society in programs that meet indigenous approval, or at least seem vaguely credible at the local level.

USING EQUALITY

> This is why they develop rather than alter, substitute rather than forgo, and give in only to try to outwit ... It is as plain as daylight that this system is still fundamentally Aboriginal in type. (W E H Stanner 1979, 62)

Pintupi have experienced what may be a short-lived coincidence between the way they conceive their relationship with government bosses, who should 'help' them, and benevolent social justice, where bosses have been ready to offer generous assistance, though for their own reasons and on their own terms. Because real self-determination for some indigenous groups does not produce equal outcomes, although this cannot be admitted, the choices on offer are limited to those believed to contribute to movement in approved directions. In this process the term 'self-determination' embraces whatever is decided to be in the interests of indigenous people.

Thus, Pintupi must negotiate in terms of the aspirations of the wider society for them, but in this largely unequal contest they have one huge advantage. As Hannerz explains, peripheral societies have usually paid far more attention to the encroaching culture than it has paid to them (1991, 109). Pintupi have had to understand whitefellas and have learnt the lessons of contact history well, whereas most whitefellas have neither needed, nor bothered, to understand them.

Pintupi 'negotiate' under the guise of equality while differences are elaborated at the settlement level where they can exert real power. The terms of this negotiation, including areas aimed at demonstrating empathy with indigenous Australians, are the only ones on offer to a people who have few alternatives to choose from in sustaining their own lifeway. As the Aboriginal and Torres Strait Islander Social Justice Commissioner, Mick Dodson, states:

> The choices available at the community level are those presented by the menu of programmes which in themselves reflect prior bureaucratic decisions as to which programmes are appropriate. In effect, community decision making takes place within the framework of decisions made by others. (1994, 112)

This brokering of indigenous lives by others, described by the Aboriginal and Torres Strait Islander Social Justice Commissioner as a process where '[indigenous] interests are interpreted by remote bureaucrats ... who have never spoken with an Aboriginal person' (1995, 9), is not necessarily antithetical to Pintupi ideals of benevolent and undemanding bosses. In their view, the relationship is not intrinsically disempowering, as there are flexibilities in the actual use of any resources once they are on their settlements. This may seem a circuitous route to a limited self-determination, but would the dominant society be willing to sustain a high level of resourcing if any but its own precepts were the goals?

Bureaucrat:	What do you think the needs of your community are?
Pintupi 1:	We got some money from ... What was it? I think it was PCDS program.
Pintupi 2:	It was for community development.
Pintupi 1:	Yes. That's right.
Bureaucrat:	What did you spend the money on?
Pintupi 1:	We got some roads and houses and money to pick up rubbish. We had some ideas but — (bureaucrat) told us to 'clean up the community'.
Bureaucrat:	Well! It's important to have a clean community.
Pintupi 2:	*Yuwa* [Yes]. Transport always gets overlooked. They wouldn't help us with transport. We were thinking you might help us.
Bureaucrat:	Our budget is really small so I'm not sure we can help with that. Is there any other project you have in mind?
Pintupi 1:	We're really thinking hard about transport.
Bureaucrat:	What sort of vehicles are you talking about?
Pintupi 1:	Everything. We need trucks and buses and cars. No help with transport.
Bureaucrat:	What do you need all those vehicles for?
Pintupi 2:	We like to go to outstations — travel around, see our families, visit country, go hunting. We play football and like to take everyone. Sometimes people have to stop here because there's no room.
Bureaucrat:	Don't you need money for health programs? Do you grow your own vegetables?
Pintupi 1:	*Yuwa* [Yes]. At Papunya we did that *irriti lingku* [a long time ago]. But we're just talking for vehicles with you mob.
Bureaucrat:	Surely you have health problems?
Pintupi 2:	Yes, kids are always sick. Lots of people get sick. Old people get sick. Maybe we could use a bus to pick up old people for the clinic.
Bureaucrat:	Other communities have vegetable gardens so they can grow their own food. Getting fresh vegetables must be difficult out here. What is it, 500 km from Alice Springs? I guess everything has to come out

by truck. Your vegetables must be old by the time   they get here.

Pintupi 1:   *Yuwa* [Yes]. We might make a garden here.

Bureaucrat: Growing your own vegetables would create jobs for people too. There must be a lot of people without jobs.

Pintupi 2:   A garden is good. For that garden we need a truck to look after it.

A demand for a motor vehicle for hunting or visiting relatives is sure to be dismissed out of hand, on the basis that this is a private resource for which the individual should be responsible and, anyway, an impoverished people should first attend to more obvious priorities. As well as equal outcomes, these also include, of course, aspects that embrace the ideal of cultural authenticity, including cultural and language maintenance.

Pintupi are subjected to various fanciful, and highly contradictory, representations of themselves, but in this they are far from victims. They may allow, or even encourage, various representations of themselves as elemental, an ancient, timeless people, environmental or heritage exemplars. They are also sometimes exploited by outside groups who claim shared interests while finding it expedient to not explore too closely the differences, as Bill Harney realised:

> ... [they had] learnt from experience of white people that many questioners are happy to get the answers they desire. It is not the truth that many want but an answer which will fall in with their theories. A leading question is fatal for that will give the informant what one requires ... I have been led up this 'blind-alley' many times ... (1995, 70)

Through acquiescence and encouragement Pintupi also benefit from these representations, because resources gained will not necessarily be used according to the intended design, just as resources gained by their inequality will not necessarily be used to redress the 'lifestyle problems' contributing to it.

Pintupi usually support equality, and most other ideals espoused for them by western society, and then re-fashion some of the services and resources provided in terms of the values of their own society. They make such judgements with confidence. My friend Tjakamarra assured me that any government decision or policy that did not meet local expectations was simply 'wrong way' because, he explained, 'that's not helping Aboriginal people'. In their version of the relationship they have with government, Pintupi insist they should be looked after, but they also firmly believe they are the best judges of how that should be achieved. Indeed, they are frequently told exactly that by the dominant society, though rarely given the opportunity to exercise the implied self-determination, at least officially.

In making claims, Pintupi are open to the characterisation of themselves as having less than other Australians. They certainly agree that
they should be equal, though they also say they do not want to *be*
whitefellas. Being level is an ideal genuinely held by Pintupi but, when
there is conflict with their immediate social imperatives, it takes second
place. That equal outcomes are rarely, if ever, achieved has no effect on
the fundamental beliefs that sustain the relationship on both sides. As
long as Pintupi remain willing to participate in programs without dis-
puting their aims, they are able to fulfil some of their real needs, despite
repeated failure of these programs in official terms.

The advantage to Pintupi of this process is that, like all previous
myopia embodied in policy down the ages, it can be harnessed to
achieve real self-determination. It enables people of a small minority
society to use the strength of a far more powerful one to their own
advantage, which is the only kind of empowerment allowed to minority societies like the Pintupi.

INSTITUTIONAL INDIVIDUALISM

> Over twenty different governmental agencies, each generally not know-
> ing what the others are planning or doing at Jigalong, or even what their
> own predecessors in the same agency have done, impinge on the com-
> munity, often repeating the same mistakes. (Robert Tonkinson, 1991,
> 171)

Although they are family-oriented, Pintupi are fully expected to act in a
unified way, plan for a collective future and confidently express the 'will
of the people', but they are already provided with abundant means for
sustenance in their own polity. The dominant society presents itself in
indigenous settlements through a multiplicity of uncoordinated and
even, at times, warring federal, state and local government bodies, as
well as non-government agencies. These groups are characterised by
oppositional policy decisions, fragmentation and overlap.

These agencies exhibit none of the unity they demand of Pintupi,
and this double standard provides opportunities for empowerment for
those Pintupi individuals who, more than others, are involved with
what King calls, 'metropolitan systems of meaning' (1991, 17). They
are adept at fulfilling their own objectives and those of their *walytja*, by
exploiting the inefficiencies and crossed purposes universally condemned as being against the interests of indigenous people.

Pintupi cultural brokers express 'whole community' needs for those
bureaucrats who believe, either simplistically or as a matter of expedien-
cy, that since Pintupi live in a 'traditional Aboriginal community' all that
is required is to talk to the leaders or 'elders'. In a process John von
Sturmer describes as 'institutional individualism' (1982, 98), indigenous brokers and their *walytja* assume a special role at the interface.

They 'represent' the community to funding agencies, while arguing to their fellows that, unlike the Canberra bosses, they are not bosses themselves but, rather, are 'working for everyone'. In this way they do not have to take the responsibilities of a boss, and are not hamstrung by the requirement that everyone reach agreement. In return, they are able to access some of the resources of both the 'community' and the outside agencies, while limiting any claims that might be made on themselves.

Where meetings are held in the settlement, the role of these 'community representatives' is aided by the value placed on personal autonomy in Pintupi society. An individual who appears to outsiders to be speaking for everyone is usually not considered by other Pintupi to be doing so and, therefore, they feel no compulsion to object to anything that is said. Representatives of agencies believe a person to be speaking for everyone, but Pintupi may consider the individual to be merely 'speaking for himself', leaving the visitor with the erroneous impression that consensus has been reached in the speaker's favour.

Institutional individualism is also abetted by the nature of the relationship Pintupi believe they have with their government bosses. Rather than feeling dismay at being denied input to either the programs or the process whereby their needs are determined, Pintupi accept such exclusion as part of their patron–client relationship with their bosses. Individuals do not challenge agency representatives when programs based on 'community' decisions they have never heard of are implemented, because it is not part of their relationship with their bosses to question their gifts.

This also suits some funding bodies, who engage in consultation as a process where decisions are taken to an elder or community representative for assent, and this is then taken to satisfactorily signal general agreement to whatever they are proposing. Given the problems of settlement consultation, and the need to implement programs that are acceptable to their western audience, this is far more expedient than actually talking to every Pintupi individual or each family. In a society where no one can speak for anyone else, this would run a high risk of never reaching a clear-cut decision, or of creating implacable opposition. Agencies can avoid the factiousness and scrutiny of settlement politics by having their own 'community representative', thereby relying on the agreement of their representative rather than a popular consensus that may be unobtainable.

Despite the stereotype view that both the disunity of government departments and the 'competitive individualism' of indigenous people disadvantages them in their dealings with the West, institutional individualism ensures that some resources are still able to be diverted to families. Paradoxically, basing social justice and self-determination ideals on 'community' rather than families, creates the potential for inequity since it facilitates the enrichment of the *walytja* of a few individuals speaking for 'everyone'. If policy were based on the real structure of Pintupi society, which would disallow that any family could speak for another, more equality among families on the settlement could be achieved.

On the other hand, in reality the multiplicity of government and non-government agencies, and their lack of coordination, counters the inequitable model by providing a diversity of opportunities for cultural brokerage, which helps ensure that the rewards are spread around the different family constellations, into which particular institutions are incorporated. If, as social justice advocates often suggest by way of remedy, there was more coordination of government, perhaps channelled through one overarching agency, the potential for inequity among Pintupi families, fuelling settlement disharmony, would be enormous.

The disorganisation and duplication of agencies involved creates additional benefits for Pintupi because this multiplicity of agencies provides a fertile ground for conflict and divisions among them. Lack of coordination and conflict are much criticised by Bennett on the grounds that competition between agencies seeking to establish a relationship with indigenous clients, in order to justify participation, 'hinders efforts to secure a concerted attack on a particular policy area' (1999, 147–8). However, such competition actually ensures that agencies need to win local political support to fight their battles, and they are therefore compelled to take into account some of the real needs and expectations of Pintupi.

Diversity and conflict weaken the centre in favour of groups like the Pintupi at the periphery, ensuring that the balance between outside and local accountability tip towards the settlement side. It is precisely the 'splintered authority', condemned in various reports, such as Griffiths', which claims that 'the proliferation of ... community-based organisations produced a factionalism which was dividing communities' (1995, 232), that has shifted resources in favour of Pintupi, whose settlements are already divided along family lines, without any influence from the outside.

Indigenous settlements may, in the words of the Aboriginal and Torres Strait Islander Social Justice Commissioner, 'peer out from the bottom of a bureaucratic process to a maze of policies and programs ostensibly designed to meet their "needs"' (1994, 11, 119). However, the conclusion that the duplication of government departments 'point to the manner in which indigenous peoples have had their ability to control their own destines taken away' (1994, 129) is not borne out by the real politics of a Pintupi settlement. Bennett may lament that 'competition has weakened the national policy of self-determination' (1999, 148), but Pintupi have never experienced self-determination, and resourcing facilitated by brokerage and agency conflict provide invaluable mechanisms for their empowerment.

According to Bennett (1999, 148), lack of coordination and fragmentation of Aboriginal affairs administration has maintained the power of outside agencies whereas, in reality, cooperation actually runs counter to the imperatives of both the agencies and Pintupi. It is little wonder, and in many respects fortuitous, that forty years of attempts to get the various agencies that deliver services to Pintupi settlements to work together have proven completely futile.

MANAGEMENT AND POWER

> One intelligent and literate young man declined the position of community manager … [which] surprised me, because it would have ensured that Aboriginal people were more fully in control of their own affairs. This job, however, would have required him to … dock [workers'] pay. Fully recognizing the likelihood of conflict, he told the councillors that 'I don't want to end up in the cemetery'. (Fred Myers 1986a, 264)

In fashioning equal outcomes on Pintupi settlements vast importance is placed on the role of western institutions. Perhaps this is not really surprising since they are often supposed to serve a social justice function in the wider society, and it is not uncommon for even greater things to be expected of them when they are situated in indigenous societies. Moreover, Pintupi are often expected to manage these western institutions for themselves, although as Stanner observed, there were no great contests for position and office in the indigenous societies he knew and the reason was clear (1979, 59). An institutional boss is responsible for many people regardless of relationship, a role Pintupi — already fully obligated to relatives — regard as an acute form of punishment.

Within my own workplace the accusation that I am the 'boss' is used in times of dissent, literally as an attack, since it conjures massive and impossible obligations. When a man kept a community-owned truck for himself it was agreed, 'We should make him boss for that truck. That way he has to do everything for us'. Another man, who was a member of a committee whose function it was to 'hold' a community institution, became angry when the administrator declared him the boss of the institutional vehicles. His retort was, 'If I'm boss, I'll take a Toyota hunting for bush turkey any time'. The administrator assumed he was fulfilling the institutional charter of indigenous control, but the Pintupi man found that role so invidious he demanded the freedom to use the vehicle for his own purposes as recompense.

Being responsible for, and to, non-relatives arouses heated complaints from one's own kin. When a man was asked why he only took his own *walytja* in his (institutional) Toyota, he explained, 'If I take others my *walytja* get angry with me'. To deny institutional resources to one's own family makes Pintupi susceptible to the accusation of being 'too hard' (lacking in compassion), as they are placed in the dangerous position of being expected to deny rightful claims from relatives in favour of institutional imperatives.

In Pintupi terms, a boss is in debt to those he has to deny and to the employees he directs. Conversely, the role of employee may be empowering, although only while workers can make claims on the boss while resisting obligations on themselves. The settling of debt incurred by a boss to employees may well lead to pressure for corruption in western terms, because bosses may be compelled to support Pintupi activities by allowing non-official and inequitable use of resources.

Bosses are simultaneously held accountable to the funding agencies they represent, and from whom they obtain the money needed to keep institutions running and, in a far more immediate sense, to Pintupi, who are themselves in no way accountable to those agencies and have a completely different worldview from them. Bosses are always vulnerable to accusations of corruption from the institution they are managing, the 'community' they are serving, and the wider society to whom they are ultimately accountable, groups whose understanding of the term can be oppositional. This generates enormous stress at the settlement/institution interface, within settlement institutions, and between them and town bureaucracies.

Whereas in western society a manager usually embraces authority, and accepts responsibility as a badge of position, Pintupi avoid telling each other what to do in a work environment and assiduously disclaim the mantle of leadership. As Myers explains:

> Faced with the threat of violence, it is not surprising that Pintupi find it difficult to be 'hard' in upholding their decisions. Nor is it easy to resist the claims on their sympathy by relatives who ask for 'one more chance'. When it is necessary to avoid the claims of sympathy and compassion, they characteristically prefer to shift the responsibility by delegating such jobs to outsiders. (1986a, 264)

When individual demands are stridently made, Pintupi say, 'We're just workers — the whitefella's the boss. Ask him'. However, they will privately make sure the 'boss' knows that he is really working for them. They will also berate the boss if decisions are made without consulting them, the responsibility for consultation being considered the administrator's, because 'He's not working for himself. He's working for Aboriginal people'.

In this work context, where Pintupi naturally avoid rather than accept managerial responsibility and its consequence of obligation, there are difficulties for all. Self-management underpins social justice aspirations for indigenous people, even though it demands a dramatic departure from the family system and shared identity between all Pintupi, where, as Myers (1986b, 443) puts it, 'overall relatedness is the structure that is reproduced through time ... rather than the structuring of difference and alliance'. In place of this destructive outcome of self-management, Pintupi seek a different path, one that is generally unrecognised and misunderstood. Like much Pintupi innovation, it is neither bound by tradition nor based on stubborn resistance to change.

They have organised a volatile, yet usually workable, compromise to their dilemma of needing to co-operate with a structure that threatens their own cultural values, by retaining control over the direction of settlement institutions while employing outsiders as 'bosses', to accept final responsibility for their day to day operation. Myers explains that the concept of *mayutju*, or boss, designates one who 'looks after' employees for which, in return, the boss 'can also expect a certain right to command' (1980, 313). That Pintupi can sustain this arrangement provides a clear demonstration of the real power relationship between themselves and the 'bosses' they employ, and an equally clear challenge to the stereotype of the overwhelming power of the state in their settlements.

A man who monopolises a settlement vehicle for his own *walytja* may be called greedy by non-relatives, but direct confrontation with other claimants is rare. Complaints are usually made to the administrator, the 'boss', rather than the perpetrator, who will be exhorted to take the resource away from the man or provide the same for others. If this does not happen it is the 'boss' who may be held responsible, thereby protecting Pintupi shared identity. Or if there are no profits to be distributed from the settlement store, the store boss may be blamed, rather than the individuals who borrowed money for their own families or those who, out of compassion, agreed to the loans.

It is outsiders who are expected to take responsibility for many decisions, in order that Pintupi do not sacrifice their shared identity, or their familial relationships. If a decision is required that must disadvantage some people, and is therefore shameful, the whitefella boss is encouraged to make it, while Pintupi reserve the right to criticise the decision and express sympathy with those who have been disadvantaged by it. In the division of 'community' money, Pintupi will publicly support, or at least not deny, each claim (though behind the scenes they will encourage the boss to exclude many of them), acceding to claims of compassion, since to do otherwise is shameful. It is the role of whitefella bosses to act 'in the interests of the community' and publicly announce the decisions reached privately, and also to be accountable for them in the face of outrage from those who have missed out.

Some years ago I was asked to select ten women representatives to attend a meeting in Alice Springs. I held a meeting with the women to tell them that, if they wanted to go, there was sufficient funding for ten of them. Not wishing to dictate their decision, I asked the women to select their ten representatives and they immediately began to tell me the names, so I could write them down. Some thirty names were dictated and then someone exclaimed that one had been left out and I was instructed to add that name as well.

Exasperated, and thinking that perhaps the women had not understood, I carefully explained once more that only ten of them could travel, and asked them to tell me the names of the ten women. The women exhorted me to show compassion for everyone who wanted to go and, again, all of them were included. To do otherwise would have been a shameful breach of the shared identity of the women who were present, it would have been unjust in their terms. As an outsider it was my job to do what the women could not publicly countenance, decide who would *not* go, while they would express compassion for those I rejected and, if necessary, anger towards me on behalf of their relatives who had missed out.

The dialogue between the two cultures is far more interesting than merely a set-piece contest between their conflicting values: whitefella bosses can be held responsible for tenets in their own culture, as well as needing to be sympathetic to those of the one they work within. For example, decisions made by the boss may be held to be absolutely binding since this is 'whitefella way' while, for themselves, Pintupi reject the bureaucratic demand that they stick to their decisions in favour of renegotiating identity according to changing circumstances and relationships. In such cases it is often the role of bosses to be accountable for the altered decision, as blaming the real decision-makers would be too divisive among Pintupi families. It is also the boss who must confront funding agencies and 'talk strong', while Pintupi reserve the right to decide whether or not he really 'talked for them' or, conversely, 'only talked for himself'.

There is no shame for Pintupi if the whitefella boss, rather than themselves, is denying a claim, and Pintupi may take requests to the boss because 'we have to ask', to avoid criticism from relatives. For example, a man may ask for the loan of an institutional vehicle to attend 'sorry business' for a distant relative, if only to demonstrate there really was no way to get there, thereby avoiding the accusation that he did not care for the deceased. In the event of refusal the applicants can deflect blame onto the boss who would not help them, a public display made all the more effective if demands are strongly made.

Pintupi defy the conventional ethnographic wisdom, expounded by Trigger, for example, with reference to Doomagee people (1992, 222), that the competitive nature of status relations in indigenous society allows whitefella bosses to take over decision-making processes. For Pintupi, empowerment often lies precisely in their ability to get bosses to make decisions and therefore to be accountable for them. Moreover, Pintupi families may be individually competitive, but unity is the shared identity of all Pintupi, where no one is subservient to any other. Individuals combine on the basis of their shared identity in the face of outsiders, 'bosses' who are not meeting each of their individual needs.

Ngayulu kutju wangkapayi walypala tjuṯaku. Ngayulu kutju nyaku-payi walypala tjuṯa. Kutjulu!
I am the only one talking for you mob about all those whitefellas. I'm the only one watching all these whitefellas. One!

Those Pintupi who stubbornly refuse to compromise their own individual and family claims in the face of collective 'equality' strive to lead the others by identifying a cause and mobilising others against the outsiders who are 'not helping', who are 'too hard', or are 'stealing from us'. Such oratory inspires a united political consciousness, exhorting all Pintupi to unite against whitefellas without sacrificing their own autonomy. Orators are not bosses themselves, they do not tell others what to do, which would be shameful, neither do they generally argue with their peers, but defer to their points of view while not acknowledging them to be superior to their own. In such a way Pintupi create an effective unity with each other that binds even fiercely competing individuals and families together.

In the art of confrontation with their local bosses, Pintupi also defy the stereotype that they are easily browbeaten by whitefellas. They say they can 'talk (argue) all night, until morning', and unlike their 'bosses', 'we don't have to stop to eat and we don't get tired'. Pintupi do not consider it wrong to cajole and 'maumau' administrators, as von Sturmer described the confrontation that sometimes flares (1982, 98). However, administrators caught on the knife-edge of the interface rarely agree that this is either an acceptable or benign means of Pintupi empowerment, and it can lead to a rapid change in management.

This contemporary arrangement of management, like all political structures on Pintupi settlements, is highly negotiable and often temporary. Whitefella bosses are expected to treat everyone the same and, in theory, since they stand outside the kinship system, this seems a realistic possibility. Yet in practice it is difficult for a boss to be fair when each individual believes that 'fair' means that what is provided for others will be given to them, regardless of need and effort. Bosses may demand that Pintupi change in official directions but distant bureaucracies cannot shield them from the threat of expulsion from the settlement, while fully expecting them to push settlement support and cooperation for their equality programs. The authority of bosses depends on Pintupi accepting it, yet Pintupi grant this only if accompanied by a great deal of nurturing, as is the basis for authority in their society.

The integration of western institutions into the hotbed of Pintupi politics makes their efficient running difficult, sometimes impossible, and the resulting frustrations ensure a steady turnover of bosses. The periodic renegotiation of relationships after each departure ensures that benefits are spread around different family constellations and that over-all relatedness or, at least, the public appearance of it, is re-established.

RELATIONS WITH BOSSES

> Suppose they do not know how to cease to be themselves? People who brush such a question aside can know very little about what it is to be an Aboriginal. (W E H Stanner 1979, 50)

It may seem that Pintupi relations with their bosses are anomalous. Cowlishaw states that the Arnhem Land community of Bulman is 'sat-urated with power from outside' and observes a 'lack of any white adaptation to Rembarrnga practice and thus the rarity of ongoing dia-logue between the two worlds of meaning' (1999, 38, 257). Indigenous societies are often rather different, but such a perspective is frequently held by those coming straight from the dominant society still wearing the mantle of protective arrogance natural to a member of the majority society. For their part, whitefella bosses on Pintupi settle-ments quickly learn that they are part of a minority society, living on another people's land and working for others who have a great deal of power over their lives. No one who has had experience of working with Pintupi would call them 'compliant' towards their local whitefella 'bosses', let alone suffering the 'entrenched Aboriginal passive depen-dency' described by Trigger (1992, 4).

Whitefella bosses cannot discount the meanings Pintupi place on roles and relationships, but they can also be a source of influence for their own benefit. Bosses can have their '*walytja*', comprising their workers, and Pintupi describe each institution as a family 'held' by the those who work for it. In this way, Pintupi have attempted to assimi-late institutions to their own system of family constellations. For some bosses this powerbase may defeat the purpose of their position, both in the view of the agencies which fund them and the 'community' which expects bosses to be fair to them each as individuals. However, Pintupi in this role can mediate on behalf of their boss, through rivalrous set-tlement politics and the quagmire of religious and cultural expectations of an order of complexity that defies whitefella pretensions to under-standing. Whitefella bosses may even be shielded when dire offence is caused.

When paintings commissioned to decorate the wall of the school reminded the old men of sacred places and caused them grave dis-quiet, because the colours were too bright and they had been paint-ed by women who they felt had no right to represent them, the outcome looked certain to be one of violent upheaval. Cameron Tjapaltjarri quickly intervened, both to ensure that whitefellas speedily erased the paintings, and to placate the infuriated old men. He told them 'the whitefellas didn't say, '*Palyala yalatji!* (Make it like this!)' — indicating sacred design — '*walypala ŋgurrpa tjuṯa* (whitefellas are ignorant)'. Fortunately for whitefella bosses, Pintupi are able to spare them the consequences of most of their offences on the grounds of ignorance, as few of their countrymen would argue to the contrary.

Whitefella bosses are not assigned authority by virtue of their positions. Nevertheless, they can choose to insist that they stand outside the relationship system and cling to the illusory authority they assume they bring with them to the settlement. Following this path they will be relentlessly informed of their obligations, told they are mad and publicly criticised for shortfalls that seem to them far removed from their official role, because bosses are considered to have infinite responsibilities. For example, I was once publicly accosted for neglect of my duties as principal because, 'You didn't take me to town to buy a car'.

As a boss for Pintupi I was forced to accept that, for them, motivation is always bound up with relationships. The value Pintupi place on their relationships with their bosses cannot be discounted for long, and since it is through those relationships that authority is expressed and institutional work done, it is self-defeating to try to do so. That I would 'hold' Pintupi in my 'employ' while I worked for the community was not negotiable, although how I did so was open to debate. In this I was perhaps fortunate because, as *Tjapaŋgaṯi*, I was uncle for many of the Pintupi workers at the school and able to make legitimate demands on these *Naŋgala*. My authority supposedly included the right to punish; at least, this is what my nieces hastened to inform me as I warily accepted the prescribed relationship with them. I discovered later that an uncle may indeed be the moral guardian of his nieces, but this is also a 'joking' relationship, characterised by much teasing.

This rich game of cross-cultural mediation of relatedness is, of course, one in which Pintupi, who start to learn the character of each of their relationships in the cradle and then devote their lives to understanding and negotiating, have enormous advantages over neophyte players. My pretensions to authority over the *Naŋgala* workers sometimes seems real enough, but my authority is often elusive or inconsequential relative to the apparently vast responsibilities of uncles to their nieces.

Goal-oriented whitefella bosses may regret the way Pintupi habitually turn even the simplest social transaction, like a school barbecue, into a playful yet tumultuous arena of relationship renegotiations and reaffirmation. However, this continual dialogue and negotiation is valued as an end in itself, beyond the issue under discussion. Refusal to enter into the process, especially when denying requests, can lead to bad feelings far beyond the expectations of over-worked, time-obsessed whitefella bosses, anxious to cut to the chase and move on to the next issue. Such interactions represent value to Pintupi and also to those bosses, who work long-term with them, most of whom look back to their relationships with great affection.

THE DESIGN AND THE OUTCOMES

> Outsiders become the instruments of the local system; councillors can ... claim they are mediating, enforcing a white boss's rules ... A Pintupi person, bound in the web of kinship ... cannot refuse a request, but a white boss can ... and [they] are used as a medium for the projection and transformation of decisions into an externalised object to which human subjects must conform ... (Fred Myers 1986a, 285)

Pintupi are frequently told that self-determination equals self-management. Because self-management is valued so highly within Australian society, and is so closely associated with progress, reports such as *Our Future Our Selves* state that 'Aboriginal concepts of community development are part of effective self determination and self-management at the local level' (Commonwealth of Aust. 1990, 21).

Like so much of the interaction with indigenous Australians, social justice policy not only allows no acknowledgment of how groups like the Pintupi strive to empower themselves, but also excludes any consideration of its own cultural bias. Pintupi concepts of settlement management produce few of the outcomes valued by other Australians, and they are the targets of continuous criticism, well-meaning advice and relentless training programs aiming to redress their obvious 'deficiencies'.

By conflating the oppositional goals of self-management and self-determination, Pintupi are precluded from openly determining that, although they want to be institutional decision-makers, it overrides many of their most important cultural imperatives to be responsible for the everyday management of them. The consummate way in which Pintupi actively negotiate the fulfillment of their own goals, rather than the ones espoused on their behalf, is ignored — except as a negative.

On their settlements Pintupi have melded contradictory ideals and systems into a workable, if tenuous, design but it is the limitations on the western outcomes, rather than the genius of that design, that remains the preoccupation of the dominant society. Pintupi management is very different from the 'glossy magazine' version, where indigenous Australians are sitting behind desks, unproblematically self-managing their settlements and being accountable to bureaucracies, while maintaining their own cultural precepts. The premise of this policy, that there is a coincidence of objectives between such different cultures, has always been fanciful.

However, it is always possible to describe their system as parasitical, or dismiss Pintupi decisions by saying they are made by whitefellas, or by a group that does not represent the 'whole community'. Of course, as von Sturmer argued, there is no such compunction for bureaucrats to 'look too closely at the basis of local decisions when they appear to coincide with their own plans, hopes and aspirations' (1982, 87). Further, the repeated failure of self-management in official terms creates a stereotype of Pintupi society's disempowerment and disintegration, when the very opposite is the case.

While Pintupi models of settlement management are no social justice miracle, able to somehow resolve all contradictions and slickly synthesise the cultural differences, they far surpass western 'two way' models and the other romances of social justice architects. This joint management is forged in the cross-cultural furnace at the interface, and is a political structure as permanent as is imaginable for a people who value family and the negotiation of a shared identity far above the demand that they embrace an alien structure. As Myers explains, their polity is a 'temporary jurisdiction among those who regard themselves as related and subordinated to a binding set of principles, (it) is not predicated on membership in groups, has no offices and no enduring structure' (1986b, 432).

In that tradition Pintupi ensure that, within any of the structures they must participate in, the usurping of their shared identity is temporary, and institutions will never work too well in fulfilling official objectives rather than their own. Thus, the scenario Cowlishaw describes, where 'many individuals seem healthy, humorous [but] there are many organisational and institutional aspects of the community which lurch from one crisis to another ...' (1999, 291), is, for Pintupi, no paradox at all.

Contrary to most interpretations, Pintupi have been far from overwhelmed and disempowered in their employment of whitefella bosses. For a people who prize individual autonomy and travel and who have many obligations to *walytja*, the perspective that their bosses have no inherent power over them and, instead, are heavily indebted to them has been invaluable in maintaining their own lifeways.

What is generally ignored, despite the dominant society's assumption of the primacy of their agencies, is that the day-to-day running of them is actually peripheral to real Pintupi concerns, busy with, and empowered by, their own cultural business. Lip service is paid by the West to the idea of indigenous societies as a viable lifeway alternative, but only when they are pursued outside office hours. The fact that management training programs proliferate, while the practice wallows, attests to both the lack of Pintupi self-determination beyond their settlements and their powerful influence within them.

On their own terms, and in the face of immense pressure, Pintupi have devised a system of family-based, cooperative — if endlessly negotiated and renegotiated — leadership with whitefellas that meets the contradictory demands that they manage alien programs and institutions while 'maintaining their culture'. In this way they have sustained their own autonomy in the face of the ideal of self-management that, against all the stated intentions, threatens to destroy it.

Above Two of Cameron's daughters and grandchildren, Kayleen Nungurrayi holding Suzette Nampitjinpa and Rosita Nungarrayi holding Aaron Tjampitjinpa, 2000.

Opposite page:
Above Cameron Tjapaltjarri's daughters, three Nungarrayi and their children at White Tree outstation, 2000.
Below Cameron Tjapaltjarri's outstation, 2000.

CHAPTER 9
AN UNEASY RELATIONSHIP

This machine is one in which everyone is caught, those who exercise
power as well as those who are subjected to it.
(Michel Foucault 1977, 156)

In western society the relationship with indigenous groups like Pintupi
tends to polarise people into two groups. On one side there are those
who pity them for their impoverished lives, and believe it is about time
they were saved; on the other are those who condemn them for their
recalcitrance, and believe it is about time they assisted in their own salvation. Although the two groups are extremely antagonistic to each
other, they both agree on the fundamental premise that things must
change for indigenous people, and assume that when this transformation happens it will inevitably be for the better. The only real difference
between them is to whom they believe the blame should be appor-
tioned for the inexplicable delay in this natural process.

The frustrations inherent in a relationship based on this control of
the discourse of progress are well publicised. They are the statistics that
refuse to budge, the grass-roots community spirit that will not kindle,
the elusive self-management forever out of reach. Yet these indicators
fail to account for both the integrity of indigenous cultures and the
complexity of the relationship with the West. However, in all the
debates that rage in western society about the plight of indigenous people, there is rarely an acknowledgment that they might have aspirations
in the relationship other than those formulated for them by outsiders,
the failure of which also cause them disappointment and frustration.

Because programs of intervention on their settlements also incidentally fulfil some of these aspirations, Pintupi participate in them,

often without questioning their directions. An arrangement that prioritises the ideals of western society, while allowing Pintupi to achieve some of their own goals, works, to a degree, in that it enables some of the felt needs of both societies to be met. Although uneasy and unstable, this cooperation is in many respects a major achievement for two such different societies to have forged, an artifice that should not be dismissed out of hand. However, the arrangement operates under severe constraints and limitations that are unacknowledged, and its fallibilities become increasingly apparent as pressure mounts for mainstream equality goals to be demonstrably achieved.

INCREDULITY AT THE INTERFACE

[Durmugan] came to terms with Europeanism ... [b]ut it never attracted him emotionally, it did not interest him intellectually, and it aroused only his material desire. (W E H Stanner 1979, 101)

Pintupi accept the precepts of social justice in exchange for continued access to resources, so the intended direction of change, though not the outcomes of it, remains monopolised by the dominant society. Because Pintupi defer to their government bosses by agreeing with the official agenda, while exercising power in their own interests on their settlements, the national political agenda is continually reinforced, despite being undermined locally.

This process creates a gulf of misunderstanding, frustration and incredulity at many levels. Pintupi have no choice but to seek much of what they cannot use in the real practice of their lives, and they receive these offerings as gifts from government bosses who 'hold' them. They may reach agreement with their bosses on the appropriateness of the gift, but this does not mean that the intent behind the decision is at all the same on each side. Pintupi understand that their role is not one of deciding exactly what they get, but they consequently do not accept any degree of responsibility, or accountability, for the lack of success, in western terms, of these gifts locally.

For example, if a social justice enterprise which delivered a vehicle founders, this may be quite satisfactory from a Pintupi viewpoint, because they prize vehicles, and the expensive failure is seen as a problem (if indeed it is one at all) for distant government bosses rather than for them. Or they may be given funding to look after themselves in one area of their lives, then use it for a different purpose. In their view, however, this does not relieve their government bosses, who 'hold' them, of responsibility for looking after them in that area. Of course, from the perspective of government, they reached 'community agreement' on a course of action, but Pintupi subsequently failed to accept accountability for the outcome.

This failure is roundly condemned, sometimes in the forthright terms used by Tatz, who is 'increasingly puzzled (and irritated) at the way some Aboriginal settlements are going about their survival' (1990, 246). Nevertheless this is a process that the dominant society instigated and perpetuates. To change this pattern would require the acknowledgment of cultural differences. In particular, it would require the acceptance that Pintupi are a family-based, rather than a settlement-based, society, and they believe they stand in a relationship with government 'bosses' in which they are 'held' in exchange for abandonment of their traditional lives, and that they do not want to be model citizens of western society, though they enjoy some of its material goods.

In a relationship with the Australian state where each failure confirms stronger representations of inequality, the confusion of deficit with cultural difference is inbuilt and has far reaching effects. While Pintupi are compelled by their own priorities to accept a low physical standard of living, they are incessantly bombarded with positive images of western television lifestyles and under constant pressure to emulate the image thus promoted, while the integrity of the way they already live goes unrecognised. These constant visions of a more materially opulent way of life makes Pintupi susceptible to external propaganda on their lack of equality, without making them any more willing to give up their own lifeways to achieve it. A false promotion of western abundance as an easy option for Pintupi can only produce negative comparisons and unrealisable expectations in their settlements, a process which, as Young observes, markedly decreases satisfaction with life, no matter what the actual circumstances of it are (1998, 357).

This representation of deficit, rather than difference, is further encouraged by the way Pintupi see the lives of other Australians. Just as many from western societies come to unfounded conclusions because they interpret indigenous cultures according to their own precepts, Pintupi view the wider society, through their own cultural experience, as a population of millionaires. This is how many Pintupi explain the tantalising materially rich lives seen on television, or in the cities they visit, or even of the whitefellas who live on their settlements. Many Pintupi have, over the years, described me as wealthy and dismissed any excuse that I cannot fulfil their requests because I lack the means as obviously ridiculous.

With their many obligations to share possessions, Pintupi would need to be wealthy beyond imagination to have the level of ownership they see me maintaining, in which, for example, I always have access to a vehicle, however decrepit. For Pintupi to have continuous ownership of a car would require not merely the purchase of a single vehicle but many, and the ability to replace each at a moment's notice. No Pintupi could be selfish, or foolish, enough to hoard a vehicle as I do, and even those who have the means to successively acquire cars are often without one. Individuals who have relatively high disposable incomes, such as internationally famous painters, continue to believe themselves to be poor in comparison with much lower income-earners in western society, and in many respects they do live comparatively materially impoverished lives in spite of their high incomes. Unlike in western society, it is very difficult to differentiate, by appearance or lifestyle, the high and low income-earners on a Pintupi settlement.

Pintupi have been given no choice but to become accomplices in a representation that defines their society in terms of what it lacks, instead of what is distinctive and workable in its own right. The wider society will always wonder why Pintupi do not seem to use its offerings as expected, and Pintupi will always wonder at the riches in the cities and the refusal of wealthier Australians to share more of them, to 'hold' Pintupi properly.

As stated by the Aboriginal and Torres Strait Islander Social Justice Commissioner, 'Policies and programs which rest primarily on a perception of need and powerlessness subtly reinforce the powerlessness of the recipients ...' (1993, 7). That this representation of victim may, in time, become self-fulfilling remains one of the possible outcomes of equality policies. Does western society really want to convince Pintupi they are merely living like 'poor whites', rather than as competent indigenous people, secure in their own ways on their own land?

RELATIONS OF POWER

> ... [w]hen policy becomes ... so certain of itself that it lays down a line, and one line only, to be walked fair weather or foul, it comes close to pre-determining what it wants or can afford to see, hear, discover, or admit. It turns its back on a life of change. It [leads] to self-defensive and self-justifying thinking ... (W E H Stanner 1979, 304)

Western conviction perpetuates a flow of resources to indigenous peoples but seeing only what a people lack creates negative stereotypes. The social organisation of a Pintupi settlement leads to an appearance of a people who are pervasively unequal with most other Australians, and this is extrapolated to represent individual, community, and cultural malaise. Yet within their remote settlements Pintupi are, in effect, the 'dominant society' and, rather than the image of a dysfunctional society portrayed in western representations, they exercise control in a competent manner to maximise the fulfillment of their own goals.

This blindness to Pintupi strength means there is a failure to acknowledge that they have viable plans for themselves. Under the assimilation policy it could, at least, be admitted that there was indigenous opposition to official goals. For example, Douglas Lockwood writing about Papunya and Yuendumu stated that '... the officers of the [NT] Welfare Branch grappling with this situation see no easy or quick solution to the many problems inherent in the social transformation being attempted' (1964, 8–9). Now the beguiling 'two way' model of cooperation between the cultures makes this acknowledgment impossible. For example, even the more grounded accounts of indigenous health fail to see that questions, such as that posed by Maggie Brady (1996, 190) — 'When should social imperatives be superseded by the requirements of health?' — are wholly theoretical, because this is not an arena in which outsiders have substantial influence. Pintupi simply do not allow the goal of equal outcomes in health, or any other area, to get in the way of their own social imperatives.

Speaking on the ABC's '7.30 Report' in 1998, on the shorter life expectancy among Australia's indigenous people, federal Aboriginal Affairs Minister Senator John Herron claimed the government 'is not going to stand for that', but government simply does not have the kind of influence on Pintupi settlements that rhetoric of this kind implies. Similarly, as Fishman makes clear (1991, 373), the reality that the family–neighbourhood–community arena is far more basic to educational outcomes than the institution of school is usually ignored. Pintupi do not, in fact, *have* to internalise western education any more than they *have* to internalise the precepts of western health.

Failing to see the primacy of Pintupi influence in their own lives leads to other manifestations of dominant society self-importance. According to Cowlishaw, even the consciousness of the Bulman mob is shaped by the moral evaluations of the whitefellas with whom they come into contact (1999, 247). However, Pintupi have their own, very busy and fulfilling, lives to lead, and they remain uninterested in the moral pronouncements of whitefellas on their lifeways, except as a source of amusement at the ignorance they exhibit. As Harney observed forty years ago, '… they just did not give a damn what we … pale creatures thought about them' (1995, 138).

The way Pintupi dismiss the evaluations of outsiders is no different from other Australians when they are subjected to the unsolicited moral judgements of foreigners — except that they (Pintupi) express a great deal more tolerance of, and less outrage at, the impertinence. This is fortunate because, if they took them seriously in the 'damned if they do, damned if they don't' dilemma policy creates, where appropriating aspects of western society is 'losing their culture' and rejecting others is 'being unequal', Pintupi might really become the confused, dispirited group they are already portrayed as being.

The belief that western society has vast importance and influence in indigenous settlements, or at least that it should have, also produces the view that the unstable and, for outsiders, highly unpredictable character of the interface and its outcomes, is merely an aberration. More than thirty years ago Tatz complained of an overwhelming 'irregularity of intent' in the relationship (1964, 271), with policies interpreted differently by every administrator and agency; while Cowlishaw in recent times sees a problem in the continual state of institutional crisis that seems to result from 'individual whims or self-interest' (1999, 291).

It never seems to be considered that the indigenous preference for, and undoubted skills in, relentless negotiation and renegotiation, where nothing is ever settled for long, may be having an impact on the western structures in their settlements. Similarly, the notion that government departments are using settlement institutions to restructure indigenous society, as Tregenza and Abbott complain, is rather presumptuous (1995, 17). While they cannot have much effect on their basic agendas, Pintupi often distort the day-to-day operation of these western institutions, and the unbearable (for whitefellas) 'chaos' between the two domains at the interface is strikingly reminiscent of many social transactions in Pintupi society.

The failure of western bureaucracies to acknowledge the strength of Pintupi society also leads to the view that 'community' control of institutions such as clinics and schools will ensure the fashioning of equal outcomes, because Pintupi will come to own these institutions and, in time, adopt their equality goals through this ownership. Mick Dodson, the Aboriginal and Torres Strait Islander Social Justice Commissioner (1994, 103), praises community control for its potential to produce 'sustainable improvement' but fails to recognise that there are limits to the resources which groups like Pintupi will apply to becoming statistically equal when they are in control of their distribution.

The advantage to achieving the stated western aims of institutions of offering an outside bureaucratic authority, onto which unpalatable decisions may be deflected, is overlooked in this model. Yet, it is only the presence of an external authority that allows Pintupi to excuse their errant whitefella bosses making decisions they themselves could neither contemplate nor defend, to ever-present critics. Such an arrangement may help to ensure that the project of the institution remains that for which it was originally intended, swinging the balance away from Pintupi goals, towards 'social justice' outcomes. Deciding whether or not community control is the best way to run an institution means acknowledging this is making a choice about which of the conflicting goals, equality of outcomes or self-determination, to favour. Of course, even the idea that these could actually be oppositional is without precedent in the rhetoric of indigenous policy.

In this rhetoric, which refuses to acknowledge that Pintupi may not want to behave like members of western society, any failure on their part to do so is interpreted as cultural weakness rather than strength, something to be overcome rather than applauded. Ignoring the strength of Pintupi within their own settlements also creates a blindness to what is already successful in realistic terms. As a consequence, there are always calls to radically change what is workable. Schooling that is ecologically useful, and judged by parents to be successful, is condemned by observers such as Keeffe (1992, 12), while Band-Aid medicine, appreciated at the settlement level, is much criticised in the wider society. The centre of focus is always on what is going wrong in the relationship, rather than what is going right.

WASTE

> Policies, programs and money will not change indigenous people from what they are — a social person, tied to others by a dozen ties which are his life — into an abstract 'individual' in order to make the facts fit a policy. (W E H Stanner 1979, 43)

A relationship where both societies espouse a rhetoric based on equality, in which Pintupi must placate, cajole, coax and eventually apologise in order to get a measure of what they really want, results inevitably in waste. The dominant society sees this in terms of resources delivered for outcomes not attained, while from the Pintupi point of view resources are wasted because much of what the government chooses to give them cannot be manipulated into what they consider useful. The former kind of waste is a problem complained of by many in the wider society, who completely ignore the structure of the relationship between themselves and indigenous people, in which they are the dominant partners.

The whitefella ways that produce this form of waste are, however, not wrong and training will not change the logic underlying them, similarly Pintupi rationality is not susceptible to re-education. The waste created by the interactions between these two societies is therefore not merely a mistake, which implies that better judgement will easily overcome it, but an inevitable consequence of two such disparate cultures attempting to operate together in the same arena. If the wasteful outcomes of this endeavour are dismissed as 'mistakes' then, surely, continually repeated 'mistakes' cannot be tolerated for long, no matter who is making them. Government may say they have had enough of indigneous 'mistakes', just as the Aboriginal and Torres Strait Islander Social Justice Commissioner says that governments have made too many mistakes in the past (1993, 94).

When asked to choose appropriate western hardware, Pintupi are expected to realise that the reality of their lives should lead them to choose things which are quite different from those whitefellas enjoy, although they have been told by social justice architects that they should have the same as other Australians. For example, the styles of houses that Pintupi want which, to varying degrees, emulate suburban Australia, are regularly constructed on their settlements where this 'health' hardware is labelled by outsiders, such as Reid and Lupton, as 'grossly inappropriate to the local environment' (1991, xvii). Such 'mistakes' are explained as indigenous ignorance of appropriate housing styles, or a symptom of government incompetence, but it is more a consequence of a fundamental contradiction inherent in the 'two ways' equality and self-determination approach.

There is an acute difference between what is 'appropriate' or practical to Pintupi lifestyles and what Pintupi, who look at the wider Australian society for their technological model, desire and use. The debris of rejected internationally acclaimed 'appropriate' technology, such as hand-operated mechanical washing machines and wood-fired water heaters, which litter their settlements, is ample testament to failed attempts at providing culturally and environmentally appropriate technology. Despite the inconvenience of such hardware Pintupi are expected to welcome it into their modern lives because it can be controlled and integrated in the same way their traditional technologies were.

Pit toilets engineered to keep flies out and odour minimal are aesthetically and environmentally friendly in a desert, and far more hygienic than wet ones because they cannot block up. However, when community decision-making is invoked, Pintupi insist they are not 'proper toilets'. Surely pit toilets are not the equality they have always been told they must have! Flush toilets inside Pintupi houses are a design disaster because frequent blocking sends excrement spilling over into the rest of the house, but whitefellas have them and the rhetoric of equality means Pintupi should have them too.

Given this relentless rhetoric, it is not surprising that when Pintupi receive 'appropriate' technology they suspect government is really trying to cheat them by giving them something second best. There are no pit toilets in the backyards of whitefella houses on their settlements, and they do not laboriously wash clothes with hand-operated washing machines. Of far more interest to Pintupi than any consideration of technological 'appropriateness' is the fact that whitefellas in their settlements live in well air-conditioned houses, while expecting most of them to swelter in unairconditioned hotboxes.

The outcome of such interactions is one of disappointment for both parties. Because Pintupi accept the propaganda of equality, without submitting to the ideology of using the inappropriate technology, western hardware given in the name of equality soon exhibits an air of disintegration. Meanwhile, the hardware delivered in the name of 'appropriateness' is unvalued with, for example, 'appropriate' houses the first to be abandoned, often to become the headquarters of petrol-sniffers.

Whether or not it is the equality or the self-determination rhetoric which take precedence in making infrastructure decisions, the goals of both societies remain unfulfilled, their desired outcomes unmet. The present approach ensures that equal results based on the provision of western resources creates a rising tide of expectations on what will be provided in the future, with no rise of commitment to use those resources in the way intended by western society. 'Ethiopia with money', as Western Desert settlements were described by one bureaucrat, is an artefact of this arrangement.

Because of the way Pintupi view their relationship with government they are not encouraged to make too many concessions in order to achieve the outcomes set for them. In their society one gives what one is obliged to give, and these obligations are so numerous that generosity can only be expressed within the kinship network. Through these cultural preconceptions Pintupi feel that what government gives them must be what they are owed within the relationship established since contact. This maintenance of their own cultural understandings has meant that, despite the best efforts of western society to 'teach' them proper western behaviour, such as self-reliance, Pintupi have continued to learn their own, rather than anyone else's, lessons from their contact history.

The more government overtly dictates targets to be aimed for by indigenous settlements, and chooses the means of their achievement, the more responsibility for apparent 'waste' must also be accepted. However, responsibility for waste is often sheeted home to indigenous people on the grounds they have asked for something, even when they have been manipulated into it in order to satisfy outside representations of their culture and aspirations.

For example, the 'outstation movement', started in the 1970s, was founded on the notion that settlement living does not suit indigenous society, which needs to be in family groups in relatively isolated locations on their own country. This worked well for some groups and the 'last contact' Pintupi, renowned for their 'authentic' culture, who had never fitted into settlement life at Papunya, were assumed to be especially good candidates for outstation living.

Soon after Pintupi moved back to Walungurru, a Commonwealth government review team (Hempel 1982) discussed with them their aspirations and expectations for the future. Officials were clearly told by Pintupi that they wanted to settle at Walungurru and use camps (outstations) in the surrounding countryside for temporary residence, such as when they went on weekend hunting trips (9). They wanted bores drilled at these camps to provide a permanent water supply. Officials told them that this would happen only if they committed to actually taking up permanent residence at these places, in line with outstation policy. Knowing this was the only way to get a water supply at their weekend camps, Pintupi acquiesced to the ideals of outstation living prescribed for them by the policy-makers.

This is how an expensive, decade-long infrastructure program on

Pintupi outstations began, designed to bribe them away from settlement life in order to fulfil the aspirations non-indigenous society held for them. By the early 1990s funding bodies expressed extreme alarm that relatively grandiose western hardware, such as solar-powered houses equipped with telephones, had been provided on their outstations, but Pintupi were still not living permanently on them. The waste of these resources was not attributed to a failed attempt to get Pintupi to conform to the ideals of the federal government's outstations policy by offering more and more resources, but to their fickle nature and lack of appreciation for the expensive infrastructure.

Pintupi, who find the hurly-burly of intense social life with their many relatives and countrymen at Walungurru too attractive to stay away long, had periodically camped at these outstations, just as they said they would back in 1982, before they expressed the dominant society's aspirations as their own in exchange for the water they wanted. They remained unswayed by the lure of the attractive infrastructure, although they welcomed it as a symbol of the degree of continuing debt owed them by government. However, they did complain bitterly when that support was, apparently arbitrarily, drastically reduced, in response to their failure to settle on outstations.

Because the western aims of programs are never questioned, only their implementation, it is assumed that when goals are not met the programs designed to achieve them have been total failures. In fact, most present efforts, and certainly all the past ones, are deemed not just to have failed but to have been actually what Keeffe calls 'locking in inequity' (1992, 67). This belief leads to a waste of accumulated expertise because there can be no learning from experience in a climate where everything must be invented anew in the chase for unattainable outcomes.

For example, many of the English reading materials produced in the 1970s, which were relevant to Pintupi students both in content and pace of learning, have been rejected out of hand because they did not result in the levels demanded of them. That is, levels equal with those of Australian students with English as a first language who live in an environment where literacy is valued and highly contextualised. Rather than learning from, and building on, the strengths of these materials with the production of more supporting resources to develop an integrated program for use in indigenous schools, it was decided the goal of equality could never be met through their use.

To fulfil this aim, new curricula and sets of materials were periodically produced at great expense. These spiralled ever further into unreality as they glossed over the real problems Pintupi students have with English and literacy, in their vain attempts to force the pace of learning to meet those of their mainstream peers. As revealed by the Collins Report, *Learning Lessons* (NT Education Department, 1999), many remote indigenous students are actually working at lower primary levels, regardless of their ages, making the focus of most of the materials that have been produced for them irrelevant. Innovation that cannot acknowledge, and therefore build on, past experiences of both success and failure, is erratic, confusing, wasteful, and undermining of programs that are ecologically successful on the ground.

The increased tempo of social justice creates a treadmill producing successive 'solutions' to indigenous 'problems', ensuring that a high proportion of resources is consumed by strategic and operational planning, monitoring and auditing, the domain of urban bureaucracies rather than remote settlements. Conspicuous 'waste' creates a powerful argument for more bureaucracy to control it, and can open the way for top-heavy programs of direct intervention. The moral justification is clear: if the achievement of equal outcomes is indeed a 'right', as the Aboriginal and Torres Strait Islander Social Justice Commissioner claims (1995), then surely it must be enacted in the interests of all indigenous Australians. This implies a return to a relationship in which there is a much higher level of government control, at least for those groups who seem unwilling and unable to move towards the desired outcomes under their own stewardship.

Waste may also be used to justify under-expenditure on indigenous settlements: if pouring in money has little effect, then why not spend only the absolute minimum? Already this line of thought has been signalled. As Phillip Ruddock, the Minister Assisting Reconciliation said, 'If you [Charles Perkins] say two billion spent on Aboriginal programs hasn't achieved outcomes, some people might say, why spend any money at all? (ABC Television, 27 September 1999). Agencies that come to believe that expenditure serves no useful purpose will devote their energies to shifting funds to areas they feel will give better value for money, because equitable distribution of resources loses its place on the moral high ground when it seems only to produce waste.

Herein lies the great advantage for the dominant society of 'two way' over the assimilation approach: if Pintupi can simply add equal outcomes to their own lives, there seems little excuse for their tardiness in doing so. After all, vast compassion is being demonstrated by the rest of Australia in throwing all manner of resources into lifting their indigenous countrymen to the elevated plane of statistical equality. When the real limitations of all the muddled policy ideals surface as waste, obviously someone must be to blame.

The expenditure of considerable funds on fine-sounding programs of social justice makes it easy to point the finger of blame away from the dominant society. Tatz argues that indigenous 'problems' have increased even though 'things can be said to be so much better than they were 30 years ago' (in Partington 1996, 144). Partington believes that the explanation is that indigenous people have insisted on their rights while declining to take responsibility (1996, 149).

ACCOUNTABILITY

> The supposed neutrality of the knower in representational models under-writes a subtle hegemony ... constituting much of the world as 'under-developed' defines those concerned as lacking, determines what they lack — the preordained goal which they have failed, but must struggle, to achieve — and specifies outside expert knowledge as the appropriate means to this end. A consequence of apotheosizing western knowledge is the dismissal of existing knowledges. One person's claim to knowledge is all too often another's condemnation to ignorance. Whatever knowl-edge is it is not neutral. (Mark Hobart 1995, 51)

The need to prioritise equality over cultural differences remains, but when programs fail it is expedient to be able to claim that it is groups like Pintupi who have been guilty of making the mistakes. The domi-nant society does not want to be held accountable for any negative consequences of its endeavours, however benevolent the intention, because avoiding this responsibility is the one lesson well learned from contact history.

The benevolent self-determination, equality-of-outcomes, approach goes some way to achieve this aim, because groups like Pintupi have become vulnerable to the claim that they have had local accountability and abused it, 'condemned as guilty when outcomes from the perspective of public expenditure are not what is expected' (Council for Aboriginal Reconciliation 1994b, 24). In western society it is illegitimate to seek resources for a particular purpose but use them for another, and it is considered especially outrageous when the official program is aimed at overcoming something as important as inequality in such areas as health, housing and education. For Pintupi this flexi-bility of intent, '... [where] negotiation is never fully concluded and decisive choices are rarely made' (Myers 1986a, 297), is a normal part of interactions within their own society and is not considered at all cor-rupt, even though it has been extended to their relationship with a dif-ferent society.

Under early social justice policy the clash between the distinct and divergent accountabilities of the two societies was rarely manifest. The response to waste, or lack of accountability, was a two-pronged approach of benevolent replacement of resources and continual educa-tion in the 'appropriate' use of them, in the hope that groups like the Pintupi would eventually adopt materialistic ideology along with west-ern goods. However, as time has passed and expected changes are still as far away as ever, the climate has chilled somewhat and there is much more talk of a lack of accountability to the western outcomes.

The response to this is to subject groups like the Pintupi to 'prop-er' accountability, with funding based on outcomes rather than need. The Aboriginal and Torres Strait Islander Social Justice Commissioner

(1994, 21) has already recommended that the provision of services be tied to 'accountable outcomes', meaning resources would be directed to those indigenous societies where 'success', defined as equality or at least the appearance of it, is attainable. Like everything else in indigenous affairs, wastefulness of resources and the lack of predicted outcomes are hardly new, and are periodically highlighted to signal and justify changes in policy.

The history of relations of the West with indigenous groups is one of unintended outcomes, yet strangely their possibility is rarely considered in the present. Most Pintupi are currently living dignified lives on their land in strong family constellations, but that should not be taken for granted. Cameron Tjapaltjarri dismisses the self-important superiority of whitefellas. He tells me that *walypala rich — Tjukurrpa wiya* (whitefellas are rich but have no Dreaming), but what if policy became so tied to outcomes and accountability that not enough money filtered into Pintupi settlements to meet their most basic felt needs?

Town may then become a powerful magnet despite all its problems. That powerful sanction in Pintupi lives, of how others judge their actions, is greatly diminished there, especially with the influence of readily accessed alcohol. Alcohol does not sit well in a society in which people carry out their own punishments, especially where there are few relatives to constrain the excesses. A man in Alice Springs may, in a drunken state, perpetrate crimes he would never contemplate in his own community, just as it is the man with no brothers to shame him who repeatedly beats his wife because 'she was jealous'. Obligations between family members do not vaporise in town, and this precludes town dwellers from many of the benefits of residence there. Just as relatives must always provide money for food they can equally sustain an endless supply of alcohol.

Town living reduces, rather than expands, the range of real possibilities available to Pintupi and there is no evidence that the subsequent disillusionment leads to a smooth adoption of an alien system in its place. Tatz reports that in a range of indigenous settlements he visited high suicide rates are essentially town-based, and there is now 'an ever readiness to misuse the "Sudden Infant Death Syndrome" or the "Failure to Thrive" terms as nicer ways of explaining the fact that a gambling and/or drinking mother hasn't cared for her child (and granny is too exhausted to do so)' (1990, 251).

This vulnerability of Pintupi to the vagaries of changing fortune is not merely theoretical. Even at a time when indigenous issues have been high on the mainstream agenda, and there has been in the 1980s and 90s an unprecedented commitment to addressing social justice issues, settlements have not been immune to sudden switches in their fortunes. A Western Desert settlement that was operating the CDEP, in which funds are made available to settlements in lieu of unemployment benefits, was judged to have wasted the funds. CDEP funds were sum-marily withdrawn, along with other grants. The settlement quickly ran out of money and Social Security refused to put anyone out on the set-tlement to help people obtain benefits, forcing the inhabitants to drift towards towns where they could obtain assistance. By the time the CDEP was reinstated, a previously vital settlement was decimated and many of its most important members had resettled as town fringe-dwellers, with all the problems of this way of life.

In basing the relationship between the two societies on a deficit model, it is expected that grafting on whatever is 'lacking' can create equal outcomes. However this approach will always fail because Pintupi society is not deficient, only different, and it already has coherent explanations in all the areas in which the dominant society hopes to teach them its own. Western society is constantly surprised at, and dis-appointed by, the resilience of other cultural lifeways, even after they have been offered, and instructed in, all the advantages of a western system. However, as these advantages cannot just be added on, but require changes that Pintupi clearly reject, they will continue to be dif-ferent, and consequently deficient, in western eyes.

The dominant society has placed itself in the role of the 'knower', and it views its material resources as a means to elevating groups like the Pintupi from their position of ignorance. Although its tactics move through a spectrum of coercion to bribery, strict accountability to self-determination, in its relationship with indigenous groups, it believes itself to be explicable, despite often antithetical strategies, in terms of its enduring agenda of westernisation.

What is problematic for Pintupi in this approach is that, because they have never internalised the underlying aims of the many programs implemented on their settlements, the sudden, dramatic changes in what they receive are, from their perspective, purely arbitrary. They do not learn the lessons in accountability that mainstream society hopes to teach them, and the lifeways of the two societies remain opaque to each other.

CHANGING FORTUNES AT WALUNGURRU

> I know enough of the facts to make me feel sure that any official or pub-lic assumption that such people can be effortlessly assimilated, on other than their own terms, is not well based. (W E H Stanner 1979, 44)

For Pintupi the past decade and a half in Walungurru has been a roller-coaster of changing fortunes. In the mid-1980s, they found that the wider Australian society suddenly became inordinately interested in them, and they welcomed this attention for the nurturing relationships it provided. Pintupi attracted support from idealistic outsiders keen to assist the 'last contact' people to create their own place, where the new and ancient ways would thrive together harmoniously. Walungurru was destined to become a showcase for a variety of health hardware, which would be constructed with the assistance of the people themselves.

'Technacy' (technical training) programs were instigated to create a pool of skilled workers who would exchange their labour to maintain the settlement infrastructure. For example, those trained to repair and renovate houses would have their work repaid by Pintupi mechanics who would fix their vehicles, and together these skilled workers would move the settlement towards self-sufficiency, reducing reliance on expensive outside labour. Since Pintupi are renowned as a 'traditional' and, therefore, communal people, this exchange system would mesh with, and reinforce, their own values. It would both strengthen the 'community' and bring its members into the modern world.

This heady mix of modernisation and cultural authenticity was orchestrated according to the assumed aim of Pintupi self-determination, in which they would literally build and take care of settlement infrastructure themselves, an interpretation of traditional culture that was so obvious to funding agencies that alternatives were never contemplated. While the commitment of outside agencies was high, programs locally flexible, and outcomes of infrastructure development and training not yet apparent, these competing views were easily accommodated. As part of their training Pintupi were able to receive wages for such things as modifying and repairing their own houses and cars, and everyone basked in the glow of success.

This era culminated in 1992 in a nationally broadcast documentary, titled *Benny and the Dreamers,* describing the ways Pintupi were taking control of their lives by blending the old and new. Shown as moving fluidly from bush ceremony to office, they appeared dedicated to community-building, living and working like whitefellas while keeping their own culture strong. Images of older and younger generations were interwoven to portray this harmony. This representation was, for a time, viable because the ready availability of funding provided high levels of support for whitefella positions, deemed trainers for Pintupi gardeners and builders, who maintained and elaborated the canvas on view to the outside world. Even blemishes such as the amount of rubbish around the settlement was, for a time, successfully accounted for as an 'environmental approach', since some rubbish degrades more quickly if exposed to the elements.

As a result of their popularity, Pintupi experienced an era where many of their own needs, such as transportation, were met. At this time western institutions were looked on favourably because they were seen as willing to fulfil their obligation to look after Pintupi, to take care of the real needs of their families, and there was a significant level of interaction between Pintupi and western institutions. A few years later the relationship with funding agencies began to change in a dramatic fashion, as expectations on both sides had been dramatically raised and then dashed. Since there is no convenient 'appropriate technology' that is acceptable to both societies, the new infrastructure was scarcely more resilient than the old, and still highly dependent upon maintenance that was underfunded. The underfunding was partly because of the mistaken assumption that the monies spent on training meant that outsiders were no longer needed.

Soon housing stock was in rapid decline, as buildings with broken-down services were abandoned and occasionally wrecked. Assumptions about the viability of housing design had been based on a representation of an ancient people keen to live as whitefellas, and the consequences of this were now apparent. Walungurru had become an eyesore, described by the local medic as a 'slum in the desert' (Alcorn 1994, 47). When a funding body that had invested heavily in technacy programs sought reassurance that Pintupi were ready to carry out the tasks for which they had now been trained, they were shocked to be told by the local builder that outside contractors must construct any new houses because local people were too unreliable for this work. The 'recalcitrant Pintupi' label, first applied at Papunya, was born anew, while Pintupi themselves despaired at the demands of maintaining a community canvas in order to obtain funding.

By the late 1990s the romantic allure of Walungurru had well and truly dissipated. The physical appearance of a rubbish-strewn settlement filled with trashed houses combined with press reports describing normal family politicking in terms of riots, and carefully controlled payback as gratuitous and random violence, made it notorious. Visitors reported that mere mention of the place brought a response of 'raised eyebrows' and a 'certain look to the eye'. Funding outside of health and education began drying up and a number of institutions faded.

Walungurru was now openly declared to be a 'chronically dysfunctional community' from which the younger generation needed to be urgently rescued. 'How can Walungurru ever change,' a representative of a training body argued, 'when the young people have seen nothing else?' This led to a program aimed at redressing this 'disadvantage' by sending young Pintupi to the town of Katherine, where they could see for themselves how a 'proper' community operated and bring new ideas home with them.

Conflict with some funding agencies inevitably produced tension between Pintupi and local administrators, to whom pressure was applied to make up the sudden shortfall from outside. Council administrators came and went in rapid succession. One of the new administrators recommended that funding be placed in the hands of a 'controller' who could bring Pintupi to heel, while denying the right of the community council to sack their appointee. Instead, Pintupi were subjected to a management plan in the hands of a non-government agency, justified on the basis that Pintupi were incapable of distinguishing between private and institutional resources. Funds for the community council would be released on the basis of a 'community plan' to be developed by the agency.

A hastily assembled team of expensive consultants was chartered in from afar, at massive cost, to conduct a series of workshops in which they sought to discover how to overcome the apparently chronic malaise of Walungurru. The new council administrator, who felt the council was being scapegoated promptly walked out. As services continued to melt down the agency assumed the role of manager, hiring out council administrators who acted as employees of the agency, rather than representatives for Pintupi.

Expensive consultants periodically reappeared, while Pintupi asked why these whitefellas kept visiting them while they could not get their toilets and showers fixed and household refuse went uncollected for more than a year, producing mountainous heaps of rubbish in front of every house. This situation did not change until an appointed administrator found it unconscionable, galvanised support in the settlement to overturn the arrangement and restored her position to that of settlement representative. Threats of withdrawal of outside funding in order to get Pintupi to renew their agreement with the organisation left them unimpressed. They had moved from Papunya to more impoverished circumstances in order to regain agency in their own lives, and they were prepared to forfeit material advantage to maintain it in Walungurru.

The pattern of their relationship with funding agencies means their wildly fluctuating fortunes were based on representations which had very few shared meanings with their own. Pintupi attributed their predicament to a change in their relationship with whitefellas, who they now said no longer liked them and apparently no longer wanted to even reside in their settlement with them. They puzzled at this sudden change, and why they were constantly being 'told off' by outsiders who lectured them endlessly on the perils of their 'lifestyle' and the need to live like whitefellas. Punishment was never part of the relationship Pintupi thought they had with whitefellas and they responded with dismay at this treachery. Many Pintupi withdrew their engagement with settlement institutions altogether.

In terms of the way they were represented, Pintupi had, in the course of a decade, moved from indigenous exemplars to accountability vandals, but although their fortunes had changed in dramatic fashion they were, throughout, the identical people. Representations of the Pintupi had been, according to the fads and fancies of the times, created by the dominant society with stupefying solemnity — despite their obvious contradictions — but they had never taken account of real Pintupi lives.

Throughout this funding see-saw, Pintupi life went on much as always because western institutions, and the whitefellas that run them, are not as critical to their lives as they presume. Feast and famine is part of the ancient pattern of life in the desert and, as always in times of hardship, Pintupi relied on the enduring strengths of their family constellations. Accountability to *walytja* remained strong; relationships were reaffirmed publicly by endless negotiation, argument and fighting. Ceremonial life burgeoned and there was a vast outpouring of creative energy focussing on community singing, with literate Pintupi writing out songs for others, while almost the entire community travelled en masse to perform all-night 'singing ceremonies' at far-flung desert homelands.

At the same time, there was an inflow to Walungurru of uncared-for 'skinny' children, some of them from the very settlements held up as exemplars to the Pintupi. Welfare agencies could always count on Pintupi families to take these children and attentively 'grow them up', and those who found a home at Walungurru were fortunate children indeed. However, as is usually the case, these strengths went unrecognised by the outside world. Pressure for change in indigenous society focussed on this, the most 'recalcitrant' settlement, where implacable cultural difference flourished and which many in the dominant society now appeared to view as the enemy within.

Author holding Shimona Napaltjarri at White Tree outstation, 2000.

CHAPTER 10
LOOKING BEYOND CHAOS

... there is often an idea that peripheral cultures come defenseless, unprepared to the encounter with metropolitan culture, that they are insufficiently organised and are taken by surprise ... this notion would frequently entail a measure of ignorance of the continuous historical development of centre–periphery contacts.
(Ulf Hannerz 1991, 109–10)

Indigenous societies are generally seen by the West to be lacking, rather than different, in need of another version of a fulfilling life. But they are actually already crammed with living principles, intricately connected to each other and difficult to extricate without damaging the entire system. Tatz expresses the frustration inherent in western society's expectation of indigenous receptivity to their own precepts when he asks, 'Can, or will, Aborigines exert a drive towards social, physical and mental well-being?' (1990, 257).

However, the lack of indigenous ability and agency implied in this question is both demeaning and misleading. Pintupi are not so incapable of transmitting their own cultural traditions that outsiders are critical to maintaining them. Nor are they so profoundly lacking in intelligence that they need endless training to produce only incremental improvement along preordained pathways. It is just that because they already have a fulfilling life they are not nearly as susceptible to re-education in the forms of western society as many whitefellas believe they should be. This is not to say that Pintupi have displayed a conservative reluctance to adjust to new circumstances, on the contrary the 'last-contact' people have changed as rapidly as any others on Earth. On that roller-coaster ride they have embraced many novel solutions without either compromising the core values of their society or drifting helplessly in a sea of despondency at the loss of old traditions. They are far too busy acquiring and deploying new resources to follow their own pursuits in a rapidly changing world to expend too much energy on wallowing in regretful nostalgia.

In this process of adaptation to their new situation Pintupi appropriate much of what many other Australians hold precious and require them to value in the name of rationality. However, they treat these appropriations as peripheral and disposable. At the same time as they commit this affront, they sacrilegiously dispense with many of the forms of their own so-called authentic culture (as it is defined by outsiders) or demand payment for their re-enactment, their 'greed' outraging the very society which preaches to them the benefits of economic self-reliance.

The one thing that is clear at the interface is that Pintupi are not exchanging their own values for those of the West, and this creates major obstacles to the achievement of the equality goals set for them. For example, Pintupi are still living their lives for the moment rather than squirrelling away for a future which may never come. Living for now has a cost, but then so does the cloistered, safe and generally insipid existence encouraged in much of the wider Australian society. Unpredictable factors can destroy the best efforts of both people and government to preserve life, and sacrificing quality for quantity is no guarantee of either increased length or value.

THE 'RIGHT' REALITY

> ... there has been little reassessment of the social anthropologist's heritage from evolutionary theory, and unexamined assumptions are still part of the framework of social anthropology. (Gillian Cowlishaw 1986, 4)

More than two decades ago, Stanner noted a wholesome fear in anthropology of overloading abstractions with reality, begging the question as to 'whether we have consulted the right reality in the first place' (1979, 63). Because of this avoidance of the reality of modern indigenous lives, anthropological explanations are often based on a paradigm of cultural disintegration, in a discipline Cowlishaw terms 'social archaeology' (1986, 9). These ethnographic descriptions should not be used to reassure us that all indigenous Australians, as a mass of wretched, passive humanity tossed on the beach of history by a tidal wave of Europeans, are ready and waiting to be redeemed. They are, instead,

> ... a highly specialised people and a contemporary people ... Unless we see both their contemporaneity and their specialisation, we set up a false model, a kind of 'generic' model in which they are depicted as 'simple' or 'earlier' or 'more primitive' than ourselves. (Stanner 1979, 59)

Because western culture is blind to the both the strengths and flexibilities of indigenous societies, its policies are often portrayed as saving or resurrecting them. However, Pintupi are not at all like the indigenous societies depicted in ethnographic accounts as helpless victims, crumbling and defeated under the pervasive influence of western culture. Hannerz claims this 'master scenario' has the great advantage of simplicity, it is appealingly dramatic and the idea that western culture may soon be everywhere makes it (and its bearers) seem important (1991, 107).

In the inevitable movement towards westernisation by indigenous societies with nothing to lose that this scenario implies, the Aboriginal and Torres Strait Islander Social Justice Commissioner believes that policy must establish 'minimum standards' which are imperative, not 'merely desirable' (1993, 6). And, according to the Council for Aboriginal Reconciliation, this move from desirable to imperative is the basis for meaningful reconciliation, and removal of inequality must be enforced (1995, 19–20). Yet calling equal outcomes an enforceable right, rather than a matter of government largesse or compassion, demonstrates no more respect for different ways of life, and may show a good deal less.

Equality policy is the latest expression of the hoped-for movement of groups like Pintupi towards westernisation. It is marketed as culturally neutral, and because Pintupi are told that it is not only their right but the government's international responsibility to deliver it to them, equality is viewed as a gift within the power of government to either bestow or withhold. Under this representation, government is inevitably placed in the position of appearing to be arbitrarily refusing Pintupi their due, and often the dialogue degenerates into a shifting of blame from one to the other. Moreover the ability of both societies to make informed decisions at the interface has been seriously eroded through this cost-negative, culturally-neutral marketing of social justice policies.

When Pintupi reflect on their lives they are constantly discouraged from weighing up the benefits and costs of equality policy, because current official propaganda is that issues of inequality and cultural distinctiveness can both be satisfied (*Social Justice for Indigenous Australians* 1991–2). Social justice policy has always shirked the question as to what Pintupi are willing to give up to gain equality. This is quite a different question from what Pintupi want. Of course, all people want the best of both worlds if only this were possible, but Pintupi can never have the best of these divergent worlds and to pretend they can does a disservice to everyone.

It is not easy to question equality goals, because their potential negative consequences are well disguised. Material gain is far more easily quantified than destructive social change, particularly when those determining the balance of benefits and costs are far distant and have no understanding — and seek none — of the particular society being evaluated. However, change in Pintupi society is not a matter of an inevitable movement towards western-style modernity, with its particular form of rationality. As Fishman demonstrates, the complexity of modern minority movements is elusive and certainly not explained by simplistic theories, according to which western processes and virtues are considered prototypical, normal and inescapable (1991, 385).

The notion that some indigenous groups may not, after all, be fitted for statistical equality, without an intrusive and unpredictable process of westernisation, is not at all the racist orthodoxy that Pettman (1987) argues it to be. The racist orthodoxy lies in the presumption that groups like the Pintupi must choose equality, at whatever cost to their own identity as a people. Therefore, programs of statistical equality are not invariably 'an affirmation of the dignity of all Australians' because they do not dignfy all indigenous lives, as the Aboriginal and Torres Strait Islander Social Justice Commissioner asserted (1993, 11).

For Pintupi, dignity is not lacking in a child playing under the ever-watchful eye of its grandparents, uncles and aunts, even if that child is naked and its playground a rubbish-strewn settlement. But it is still impossible for the dominant society to contemplate the possibility that, rather than being just outward signs of degradation, the striking appearance of poverty and dysfunction presented by a Pintupi settlement is in fact a monument to the strength of a way of life still unacknowledged by the West.

However, like many other indigenous societies, Pintupi have never been merely a repressed people fighting a desperate rearguard action against a globalising world. Throughout contact history, rather than being rescued by policy, Pintupi have always sought to use its vagaries to find the right balance in their own lives. 'Protection' at Haasts Bluff, 'assimilation' at Papunya and, more recently, 'self-determination' have all served as resources for cultural vitality. Pintupi use the ambivalence and contradictions of policy not merely to persist, accommodate or resist, as Keeffe has claimed (1992, 96–103), but to explore, seize, reinvent, transform and invigorate their lives. They have taken western rhetoric and turned it to their advantage, demonstrating in the process that they are a vigorous part of the worldwide burgeoning of what Wuthnow called 'cultural heterogeneity' (1983, 66).

An obstacle to understanding the relationship between Pintupi and the West is that it is complex and utterly challenging, rather than simple and slipping easily into politically sound convictions. Hannerz observes that theories contending that peripheral groups (like the Pintupi) are *not* just being overwhelmed, or are *not* simply corrupting of all the best ideals from the centre, have the disadvantage of being far more demanding of patience (1991, 110). But the differences both societies struggle with are fundamental and profound, and only patience will achieve a greater acceptance of this diversity than is suggested by the condemnation of much of the practice of indigenous lives as human rights abuses and breaches of international covenants (Aboriginal and Torres Strait Islander Social Justice Commissioner 1995).

BEYOND CHAOS

> I doubt if we could now bear to face the truth if we found we had been
> hallucinated. (W E H Stanner 1979, 132)

Pintupi will certainly continue to live their lives as they see fit, irrespective of the effects on statistical measures, and regardless of whether
their right to do so is acknowledged. By resisting in some instances, by
seizing useful elements in others, and by embracing the ideology of
equality but not the practice, Pintupi are able to exert more control
over social change in their own society than many Australians feel comfortable with. What happens 'on the ground' can never be completely
controlled by outside agencies, and it is not in the interests of Pintupi
for that to happen. Within their settlements, whitefella 'bosses' are left
in no doubt when real 'self-determination' has been infringed, and
they repeat the mistake at their own peril.

Each society in the relationship has both strength and integrity and
rather than overturning its own tenets to placate the other, each will
continue to bring pressure to bear to exert their own will at the interface. Just as it is unrealistic to expect Pintupi to unlearn being Pintupi,
it is unthinkable that the dominant society will unlearn being western
in its dealings with them. Therefore, Pintupi will not adopt western
values carte blanche, and there will not be the much-vaunted recognition by the West of cultural diversity on which indigenous survival is
alleged to depend (Tonkinson 1991, 181; Howitt 1998, 28). Not that
Pintupi will despair at this. The West's disapproval of their life choices
has no power to cause the abandonment of the value they place on
things such as *walytja,* which are the core of their wellbeing. Similarly,
the dominant society will not cast out its core ideal of equality merely
because recalcitrant groups like Pintupi repeatedly fail to achieve it,
despite numerous programs of intervention.

Both sides have come to expect so much yet this is, after all, an uneasy
relationship forged between a western and indigenous society, both self-
assured in the self-evident rationality of their own lifeways. This clash of
conflicting wills is a recipe for chaos, a state with which Pintupi are much
more comfortable than western society, which has a need for control and
structure and tends to interpret any other situation as anarchy. As long as
the dominant society is focused only on the chaotic nature of the interface, Pintupi and the institutions serving them will always be seen to be
failing because they do not accept, or impose, the order and structure necessary to achieve western aims. Both societies are thus locked into a frustrating relationship where all they seem to share is an aptitude for mutual
failure. However, despite — or because of — the apparent chaos much is
already working in the volatile arena of the interface.

If the dominant society came to accept that Pintupi are not merely
failed whitefellas, and that there are two coherent and competent societies

in the relationship, perhaps there would be less angst at the interface. The local effectiveness of its institutions may become clearer if their true context could be acknowledged, as they juggle the delivery of alien, western services against unwanted intrusion into Pintupi lives. A paradigm of mutual competence also promotes a shift away from a focus on accountable equality to one of providing equal opportunities for its achievement, in a partnership of peers. If the focus is on opportunities rather than outcomes then, implicitly, Pintupi have the freedom to select what they want without their life choices sparking reports of their imminent 'collapse', a slashing of funding or a crisis of programs (though never of policy).

Through all the caprices of policy, and despite a relationship between the two societies which could often be described as one of mutually outraged sensibilities, Pintupi have retained a resilient sense of humour about western culture and its strange ways. Because of this its representatives still find themselves warmly welcomed by a self-assured people, who believe that it is whitefellas who stand in need of guidance, if only they would listen. When they depart the settlement Pintupi say they must be crying for what they are leaving behind because, like many other Australians, Pintupi cannot comprehend a more fulfilling life than their own.

ACKNOWLEDGING ACHIEVEMENT

[W]e fail to grasp the zest for life which animates them ... Some of our general ideas may thus need drastic revision. (W E H Stanner 1979, 49)

The purpose of this account has not been to elaborate the irreconcilable differences between the cultures in order to conclude that no rapprochement is possible. My argument is that it is only through an acknowledgment of the collision of values at the interface that the achievements of both sides of the relationship will ever be seen and appreciated. It is other Australians who often despair at the outcomes of Pintupi life choices, because what can be seen disintegrating on their settlements is not Pintupi culture, but western infrastructure and, sometimes, the whitefellas sent out to oversee it.

Pintupi are an innovative, modern people, engaging selectively and creatively with the contemporary world while living their lives with great exuberance on their settlements. They do so in settlements founded on a complex polity which accommodates a conglomeration of strong *walytja* and alien western institutions, which in their turn balance the demands of mainstream bureaucracy and their Pintupi constituency. This is no small accomplishment. It is a feat of reconciliation between two fundamentally discordant cultures that deserves recognition.

To have known these people, to have talked with them and lived with them and to have come to understand something of their strength, was one of the great experiences of my life. (Donald Thomson 1975, 154–5)

REFERENCES

Aboriginal and Torres Strait Islander Social Justice Commissioner (1993) *First Report*. Australian Government Publishing Service, Canberra.

—— (1994) *Second Report*, Australian Government Publishing Service, Canberra.

—— (1995) *Third Report*, Education and Training, Australian Government Printing Service, Canberra.

Aboriginal Education Policy Task Force (1988) *Report of the Aboriginal Education Policy Task Force*, Department of Employment, Education and Training, Australian Government Publishing Service, Canberra.

Alcorn, G (1994) Born to Lose, *Time*, 11 April, pp. 46–51.

Altman, J C (1985) Aboriginal Outstation Communities: Some economic issues. Submission to the House of Representatives Standing Committee on Aboriginal Affairs, *Official Hansard Report*, 20 November.

—— (1987) *The Economic Viability of Aboriginal Outstations and Homelands*, Australian Government Publishing Service, Canberra.

Amadio, N and Kimber, R (1988)*Wildbird Dreaming*, Greenhouse, Melbourne.

Appadurai, A (1990) Disjuncture and difference in the global cultural economy, in M Featherstone (ed.) *Global Culture: Nationalism, Globalization and Modernity*, Sage, London.

—— (1995) The production of locality, in Richard Fardon (ed.) *Counterworks, Managing the Diversity of Knowledge*, Routledge, London.

Australian Reconciliation Convention (1997) *The Path to Reconciliation, Renewal of the Nation*, Australian Government Publishing Service, Canberra.

Bardon, G (1991) *Papunya Tula Art of the Western Desert*, McPhee Gribble, Melbourne.

Barnett, J, Kemelfield, G, Muhlhausler, P, Burton, J, Clayton, J, (1995) Desert Schools, An Investigation of English and Literacy among young people in seven communities (unpublished draft). National Languages and Literacy Institute of Australia, Canberra.

Begley, S (1998) Science Wars, *Bulletin*, Dec/Jan, pp. 80–81.

Bell, D (1993) *Daughters of the Dreaming*, 2nd edition, Allen & Unwin, Sydney.

Bennett, S (1999)*White Politics and Black Australians*, Allen & Unwin, Sydney.

Benny and the Dreamers (1992) CAAMA and ABC, film produced for 'The Big Picture'.

Bucknall, J (1995) Social Justice Directions in the Aboriginal Independent Schools (WA), *The Aboriginal Child at School*, 23(2): 33–44.

Carnegie, D W (1989) *Spinifex and Sand*, Pearson, London.

Clifford, J (1988) *The Predicament of Culture. Twentieth-Century Ethnography, Literature, and Art*, Harvard University Press, Cambridge, Mass.

Commonwealth of Australia (1989) *A Chance for the Future. Training and Skills for Aboriginal and Torres Strait Islander Community Management*, Report of House of Representatives Standing Committee on Aboriginal Affairs.

Commonwealth of Australia (1990) *Our Future Our Selves*, Report of House of Representatives Standing Committee on Aboriginal Affairs.

Community Aid Abroad (1997) *How your donation could change someone's world*, CAA–Oxfam in Australia, Melbourne.

Cooke, M (1988) Two-faced, Two-Ways Teacher Education with a Maths/Science Focus, unpublished paper, Batchelor College, Batchelor, NT.

Council for Aboriginal Reconciliation (1993) *Addressing the Key Issues for Reconciliation*, Overview of Key Issues Papers nos 1–8, Australian Government Publishing Service, Canberra.

—— (1994a) *Improving Relationships: Better Relationships between Indigenous Australians and the Wider Community*, Australian Government Publishing Service, Canberra

—— (1994b) *Addressing Disadvantage: A Greater Awareness of the Causes of Indigenous Australians' Disadvantage*, Australian Government Publishing Service, Canberra.

—— (1994c) *Controlling Destinies: Greater Opportunities for Indigenous Australians to Control Their Destinies*, Australian Government Publishing Service, Canberra.

—— (1995) *Going Forward. Social Justice for the First Australians*, Australian Government Publishing Service, Canberra.

Cowlishaw, G K (1986) Aborigines and Anthropologists, *Australian Aboriginal Studies*, 1: 2–11.

—— (1999) *Rednecks, Eggheads and Blackfellas*, Allen & Unwin, Sydney.

Cox, E (1998) Measuring Social Capital as Part of Progress and wellbeing, in Richard Eckersley (ed.) *Measuring progress. Is life getting better?* CSIRO Publishing, Melbourne.

Davis, K, Hunter, J and Penny, D H (1977) *Papunya: History and Future Prospects*. A report prepared for the Ministers of Aboriginal Affairs and Education, Northern Territory Administration, unpublished.

Duguid, C (1963) *No Dying Race*, Rigby, Adelaide.

Edmunds, M (1989) *They Get Heaps. A study of attitudes in Roebourne, Western Australia*, Aboriginal Studies Press, Canberra.

Egan, T (1997) *Sit Down Up North*, Kerr Publishing, Sydney

Elkin, A P (1944) *Citizenship for the Aborigines: A national Aboriginal policy*, Australian Publishing Company, Sydney.

Fishman, J (1991) *Reversing Language Shift: theoretical and empirical foundations of assistance to threatened languages*. Multilingual Matters (series): 76, Multilingual Matters, London

Foucault, M (1970) The Order of Discourse, in Robert Young (ed.) *Untying the Text: A Post-Structuralist Reader*, Routledge & Kegan, London.

—— (1977) The Eye of Power, in Colin Gordon (ed.) *Power/Knowledge Selected Interviews and Other Writings 1972–1977*, Pantheon, New York.

Gartrell, M (1957) *Dear Primitive. A Nurse Among the Aborigines*, Angus & Robertson, Sydney.

Gill, W (1968) *Petermann Journey*, Rigby, Sydney.

Graham, R and Thorley, P (1996) Central Australian Aboriginal stone knives — their cultural significance, manufacture and trade, in S R Morton and D J Mulvaney (eds) *Exploring Central Australia: Society, the Environment and the Horn Expedition*, Surrey Beatty, Chipping Norton, Australia.

Greenway, J (1973) *Down Among the Wild Men*, Hutchinson, Melbourne.

Griffiths, M (1995) *Aboriginal Affairs. A Short History 1788–1995*, Kangaroo Press, Melbourne.

Hannerz, U (1990) Cosmopolitans and Locals in World Culture, in M Featherstone (ed.) *Global Culture: Nationalism, Globalisation and Modernity*, Sage, London.

—— (1991) Scenarios for Peripheral Cultures, in Anthony King (ed.) *Culture, Globalisation and the World-System*, Macmillan, New York.

—— (1992) *Cultural Complexity. Studies in the Social Organisation of Meaning*, Columbia University Press, New York.

Hargrave, J C (1957) Medical Survey of the Nomadic Natives in the Lake Mackay Area of the Northern Territory and Western Australia, Dept of Aboriginal Affairs Archives, Darwin.

Harney, B (1995) *To Ayers Rock and Beyond*, Lansdowne, Sydney.

Heffernan, J A (1977) The Provision of Visiting Teachers for some Papunya Outstations. A Feasibility Study, unpublished, Alice Springs.

Hempel, R (1982) *Review: Kintore Outstations Movement*, Dept of Aboriginal Affairs and Dept of Community Development, Darwin.

Henson, B (1992) *A Straight-out Man: F. W. Albrecht and Central Australian Aborigines*, Melbourne University Press, Melbourne.

Herbert, J (1995) Gender Issues for Torres Strait Islander Girls: Exploring Issues for Aboriginal and Torres Strait Islander Boys, *The Aboriginal Child at School*, 23(2): 23–32).

Herron, J (1998) ABC-TV '7.30 Report', 24 March.

Hirst, J (1994) Five Fallacies of Aboriginal Policy. *Quadrant* July/August pp.11–16.

Hobart, M (1995) As I Lay Laughing: encountering global knowledge in Bali, in Richard Fardon (ed.) *Counterworks: Managing the diversity of knowledge*, Routledge, London & New York.

Hoogenraad, R and Robertson, G J (1997) Seasonal calendars from Central Australia, in Eric Webb (ed.) *Windows on Meteorology: Australian Perspective*, CSIRO Publishing, Melbourne.

Howell, S (1995) Whose Knowledge and Whose Power? A new perspective on cultural diffusion, in Richard Fardon (ed.) *Counterworks: Managing the diversity of knowledge*, Routledge, London & New York.

Howitt, R (1998) Recognition, Respect and Reconciliation: Steps towards decolonisation, *Australian Indigenous Studies*, 1: 28–39.

Howson, P (1996) Separatism: A shortcut to Aboriginal tragedy, *Weekend Australian*, 29–30 June, p. 4.

Hunter, E (1993) *Aboriginal Health and History: Power and prejudice in remote Australia*, Cambridge University Press, Cambridge.

Keeffe, K (1992) *From the Centre to the City: Aboriginal education, culture and power*, Australian Institute of Aboriginal Studies, Canberra.

Kidd, R (1997) *The Way we Civilise. Aboriginal Affairs – the untold story*, University of Queensland Press, Brisbane.

King, D (ed.) (1991) *Culture, Globalisation and the World-System: Contemporary Conditions for the Representation of Identity*, Macmillan, New York.

Lockwood, D (1664) *The Lizard Eaters*, Cassell Australia, Sydney.

Long, J (1964a) Papunya: Westernization in an Aboriginal Community, in Marie Reay (ed.) *Australia Now. New Perspectives in the Study of Aboriginal Communities*, Angus & Robertson, Sydney.

—— (1964b) Desert Aborigines: The later phases. *Australian Territories* 4(6): 25–31.

—— (1970) *Aboriginal Settlements*, ANU Press, Canberra.

Maddox, J (1998) *What Remains to be Discovered?* Macmillan, London.

Mant, A (1997) *Intelligent Leadership*, Allen & Unwin, Sydney.

Mathers, C (1998) Measuring Progress in Population Health and wellbeing, in

Richard Eckersley (ed.) *Measuring progress. Is life getting better?* CSIRO Publishing, Melbourne.

Mehan, H (1989) Beneath the skin and the ears. A case study in the politics of representation, unpublished, University of California, San Diego, CA.

Morice, R D (1976) Woman Dancing Dreaming: Psychosocial Benefits of the Aboriginal Outstation Movement, *Medical Journal of Australia*, 2: 939–42.

Myers, F (1980) A Broken Code: Pintupi political theory and temporary social life, *Mankind*, 12(4): 311–326.

—— (1982) Ideology and Experience: The cultural basis of politics in Pintupi life, in Michael C Howard (ed.) *Aboriginal Power in Australian Society*, University of Queensland Press, Brisbane.

—— (1985) Illusion and Reality. Aboriginal Self-Determination in Central Australia, in C Schire and R Gordon (eds) *The Future of Former Foragers*, Cultural Survival, Cambridge.

—— (1986a) *Pintupi Country Pintupi Self. Sentiment, Place and Politics among Western Desert Aborigines*, Australian Institute of Aboriginal Studies, Canberra.

—— (1986b) Reflections on a Meeting: Structure, language, and the polity in a small-scale society, *American Ethnologist*, 13(30): 430–47.

—— (1988) Burning the Truck and Holding the Country: Property, time and the negotiation of identity among Pintupi Aborigines, in Tim Ingold, David Riches and James Woodburn (eds) *Hunters and Gatherers Vol 2, Property, Power and Ideology*, Berg, New York.

National Aboriginal and Torres Strait Islander Education Policy (1989) Australian Government Publishing Service, Canberra.

National Aboriginal Health Strategy (1989) Report for the National Aboriginal Health Strategy Working Party, Australian Government Publishing Service, Canberra

National Review of Education for Aborigines (1994) Australian Government Publishing Service, Canberra.

Nolan, Billy Tjapangati (1989) *Kunki*, sound recording by Peter Thorley, Walungurru Literacy Centre, Walungurru, NT.

Northern Territory Administration (1933, 1936, 1937, 1938, 1949–53, 1957–58, 1958–59) *Annual Report*, Commonwealth Government Printer, Canberra.

Northern Territory Administration, Welfare Branch (1961) *Pintubi Aboriginal Reserve, Central Australia*, Northern Territory Administration, Darwin.

Northern Territory Administration, Welfare Branch (1971–72) *Annual Report*, Darwin.

Northern Territory Education Department (1999), *Learning Lessons: An independent review of indigenous education in the Northern Territory* (Collins Report), Darwin.

O' Donoghue, L (1992) *Aboriginal and Torres Strait Islander Commission Corporate Plan 1992–96*, Australian Government Publishing Service, Canberra.

Our Futures Our Selves (1990) Aboriginal and Torres Strait Islander Community Control, Management and Resources, House of Representatives Standing Committee, Australian Government Publishing Service, Canberra.

Parkin, D (1995) Latticed Knowledge: Eradication and dispersal of the unpalatable in Islam, medicine and anthropological theory, in Richard Fardon (ed.) *Counterworks: Managing the Diversity of Knowledge*, Routledge, London and New York.

Partington, G (1996) *Hasluck versus Coombs: White politics and Australia's Aborigines*, Quakers Hill Press, Sydney.

Peterson, N (1998) Welfare Colonisation and Citizenship: Politics, Economics and Agency, in Nicolas Peterson and Will Sanders (eds) *Citizenship and Indigenous Australians. Changing Conceptions and Possibilities*, Cambridge University Press, Cambridge.

Pettman, J (1987) Combating racism within the community, in A Markus and R Rasmussen (eds) *Prejudice in the Public Arena: Racism*, Monash University Press, Melbourne.

Pintupi Homelands Health Service (1985) *Annual Report*, PHHS, unpublished.

—— (1994) *Health on the Homelands*, PHHS, unpublished.

—— (1996–97) *Still Battling*, PHHS, unpublished.

Pollard, D (1992) *Give and Take: The losing partnership in Aboriginal poverty*, Hale & Iremonger, Sydney.

Reid, J and Lupton, D (1991) Introduction, in Janice Reid & Peggy Trompf (eds)*The Health of Aboriginal Australia*, Harcourt, Brace Jovanovich, Sydney.

Report of the Aboriginal Education Policy Task Force (1988) Australian Government Publishing Service, Canberra.

Report on the Administration of the Northern Territory (1932, 1944–45, 1958–59, 1961) Commonwealth Government Printer, Canberra.

Rowley, C D (1971) *The Remote Aborigines: Aboriginal policy and practice*, vol. III, ANU Press, Canberra.

—— (1978) *A Matter of Justice*, ANU Press, Canberra.

Rowse, T (1993) *After Mabo: Interpreting indigenous traditions*, Melbourne University Press, Melbourne.

—— (1998)*White Flour, White Power*, Melbourne University Press, Melbourne.

Said, E W (1979) *Orientalism*, Vintage, New York.

Sheehan, P (1998) *Among the Barbarians*, Random House, Sydney.

Social Justice for Indigenous Australians (1991–92) 1991 Budget related paper no. 7, Australian Government Publishing Service, Canberra.

—— (1992–93) 1992 Budget related paper no. 7, Australian Government Publishing Service, Canberra.

—— (1993–94) 1994 Budget related paper no. 7, Australian Government Publishing Service, Canberra.

Stanner, W E H (1964) Foreword, in Marie Reay (ed.) *Aborigines Now*, Angus & Robertson, Sydney.

—— (1979) *The Aborigines: White man got no Dreaming, Essays 1938–73*, ANU Press, Canberra.

Stead, J (1986) *Pintupi Review*, Central Land Council, Alice Springs.

Stockton, E (1995) *The Aboriginal gift. Spirituality for a nation*, Millennium Books, Sydney.

Strehlow, T G H (1966) *The Sustaining Ideals of Australian Aboriginal Societies*, Aboriginal Advancement League Inc, Adelaide.

Tatz, C (1964) Aboriginal Administration, unpublished PhD dissertation, Australian National University, Canberra.

—— (1982) *Aborigines and Uranium and Other Essays*, Heinemann, Melbourne.

—— (1990) Aboriginal violence: a return to pessimism, *Australian Journal of Social Issues* 25(4): 245–60.

Thomas, N (1994) *Colonialism's Culture. Anthropology, travel and government*, Polity Press, Cambridge.

—— (1999) *Possessions. Indigenous Art/Colonial Culture*, Thames and Hudson, London.

Thomson, D (1964) Some Wood and Stone Implements of the Bindibu Tribe of Central Western Australia. Proceedings of the Prehistorical Society, Cambridge University, 30: 400–22.

—— (1975) *Bindibu Country*, Nelson, Auckland.

Tickner, R (1992) *ATSIC Corporate Plan 1992–96*, Australian Government Publishing Service, Canberra.

Tjapaltjarri, B (1989) *Mitjinirrikutu*, story recorded by Peter Thorley, Walungurru Literacy Centre, Walungurru, NT.

Tjapaltjarri, M (1989) *Waru*, in P Thorley (ed.) *Kuka: Pintupi animal foods*, Walungurru Literacy Centre, Walungurru, NT.

Tjapanangka, P P (1989) Malu red kangaroo, in P Thorley (ed.) *Kuka: Pintupi animal foods*, Walungurru Literacy Centre, Walungurru, NT.

Tonkinson, R (1991) *The Mardu Aborigines. Living the Dreaming in Australia's Desert*, 2nd edition, Holt, Rinehart, Winston, London.

Tregenza, J and Abbott, K (1995) *Rhetoric and Reality, Perceptions of the roles of Aboriginal health Workers in Central Australia*, Central Australian Aboriginal Congress, Alice Springs, NT.

Trigger, D S (1992) *Whitefella Comin'. Aboriginal responses to colonialism in northern Australia*, Cambridge University Press, Cambridge.

Vitebsky, P (1995) From cosmology to environmentalism, in R Fardon (ed.) *Counterworks, Managing the diversity of knowledge*, Routledge, London.

Von Sturmer, J R (1982) Aborigines in the Uranium Industry: Towards self-management in the Alligator River region? In Ronald Berndt (ed.) *Aboriginal Sites, Rights and Resource Development*, University of Western Australia Press, Perth.

Williams, N M (1985) On Aboriginal decision-making, in D Barwick, J Beckett and M Reay (eds), *Metaphors of Interpretation: Essays in honour of W E H Stanner*, ANU Press, Canberra.

Wilson, J (1964) quoted in K Davis, J Hunter and D H Penny, 1977, *Papunya: History and future prospects*. A report prepared for the Ministers of Aboriginal Affairs and Education NT Government, Darwin.

World Council of Churches (1991), *Between Two Worlds: Report of a WCC Team Visit to Aboriginal Communities in Australia*, World Council of Churches, Geneva.

Wuthnow, R (1983) Cultural Crisis, in A Bergesen (ed.) *Crisis in the World System*, Sage, Beverly Hills, CA.

Young, M (1998). General Discussion, in Richard Eckersley (ed.) *Measuring progress. Is life getting better?* CSIRO Publishing, Melbourne.

Young, R (ed) (1986) *Untying the Text: A Post-Stucturalist Reader*, Routledge & Kegan, London.

INDEX